The End(s) *of* Community

Laurier Studies in Political Philosophy

Laurier Studies in Political Philosophy Series

Global migration, MTV, transnational capital, and colonialism have given birth to a new and smaller world. To a greater degree than at any other time in remembered history, different cultures are brought together to live side by side. This close proximity has brought new mixtures and exciting possibilities—and also new struggles and conflicts. From many quarters comes an urgent call to build a sense of political belonging and unity in a diversity of voices. The call to unity is not, however, for uniformity or hegemony in one particular way of life. The unity to which we refer requires a rethinking and reconceptualization of existing philosophical paradigms that guide our relationships with others. In the spirit of intercultural dialogue, our Laurier Studies in Political Philosophy series is dedicated to exploring key challenges to our changing world and its needs. We are particularly interested in submissions that challenge dominant existing frameworks and approaches. We invite submissions in areas including Multicultural Theory, Aboriginal Studies and Philosophy, Post-colonialism, Globalization, Critical Race Theory, Feminism, and Human Rights Philosophy.

Editorial Committee:

James Tully, Political Science, University of Victoria
Rhoda E. Howard-Hassmann, Canada Research Chair in International Human Rights, Wilfrid Laurier University
Frank Cunningham, Philosophy, University of Toronto
Lynda Lange, Philosophy, University of Toronto
Audra Simpson, Anthropology, Columbia University
Sonia Sikka, Philosophy, Ottawa
Bidyut Chakrabarty, Political Science, University of Delhi
Allison Weir, Philosophy, Wilfrid Laurier University
Chandrakala Padia, Political Science, and Director of Women's Studies, Banaras Hindu University
Dale Turner, Native American Studies, Dartmouth
Michael Murphy, Political Science, University of Northern British Columbia
Kimberly Rygiel, Political Science, Wilfrid Laurier University
Ashwani K. Peetush, Series Editor, Philosophy, Wilfrid Laurier University

For more information, please contact the **Series Editors:**

Ashwani K. Peetush
Associate Professor of Philosophy
Wilfrid Laurier University
75 University Avenue West
Waterloo, ON N2L 3C5
Phone: (519) 884-0710 ext. 3874
Fax: (519) 883-0991
Email: apeetush@wlu.ca

Ryan Chynces
Acquisitions Editor
Wilfrid Laurier University Press
75 University Avenue West
Waterloo, ON N2L 3C5
Phone: (519) 884-0710 ext. 2034
Fax: (519) 725-1399
Email: rchynces@wlu.ca

The End(s) *of* Community
HISTORY, SOVEREIGNTY, AND THE QUESTION OF LAW

Joshua Ben David Nichols

WILFRID LAURIER
UNIVERSITY PRESS

This book has been published with the help of a grant from the Canadian Federation for the Humanities and Social Sciences, through the Awards to Scholarly Publications Program, using funds provided by the Social Sciences and Humanities Research Council of Canada. Wilfrid Laurier University Press acknowledges the financial support of the Government of Canada through the Canada Book Fund for its publishing activities.

Library and Archives Canada Cataloguing in Publication

Nichols, Joshua Ben David, 1978–
    The end(s) of community : history, sovereignty, and the question of law/ Joshua Ben David Nichols.

(Laurier studies in political philosophy series)
Includes bibliographical references and index.
Also issued in electronic format.
ISBN 978-1-55458-836-7

    1. Law—Philosophy. I. Title. II. Series: Laurier studies in political philosophy series.

K230.N52 2013   340!1   C2012-904292-7

Electronic monograph issued in multiple formats.
Also issued in print format.

ISBN 978-1-55458-870-1 (PDF).—ISBN 978-1-55458-871-8 (EPUB)

    1. Law—Philosophy. I. Title. II. Series: Laurier studies in political philosophy series (Online).

K230.N52 2013   340!1   C2012-904293-5

Cover design by Blakeley Words+Pictures. Front-cover image: *Monastery Graveyard in the Snow*, by Caspar David Friedrich (1774–1840), from Wikipedia, http://en.wikipedia.org/wiki/File:Caspar_David_Friedrich_049.jpg. Text design by Angela Booth Malleau.

© 2013 Wilfrid Laurier University Press
Waterloo, Ontario, Canada
www.wlupress.wlu.ca

Every reasonable effort has been made to acquire permission for copyright material used in this text, and to acknowledge all such indebtedness accurately. Any errors and omissions called to the publisher's attention will be corrected in future printings.

No part of this publication may be reproduced, stored in a retrieval system, or transmitted, in any form or by any means, without the prior written consent of the publisher or a licence from the Canadian Copyright Licensing Agency (Access Copyright). For an Access Copyright licence, visit http://www.accesscopyright.ca or call toll free to 1-800-893-5777.

CONTENTS

Acknowledgements	vii
Introduction	1

SECTION I AT THE END(S) OF COMMUNITY

1. "Community, Number," and Democracy: An Excursus on the Politics of Fraternity — 17

SECTION II WRITING AND RESISTANCE

2. Keeping Time beneath a Canopy of Skins: Reading at the Limits of Sense and Sign(s) in Augustine and Bataille — 59

3. The Way Out Is Through: Sade's Novel and the Crime of Writing — 87

SECTION III BODIES OF RESISTANCE

4. Between Law and the Slaughterhouse: Kant, Fichte, and the "Absolute" Right of Punishment — 107

5. Between the Judge and the Executioner: Revisiting the Silent Foundations of Hegel's Moral Point of View — 129

6. To Read the Writing of Right: An Excursus on Death and the Foundations of Law in the Penal Colony — 139

Notes	163
Bibliography	193
Index	199

ACKNOWLEDGEMENTS

THE MAJORITY OF THIS BOOK was written while I was a postdoctoral fellow at the University of Victoria's Faculty of Law. During that time I had the good fortune to be able to work with both James Tully and Rebecca Johnson. Their kindness, patience, and wealth of knowledge were and are a source of constant inspiration to me.

Of course, the book did not come suddenly. Its beginnings are found in the network of the small, winding paths and long, arching trajectories that precede it. In my case this journey has been marked by the invaluable contributions of many generous guides. My studies took me from the Departments of Political Science and Sociology at the University of Alberta to the University of Toronto's Department of Philosophy. I would like to express my deepest gratitude to Rebecca Comay, Robert Gibbs, and Mark Kingwell for all of their philosophical insight, incisive criticism, and unending hospitality throughout the course of my dissertation and beyond. This work would not have been possible without the indispensable instruction, advice, and friendship of Doug Aoki, Catherine Kellogg, George Pavlich, Derek Sayer, and Yoke-Sum Wong while I was a student at the University of Alberta. Their continuing influence extends throughout my work.

I would be remiss not to acknowledge my friends and colleagues, in particular Sagi Cohen, Pablo Ouziel, and Amy Swiffen, for their conversation and companionship. Of course, my mother Linda, brother Zach, and the entire Joensuu family for their ever-present support and for showing me the meaning and value of family.

Finally, I must thank my loving Eleonora. Her unending kindness, love, and willingness to read (not to mention painstakingly edit) basically every word I have written marks every page of this book and, quite simply, makes life worth living.

INTRODUCTION

WHAT ARE THE LIMITS OF LAW? At first glance this question seems commonplace. After all there is no law without limitations. In order for law to function, its limits must be either determined or determinable. They are, quite simply, conceptually co-determined. Given this relation, it seems one could simply respond with a basic indicative "here" or "there," as if responding to a tourist asking for directions. But if we pause and begin to consider this question a little more carefully, it quickly loses its everyday veneer. There is a troubling undercurrent to this question, one that echoes Antigone's animal-like cry, Leontius' irrepressible desire to see, or the ultimate fate of the officer in Kafka's "In the Penal Colony."[1] This undercurrent shifts the very force and character of the question from the simple, everyday point of reference (i.e., from the specific legal limits for a given activity to the imaginary lines that define a jurisdiction and the set of qualities that determine the "common" of community) to a radical contestation of the power to make law. As soon as we begin to attune our ear to this undercurrent, the simple response of "here" or "there" suddenly becomes abstract to the point of absurdity. We are drawn towards that which is set outside of the law—the king, the outlaw, and the scaffold—in an attempt to find the stakes of the question itself. However one chooses to answer this question—and we should note that it is one always already being both asked and answered—determines the line that both unites and divides sovereignty and democracy, force and law.

This text addresses the philosophical genealogies of these fundamental concepts in order to respond to the question. In particular it sets out to examine how the tradition of Western philosophy has accounted for the foundations of law, that is, for the movement from a "state of nature" to political order. Traditionally, the character of the "sovereign" or "lawgiver" has provided the solution to this problem. The sovereign sets the limits of the law by presenting its authority as natural or at the very least necessary, but this solution simply suspends or defers the question of the limits of law (i.e., the line between force and law). Effectively, by proclaiming law, the sovereign faces the problem of responsibility. The solution to this problem has been the claim that the sovereign's relationship to the law is exceptional, that is, it may both found and enforce law, but it is not bound by it. This exceptional status requires an explanatory framework, as without one the claim to the rule of law is impossible to maintain. Quite simply, sovereignty requires a unified historical narrative to contextualize its foundations (i.e., fate), give meaning to its future (i.e., messianism), and thereby preserve its authority within the present. This requirement has effectively tied sovereignty to universal history—or, to borrow Lyotard's terminology, "grand historical narratives"—at the conceptual level.

This line of inquiry is by no means easy. When we begin to question the historical foundations of the relationship between sovereignty and law, we are immediately confronted with a convoluted mixture of jurisprudence and theology. While it is possible to argue that this metaphysical component is merely a distraction, and that the true basis of both sovereignty and the legal order is simply violence, such a hypothesis is fundamentally incomplete. Simply dismissing metaphysics as a façade renders one unable to account for the series of structural effects the foundational myth has within the system.

Myth serves to bind the sovereign and the community together—a classic example being the so-called "noble lie" in the *Republic*—and thus set the stage for the proclamation of laws that are received as more than a set of externally imposed limits. In the twinkling of an eye, individuals become moral subjects and the rule of the strongest becomes the rule of law. And this is not the end of the story. While any given mythology may serve to found law and convert force into law, it cannot simply be dispensed with once the foundation is in place, for it introduces a set of relationships and rules that must be maintained. Like the script for an elaborate stage play, it defines the scenes and sets the actors in motion.

Nevertheless, when one starts to question the logic of the play itself, it begins to unravel. When we leave the script and pose a simple and direct question, such as "Who are you to proclaim the law?" the sovereign is forced either to make the obvious tautological assertion "I am the King"—a kindness to remind us of our place within the script—or to simply change the scene and have us arrested and executed for high treason. It is violence that both founds and maintains the relationship that binds the play to the script. And yet, paradoxically, it is acts of violence—and here I draw directly on Benjamin's use of the German term *Gewalt*—that strain this relationship to the point of unworking it. The magic circle that leads from the subject to the sovereign draws itself towards the limit in and through exercising the right to kill. Foucault puts his finger on precisely this in *Abnormal* when he marks out the historical-political category of the "grotesque" or "Ubu-esque":

> At its extreme point, where it accords itself the right to kill, justice has installed a discourse that is Ubu's discourse; it gives voice to Ubu science. To

express things more solemnly, let's say that the West, which, no doubt since Greek society, since the Greek city-state, has not ceased to dream of giving power to the discourse of truth in a just city, has ended up in a system of justice conferring unrestrained power on the parody, on the parody that is recognized as such, of scientific discourse.[2]

This is left as a possible course or an aside within Foucault's lectures in 1975. He states that he had "neither the strength, nor the courage, nor the time" to devote the course to this theme.[3] By the following year, his approach to the question of sovereign power had shifted from the "grotesque" to the "manufacture of subjects."[4] Despite this fact—and the fact that I will not be directly addressing Foucault's work in this text—the category of the "Ubuesque" remains directly relevant to the question of sovereign power and the right to kill. It draws our attention to the undercurrent of the historical-political relationship between the subject and the sovereign. In Marx's *Eighteenth Brumaire* this undercurrent flows from high tragedy to low farce. Louis Bonaparte is sovereign, and yet,

> driven by the contradictory demands of his circumstances, and having to keep in the public eye as a substitute for Napoleon, hence executing a coup in miniature every day, Bonaparte, like a conjuror who has come up with constant surprises, brings the whole bourgeoisie economy into confusion, violates everything that seemed inviolable during the revolution of 1848, makes some tolerant of the revolution and others desirous of it, and produces anarchy in the name of order, while stripping the halo from the whole machinery of state, profanes it, and makes it loathsome and laughable.[5]

By operating under the name of those that came before, he exposes the palimpsest of sovereignty. In his repetition he stands out like an actor whose performance fails, and thereby exposes the artificiality of the entire play or a sign repeated to the point at which it can no longer maintain its claim to significance. Here the pageantry of sovereign power undoes itself by asserting itself. Each act, and, in particular, each use of its right to kill, draws out the grotesque logic that lies at its core. By following this undercurrent through a number of texts, we will be taken to the limit at which violence undoes the "mystical foundations of law" and with it the spell of subjectivity, leaving the sovereign in the open, as absurd, as parody, and exposed to the possibility of radical contestation. The outcome of this contestation is by no means assured—a naked sovereign is perhaps even more dangerous than one with imaginary clothes—but there is, at this point, the possibility of redefining the limits of political order. My line of inquiry sets out to trace the structural dynamics that exist between violence and the metaphysical infrastructure that binds sovereignty to community and thus founds the legal order.

A NOTE ON METHOD(S)

Now that I have outlined the general field of relations I will be addressing, there remains the question of approach. While the breadth of the field—which might well be said to be the entire history of political thought—presents us with any number of possible lines of approach, I have chosen to adopt a non-linear one. This being so, the text does not present the reader with a series of chapters that directly build upon one another in an interlocking series. This does not mean that the text is simply a set of essays whose only commonality is their physical proximity. Rather, each shares what might be referred to as a point of dispersion or common problematic. We can relate this problematic in the form of either a question ("What are the limits of law?") or a sequence of basic relations (sovereignty/democracy, force/law, community/number, etc.). But the precise arrangement of the problematic will shift in each case as each chapter takes on a distinct text. The text is thus neither a building (an ordered sequence of layers) nor a straight path from one point to another. It does not establish a genealogy or construct a family tree. It is dispersive. It is composed of a number of paths, which break off from a shared point. In this sense I have tried to practise a "blind tactics." As Derrida states in *Margins of Philosophy*,

> In the delineation of *différance* everything is strategic and adventurous. Strategic because no transcendent truth present outside the field of writing can govern theologically the totality of the field. Adventurous because this strategy is not a simple strategy in the sense that strategy orients tactics according to a final goal, a *telos* or theme of domination, a mastery and ultimate reappropriation of the development of the field. Finally, a strategy without finality, what might be called blind tactics.[6]

Given this approach readers may well find themselves following a particular line of inquiry in the text only to find it suddenly veers off course. This does not mean that the course is somehow "incomplete." My aim is not to determine, define, and close off a field, but to open up paths. Plurality is of the utmost importance here. While these paths might be said to share a common dispersion point, they do not thereby become tokens of *the* path (the path that would lead to the resolution of the problematic). Their plurality problematizes the very possibility of such an ultimate or final resolution. This is reflected in the very structure of the text. There is no conclusion, no masterful resetting of the stage, no reestablished genealogical order; it is left open. The text is thus not written as a series of ends, but a series of openings. This is also reflected in the internal structure of the chapters and the style of writing. Each chapter engages with a text or series of texts by following their internal dynamics to the point at which they begin to rupture.

Reading a text (i.e., reading it carefully) is much like watching a play. We must attend to both what is presented on stage—the acting-out of the script—and the staging of the play itself. Each of those elements we are not supposed to see—the stagecraft, the artificiality of the props, forgotten lines, slips in dialogue, and glimpses behind the curtain—act as a reminder of the separation of the play and the script. By stepping back and patiently attending to the progression of the text, we can begin to appreciate both the richness of the given moment and the fundamental strangeness of the scene change. To read carefully is to slow the pace of the text: to take a step back and follow.

Due to this need for slowness I rely extensively on the tactical resources of commentary and close reading. I take up a line and follow the text closely. I take up concepts as needed, deploy them, and refine them to suit a particular purpose or draw out a certain set of relations, only to leave them and take up another. In short, I take the practice of *bricolage* seriously. The reader expecting a clear, concise, and exhaustive survey or map of the field or fields touched on will be disappointed. For such a reader what I offer here can only ever appear as the notes for a "real" or "complete" text. This reader will enter the text, follow its course, and examine its contents only to demand a series of changes. Like a self-appointed building inspector he or she will arrive with a thorough to-do list for me. Such readers would assure me that if I only follow the list and make the corrections, my text will be up to "code."

While these readers might be driven by the best of intentions, the effect of such changes would be fundamental. I would have to shift from opening to closing, defining, and walling off. Every point would set through an elaborate survey of the author's oeuvre and the canonical secondary literature. It would no longer be a text that practises *blind tactics*: rather, it would become one that merely sets out to talk about said practice in order to define, capture, and eventually exhibit it in a *serious* "academic" setting. Despite all claims to the contrary, the "code" that this reader would seek to impose is methodological. The differences between my text and the "code" are thus not indicative of a failure or lack, but a difference in method.

I do not set out to follow only the course that the author may have in some sense intended the reader to follow. Such a practice is often simply a repetition in which a reader seeks to come to the aid of the author—or their imaginary version thereof—by covering their tracks (i.e., by trying to erase or perhaps explain away the fissures and gaps that can, and often do, confuse readers). This type of reader progresses too quickly through the very moment in the text that may disrupt their reading. For them the play becomes a film; the transitions are effectively lost in the blurring succession of moments. This mode of reading is, in and of itself, a sovereign act: a territory is set, defined, and mastered by a reader who claims the right to set the intended or actual meaning of the text in the name of the author. Adopting such a role while attempting a critique of the logic of sovereign power would be a performative contradiction. By taking a slow and indirect approach to the text, I am attempting to follow the characters and scenes that are missing—and yet, like pages missing from a play, their traces remain. Beckett evokes a similar practice while expressing his own frustration with attempting to write in formal English, in a letter he wrote in 1937 (in German): "More and more my language appears to me like a veil which one has to tear apart in order to get those things (or the nothingness) lying behind it.... To drill one hole after another into it until that which lurks behind, be it something or nothing, starts seeping through—I cannot imagine a higher goal for today's writer."[7]

My aim is not to draw them out and thereby somehow fill the text, but to question how these gaps, these missing pages, colour the very structure and logic of the play we believe we are looking at. Only by slowing down and attending to the precise details of the text do we begin to see the practical absurdity of the logical transitions. Nowhere is this truer than in the texts that set out to found the sovereign's right to kill. Following the logic that leads from the throne to the gallows is not an attempt to get beyond silence—to somehow *sound-it-out*—or even to tarry within it and thereby somehow *know* it, but rather, to attend to it. To do this is to take the stakes of the game of sovereign power seriously. This entails asking not only *what* is at stake (i.e., the boundaries, costs, interests, and claims involved), but *who*.

This is meant not to discourage the reader from taking the text seriously, but to encourage him or her to be aware of my approach and attentive both to the text at hand and to those I am working within. These texts—which range from the canonical to the apocryphal—all struggle, in their own manner, with the question of the foundations of law. Some do so by attempting to find the voice of God or Nature in ecstatic experience and then set it down in language in order to finally found *the* community. Others point towards the execution of a murderer as a manifestation of the law. Still, each offers a path to the law. Each offers a foundation for community. If a reader accepts this path as it is and follows without question, the law is set and determined and the possibility of dialogue is thus closed. My aim is to open the question of law within these texts by practising an ethics of reading, which opens up the possibility of dialogue. The course of this dialogue is not set. There are always many paths yet to be taken.

MAPS AND GUIDELINES

While the reader might very well choose to begin anywhere, there is a rationale behind the order I have selected. As I have stated above, the text is composed of a series of trails that break off from a shared point of dispersion. While I cannot tell you precisely where these trails end—or, for that matter, where *we* are left once they have been followed—I can provide a reader with their starting point. They begin with the same question: What are the limits of the law? As we have seen, this is not simply a straightforward jurisdictional question. To point towards a border and answer "here" is, perhaps, an answer, but it is by no means a solution. It requires that we ask a seemingly endless series of questions: Who can make law? Where do they derive this power from? Are the limits of the law the limits of community, and if so in what sense? Jurisdictional boundaries? Moral limits? Is there a limit to what can be made into a law? What occurs when this limit is breached? Does a law that goes beyond this limit still remain law? What is outside of the law—the sovereign, the outlaw, the scaffold or war? Is there community outside of the law?

This list is by no means exhaustive, but it serves to remind us of the labyrinthine nature of this problem. To simply abandon the reader at this point without some sense of orientation is, at the very least, irresponsible. In fact, doing so would confuse the very purpose of the text itself. My invitation to the reader is not a ticket to a carnival or circus. My intent is not to dazzle or confuse the reader with a display of semantic acrobatics. The structure and style of the text is not the expression of an aesthetic. The sudden movements of the text are not a theatrical display; rather, they are signs of a struggle with the "Ubu-esque" logic of the sovereign's "right to kill."

The reader might wonder why I selected these texts specifically. This is an interesting question, but its precise nature depends on the expectations of the reader. If readers expect an answer that would transform my selection of texts into a necessary line through or reconfiguration of the canon of political philosophy, they will once again be disappointed. A series of other texts, or even other selections from the texts that I do engage with, might have to be taken on with the same initial set of questions. I chose these texts and selections because they all struggle with the problem of the foundations of the law. I did not choose them because they are the only texts that do so, nor did I choose them because they are essential texts within the canon for this question. They are all important texts—indeed each is canonical within one or more lines of thinking—but they are not often juxtaposed. I chose them because I have encountered them and struggled with them, and because in each the stakes are absolute.

In each text or selection there is an attempt to find a way to get beyond the undecidable plurality of laws and ground *the* Law (i.e., *the* Law that would for once and for all close the site of the political—the open site of agonistic contestation—and found *the* Community). By following these attempts to found *the* Law—to collapse the distinction between laws and law, to make laws that would be immune to all contestation, immune to the question of justice—to the point at which they begin to unravel themselves in mysticism and silence, is to encounter a limit. This limit does not simply undo law. It does not unmask law to reveal the sovereign's "Ubu-esque" self-authorization, *"L'État, c'est moi."* As Derrida states in *Force of Law*:

> [L]aw is essentially *deconstructible*, whether because it is founded, that is to say constructed, upon interpretable and transformable textual strata (and that is the history of law, its possible and necessary transformation, sometimes its amelioration), or because its ultimate foundation is by definition unfounded. The fact that law is deconstructible is not bad news. One may even find in this the political chance of all historical progress.[8]

The fact that the disjunction between laws and law (i.e., between positive determinations of law and law as a concept) cannot be closed does not mean that the only choice is between the arbitrary will of the strongest and lawlessness. The unbridgeable interval is not "bad news." Rather, it means that law is fundamentally contestable; that law cannot be separated from the question of justice. It means that the foundations of law are *open*. Returning momentarily to *Force of Law*: "the operation that amounts to founding, inaugurating, justifying law, to making law, would consist of a *coup de force* of a performative and therefore interpretive violence that in itself is neither just nor unjust and that no justice and no earlier and previously founding law, no preexisting foundation, could, by definition, guarantee or contradict or invalidate."[9]

This is the silence that is "walled up in the violent structure of the founding act": the sovereign's authority is not *necessary*—it does not bridge the divide between law and justice—it is *subjective*.[10] Silence is its response to those who contest its foundations because it has no answer to offer them aside from the choice between the mythology and a death sentence. All that the sovereign can offer to the subject is summarized in the inscription the tomb of the Old Commandant in Kafka's "In the Penal Colony"; "Have faith and wait!"[11] Outside of that faith—the faith that, as Nancy notes, sets the limits of community as communion—the sovereign would have us believe there is only the silence of the scaffold and war. But does this silence leave the scaffold intact? Does it have more to offer? Is this silence the point at which we begin to touch on the politics of the political? A *community-of-those-without-community*? *Democracy-to-come*? The question is open.

The texts I am engaging with either draw out this silence (Nancy, Derrida, Benjamin, Kafka) or attempt to fill it (Augustine, Sade, Kant, Hegel). By bringing the latter set of texts into question, I am not attempting to simply indict them; rather, I engage with them because I believe they must be read with care. We, as readers, must remember that texts that we approach do not slumber innocently on their shelves. Their words, no matter how abstract and rarified, have lived consequences, and thus our duty as readers cannot be one-sided. We cannot blindly defend a text without bearing some responsibility for the acts it condones. Nor can we flatly condemn a text without bearing some responsibility for the words that it contains. Every act of interpretation is thus doubly responsible. This does not mean we should simply abandon a text or pronounce it dead; rather, it should serve as an impetus to read it with ever-greater care. The practice of this care cannot simply be extended to those aspects of the text that we admire or that bring us to wonder; it must bring us to those moments of the text that we find the most difficult to face.

Given this twofold duty, I owe the reader some basic guidelines to orient them. The text itself is organized into three sections, each with a set number of chapters. The first section has a single chapter, the second two, and the third three. What I need to do, at the very least, is to clearly connect the trails carved out in each chapter to the question they begin with. In order to do this I have written a short guide to each section below. In each I introduce the general parameters of the chapters, how they fit together as a section, and how they relate to the text as a whole. The progression of the sections themselves is also purposeful. I begin with the question of community as played out between Derrida and Nancy, because it is this exchange that gives shape to my own line of inquiry. For me this is the central path of the text. The sections that follow both branch off from it and return to it. The resistance of both writing and bodies—indeed the very concept of *resistance* as such—are constant themes for both Derrida and Nancy. But my exploration of them here is not an attempt to refine, clarify, survey, or expand their thoughts on these issues. My aim is to try to make use of their work in order to follow the question of law and community through the texts that I engage with.

Each chapter struggles with moments that we would often simply rather not see, from Sade's injunction to follow desire beyond all limits to the pale logic of execution drawn out by both Kant and Hegel. These moments are, in many ways, the most difficult moments to attend to, but it is precisely because they are unsettling that they demand our attention. There is a twofold ethical duty in reading these moments. On the one hand, they deal with the legitimation of the right to kill, and consequently as readers we face the ethical duty of seeking out the principles and arguments that ground this claim to legitimacy. It is not a duty to refine the argumentative machinery of the text, but to attempt to map its routes, no matter how convoluted and paradoxical. On the other hand, we have an ethical duty to the text: to present the arguments to the very best of our ability. These duties are inseparable. If we simply dismiss or omit these moments, we not only fail to read the text; we fail those condemned by it.

SECTION I

What is the relationship between law and community? On an elementary level the mere fact that law applies within a determined area implies something that might be loosely referred to as a "community." In this sense "community" would be the enclosure formed by the spatial limits of the law. But how are they related? Does one precede and therefore generate the other? Is there law before "community"? Can there be a "community" without law?

The answers hinge on what we mean when we say "community." The concept itself is ambiguous. Generally speaking, it is used to refer to a quality all members share. As such, it ranges in application from specific (i.e., a common location, ethnicity, language, culture, etc.) to universal (i.e., humanity, rationality, etc.) qualities. But even here we face the fact that these qualities themselves are contested, riven by divisions and a seemingly endless series of stakeholders. Do we take from this that law is, despite its claims to universality, merely local? Conversely, is law more than simply the determination of rules that apply within a bounded jurisdiction? Does it, in fact, imply a universal or universalizable community? Or, alternatively, is the relation between law and community irretrievably paradoxical? And, as such, is it locked in an antinomy or double bind that prevents it from being either absolutely determined or determinable?

We begin our inquiry with a lengthy and deeply nuanced exchange between Derrida and Nancy on the question of community and fraternity. In general terms, this exchange centres on the meaning of community. That is, is it simply a set of regional qualities (real or imagined) used to distinguish one group from another, or is it universal? Of course, neither Derrida nor Nancy sees this as a simple either/or problem. Rather, the question is whether the concept of community is inextricably complicit with exclusion and messianism, or whether it holds within it the possibility of something else entirely. For Derrida, the word "community" is too entangled in the logic of race and ethnicity (i.e., the *Blut und Boden* of the Third Reich) and Christian eschatology (i.e., the many-membered body). It is synonymous with closure and totality. This being so, Derrida turns to democracy or in his terms "*démocratie à venir.*" But Nancy's work charts a different course. He does not hesitate to use the word "community," or even "fraternity," but this does not mean he is simply ignoring the problems associated with these terms. Nancy openly acknowledges the risks of employing these terms. In fact, his strategy is to raise the stakes of this risk. This strategy brings Derrida to ask a series of questions: Does Nancy's "inoperative community" form a closed community (i.e., a "fraternity" in Derrida's terms) or does it resist closure? If community is, as Nancy suggests, "resistance itself," how does it resist the movement towards the absolute closure of the "common"?[12] And while Nancy does not necessarily respond to these questions directly (i.e., in response to Derrida's "x"), a dialogue can be traced between them through a series of their respective texts. Our aim here will be to attend to that dialogue.

This thinking of community, process, event, and democracy brings us to the question of political violence. It is in and through the enforcing of the boundaries of community (i.e., attempting to end the play of *différance* by force) that the stakes of the political are exposed. By pursuing this line of questioning, I will provide a reading of the relationship between violence, community, and democracy in both Nancy's and Derrida's work. This serves as the starting point for a series of related textual engagements that can be broadly divided (and I specify "broadly" precisely because they are neither entirely separate nor entirely the same) into the resistance of writing and the resistance of the body.

SECTION II

What is the relationship between law and writing? If we take it as a given that in order for law to be recognized as law it must be determined or determinable, then it requires some form of codification to disseminate it. This introduces an interesting problem: How does one guarantee that the law as written is *the law* as intended? How does one fix the intent or even the identity of the lawgiver? Is not the written law exposed immediately to the possibility of misinterpretation, fraud, and falsification?

This problem is what animates the texts that the following two chapters engage with. Each struggles, in its own manner, with the problem of reading and writing the law. While it might seem that the several authors are incommensurable—What could Saint Augustine have in common with the Marquis de Sade or Georges Bataille?—each of them struggles, in his own way, with the problem of writing and the question of law. Each discovers the origin of the law in a certain manner and from that point develops, refines, and systematizes a series of hermeneutic techniques.

In the *Confessions* Augustine attempts to suspend the very question of writing—and thus secure the context and meaning of the Law as the Word of God—by developing a systematic combination of religious experience (the paradoxical memory of what is forgotten in Book X) and messianism. Sade finds the Law of Nature in sensation and he seizes upon writing—in particular, the form of the novel—as a mechanism for organizing, for amplifying, and for disseminating this Law. The Sadean novelist is not an author; he is a translator. The text is arranged as a way of transmitting a charge. Connections are tested and rearranged in accordance with a system whose ultimate end is to transcribe the Law of Nature once and for all. While both the source of the law and the techniques used to decipher it are distinct, the ultimate end to each of these two authors is the same: both set out to overcome the problem of writing, and absolutely determine *the Law*.

Bataille's work charts a different course. While he is no stranger to the mysteries of gnostic texts, religious ecstasies, or the excesses of libertinage, the ends of his project are distinct from those of both Augustine and Sade. He does not seek to close the gap between the sign and the referent; rather, he attends to the consequences of this closure. No experience can serve to stabilize and ultimately determine the authorship, intent, context, or meaning of law. Bataille seizes upon this as a principle, and writes in an effort to communicate this inadequacy. To "communicate" it is not to somehow bridge the gap between the sign and the referent and secure absolute meaning; rather, "communication" in his terms is to communicate the inadequacy as inadequacy. For Bataille, the only truth is the impossibility of absolute truth. His understanding of temporality is thus centred on the moment. The "now" is not that of expectation but that outside of the possibility of messianic salvation. The struggle is thus not to await the coming of the messiah or of the perfect novel, but to *live the impossibility of meaning*.

The terrain that will be covered in the following two chapters is not easily traversed. The texts addressed are difficult, and the course taken through them is, at times, less than direct. As a result, much is being asked of the prospective reader. I want to take this opportunity to assure you that there is a purpose for this difficulty. My guiding aim is to practise what I have referred to as an *ethics of reading*. By this I do not mean to merely rename the fastidious care and discipline of the scholar. Rather, the aim is to attend to the fact that the text is not strictly contained within the covers of the book. Nowhere is this clearer than with the question of law. This being so, an ethics of reading simultaneously entails care for the text and for those whose fate the texts circumscribe—that is, those others who are placed outside the law, beyond the pale, whose bodies bear the mark of authorized violence. While the stakes may not be immediately apparent in the following two chapters, they do remain (always and already) in play.

SECTION III

What is at stake in questioning the limits of law? To answer this we must first address the ambiguity of the meaning of the term "stake." It can function as both a noun and a verb. In its verb form it is used to refer to marking out the boundary of either a territory or claim (i.e., to "stake out" or "stake off" land, title, shares, profit, credit, etc.), to fastening or securing something in a fixed position (i.e., to stake or put to the stake), and to risking or defining the limits of risk (i.e., to put one's reputation "at stake," to set or to increase the stakes). As a noun, it refers to a stick or pole used both to mark out boundaries and as a post to which a person is bound for execution.

Given this series of associations, asking what is "at stake" in questioning the limits of law is effectively relating (or even binding) two questions. First, what are the limits in the sense of a determinable boundary; and second, what, or more precisely who, is at risk in this determination? We cannot ask one without asking the other. This section sets out to expose the stakes of writing by turning our attention to the body. More specifically we will be following the course of the relationship between law and the death penalty in Kant and Hegel. Both see it as a foundational component of the law, as the necessary expression of an *a priori* demand, but one that must be carefully regulated. It resides on the fine edge between justice and vengeance. Therefore, for both Kant and Hegel the question of the death penalty is a question of measure. In order for there to be a "just" or "proper" execution it must apply to the right crime (i.e., the exchange of crime and punishment must be balanced) and it must not be excessively cruel (i.e., the suffering must not make the condemned into something abominable). But how can we establish a measure or value for death? Furthermore, what method or procedure of execution can be possibly accepted as "just"? Despite all of these issues, both Kant and Hegel affirm the *necessity* of the death penalty. It is a demand given by rationality itself. If the formula is followed, the execution becomes akin to a miracle: the most extreme act of violence becomes the very manifestation of justice.

Kafka and Benjamin (and, in many respects, Fichte) depart from this course by questioning this claim of *necessity*. Instead of finding the demand for the death penalty in the recesses of some metaphysical foundation, each sees it as the product of subjective judgment. That is, it is not rationality or fate that demands the death penalty, but merely those who call for it. The complex metaphysical framework is thus an elaborate play staged in order to wash the hands of those who would put another to the stake in the name of law. The miraculous conversion of violence into law becomes little but a shell game designed to make the sovereign appear *as if* he were crowned by necessity.

From this perspective the truth of the game is given in the design and operation of the apparatus in Kafka's fictional "Penal Colony." It is designed to fulfill the impossible measure of justice, but all it can really do is repeat the same sentences, leaving us to face the fact that there is no death without responsibility. It is neither fate nor necessity that spills the blood of the condemned.

Does this mean that lethal violence cannot occur within the law? And following from this, that there is no possibility of a legal exception to responsibility? If this is the case, how do we come to grips with the so-called mystical foundations of law?

Section I

AT THE ENDS(S) OF COMMUNITY

In common we have: burdens. Insupportable, immeasurable, unsharable burdens. The community does not secure itself against such disproportion; it has always left behind the mutual exchange from which it seems to come. It is the life of the nonreciprocal, of the inexchangable—of that which ruins exchange.
—Maurice Blanchot, *The Writing of the Disaster*

Chapter 1

"COMMUNITY, NUMBER," AND DEMOCRACY
An Excursus on the Politics of Fraternity

Community is, in a sense, resistance itself: namely, resistance to immanence.
—Jean-Luc Nancy, *The Inoperative Community*

I was wondering why the word "community" (avowable or unavowable, inoperative or not)—why I have never been able to write it, on my own initiative and in my name, as it were. Why? Whence my reticence?
—Jacques Derrida, *Politics of Friendship*

IN *POLITICS OF FRIENDSHIP* Jacques Derrida engages with a series of texts that correspond with the work of Georges Bataille. This series extends from Bataille to the work of Jean-Luc Nancy and Maurice Blanchot. With regard to the latter two, the specific texts most frequently referred to are Nancy's *The Inoperative Community* and Blanchot's *The Unavowable Community*, *The Writing of Disaster*, and *Friendship*. Derrida's relationship to these texts is complex, as he, at one and the same time, maintains a cautious distance while noting his own proximity to them. As he states in a footnote from Chapter 2, "these works are no doubt among those that count the most for me today."[1] He goes on to qualify his relationship to these texts within the same footnote, "There is still perhaps some brotherhood in Bataille, Blanchot and Nancy, and I wonder, in the innermost recess of my admiring friendship, if it does not deserve a little loosening up, and if it should still guide the thinking of the community, be it a community without community, or a brotherhood without brotherhood."[2]

His concern here is as puzzling as it is important. It is puzzling precisely because there is a distance here, but he is reticent to make this distance anything more than provisional (i.e., the function of the terms "perhaps" and "wonder"). In a parenthetical remark in the final chapter of the *Politics of Friendship*, he calls this intimate distance into question, "I was wondering why the word "community" (avowable or unavowable, inoperative or not)—why I have never been able to write it, on my own initiative and in my name, as it were. Why? Whence my reticence? And is it not fundamentally the essential part of the disquiet which inspires this book?"[3]

He situates his *reticence to write* the word "community" at the very heart of the text.[4] And yet, why this word? Why "community"? What is it about "community" [*commūnitās*] or the "common" [*commūnis*] that brings this sense of disquiet? As Derrida states, "affirmed, negated or neutralized, these 'communitarian' or 'communal' values always risk bringing the brother back."[5] Here the cause of his "disquiet" is named: "community"—as the desire for *belonging to* and *sharing in* that which is *common*—always comes with a risk of a return to the logic of fraternity (i.e., the logic of affiliation by blood, soil, and/or spirit). He is more explicit in *Rogues* where he directly connects community to his work on auto-immunity, "community as *auto-co-immunity* … the common of community having in common the same duty or charge [*munus*] as the immune."[6] Consequently, "community"—like friendship and fraternity—is placed within a kind of messianic constellation. It is one of many terms that give expression to the desire for an absolute *immunity* to all that is "other." Derrida continues:

> Perhaps this risk must be assumed in order to keep the question of the "who" from being politically enframed by the schema of being-common or being-in-common, even when it is neutralized, in a question of identity (individual, subjective, ethnic, national, state, etc.). The law of number and of the "more than one" which goes all through this book would not be any less crucial and ineluctable but it would, then, call for an altogether other language.[7]

A lot hinges on this "perhaps." On the one hand the value of putting "community" into question is recognized (and with it the work of the authors whom he refers to as both friends and as Nietzsche's sons), but this recognition is conditional.[8] Derrida seems to suggest that while we might have to critically engage with community we must ultimately abandon the name, because unlike democracy it cannot be separated from the history of autochthony, eugenics, myth and fraternity.[9] This leads us to two related lines of questioning:

1. First, with regard to Nietzsche's sons—those authors that attempt to take the concept of community to its limit—are they all simply sowing dragon's teeth? That is, despite all their intentions are they simply bringing the brother back in another guise? Is the "community of those without community" yet another fraternity? This is a difficult question to properly address, as it requires an exhaustive engagement with the entire series of authors from Nietzsche to

Bataille, Blanchot, and Nancy (not to mention Heidegger). Derrida takes this task on—at least in part—in *Politics of Friendship*, but the actual textual engagement is centred heavily on Nietzsche and Blanchot. There is much less direct engagement with Bataille, and virtually none with Nancy (this engagement is carried out, in part, in *Rogues* and more extensively in *On Touching—Jean-Luc Nancy*, but in each case the focus is on other texts).[10] And so we will set ourselves the more limited task of examining the relationship between Nancy's *The Inoperative Community* and Derrida's critique of the "community of those without community." Our aim here is not to act as a kind of forensic moderator who arrives late to the scene simply to make a final judgment or ruling in order to somehow close the case; it is rather to trace the boundaries that serve to both separate these texts and put them in communication with one another. This will hopefully enable us to reach a better understanding of this boundary and open up the possibility of unexplored points of communication.

2   Second, how does this movement from or through community occur? For Derrida, the short answer is that the *law of number*—"the abstract and potentially indifferent thought of number and equality" that marks democracy with an auto-deconstructive force—marks out a trajectory that goes beyond the limits of "community."[11] This trajectory takes us from the community (avowable or unavowable, inoperative or not) to the democracy-to-come. But, if this is the case, what is the difference between this account and that offered by Nancy? What is the relationship between democracy and community in Nancy? Does the "inoperative community" form a closed community (i.e., a "fraternity" in Derrida's terms) or does it resist closure? How does its trajectory begin or, for that matter, end? How does the law of number (the "more than one" or *plus d'un*) relate to the "inoperative community"? If community is, as Nancy suggests, "resistance itself" then how does it resist the movement towards the absolute closure of the "common"?[12] What is the historical logic or process of this resistance? If this logic is analogous to what Derrida will call *auto-immune*, that is, if Nancy's "inoperative community" parallels Derrida's characterization of community as *auto-co-immunity*, how are we to read Nancy's persistent use of "fraternity"—that is, his own resistance to Derrida's *call* "for an altogether other language"? This thinking of process, event, and democracy brings us to the question of political violence. It is in and through the enforcing of the boundaries of community (i.e., attempting to end the play of

différance by force) that the stakes of the political are exposed. By pursuing this line of questioning, we will provide a reading of the relationship between violence, community, and democracy in both Nancy's and Derrida's work.

By taking up these two lines and following them through the text, we will be tracing the contours of the boundaries that exist between Derrida's work on the democracy-to-come and the unworking [*désoeuvrement*] of community in Bataille, Blanchot, and Nancy. Our trajectory will begin with a brief outline of Derrida's reservations regarding the "community of those without community." From this basis we will turn our attention to Nancy's *The Inoperative Community*—making the occasional detour through Bataille and others when necessary—and the distinction between communion and community. The point of following this more limited or constrained line of questioning is not simply to survey a contested area and demarcate two distinct territories. Rather, it is to place the question of community (with all of its cruel and suicidal *risks*) in communication with that of democracy. By placing them in communication we will be able to begin to trace the relational arc—the arc formed by the tension between the question of community (what *being-in-common* means) and the desire for a final answer to this question—that inevitability draws community to its limit. And it is in this encounter with the limit—with the *im-possible*—in the singular urgency of *here and now* that community is exposed to the alterity of the *other* [*autrui*]. Here in this exposure we enter the question of the political, of the "*more than one*": what is to be done *now*? Perhaps the possible responses to this question (one that can never be done with or somehow finalized, as it always returns, always remains in play) can be pared down to two basic forms that, following Blanchot, we can summarize as "speech or death."[13] If we modify the terms of this alternative from "speech or death" to "democracy or community," are we faced with a repetition of the same problematic, or is there a difference we have yet to account for?

DERRIDA AND NIETZSCHE'S SONS

In order to provide an account of Derrida's engagement with the "community of those without community," we will follow his reading of Nietzsche—and "sons"—in *Politics of Friendship*. Our focus will be constrained to two related terms and their derivations. The first, *teleiopoesis*, addresses the messianic logic of Nietzsche's text. It traces the teleological call of his poetics, his use of allocution and the vocative case (i.e., addressing the "philosophers of the future," his "friends" as the "we" and "you" that are *not-yet*). This *call*—always suspended by the "perhaps"—carries with it the possibility of a limiting, a selecting, or to use a more theologically loaded term, an "electing" of those that are *yet-to-come*. According to Derrida it runs the risk of being a fraternal call, that is, of being *auto-teleiopoetic* (a call issued by and addressed to the *autos*, the self, and thus closing or sealing off the infinite possibility of the other). The second term takes the form of a logical contradiction: "X without X." This is simply a formalization of the logic expressed in a series of impossible sentences. From Bataille's "community of those without community," to Nancy's "inoperative community" and Blanchot's "unavowable community," each follows the other in a dizzying progression of predicates that cancel, suspend, or annul the word "community." As Derrida states, "they belong—but the word is not appropriate—they belong without belonging to the untimely time of Nietzsche."[14] Each is bound by the impossibility of the "X without X." Like Bataille, each responds to Nietzsche's untimely call: "Nietzsche is the only one to support me: he says *we*. If *community* doesn't exist, Mr. Nietzsche is a philosopher."[15]

By responding to this call to *being-in-common*, the *teleiopoetic* "we," each takes the thinking of community to its limits. This "thinking" that they hold in common is not a dispassionate academic exercise. There is an almost frantic urgency to this thinking of community. As Derrida notes, it is both a response to the question of community and a warning:

> Yes, these warnings turn endlessly. Yes, like searchlights without a coast, they sweep across the dark sky, shut down or disappear at regular intervals and harbour the invisible in their very light. We no longer even know against what dangers or abysses we are forewarned. We avoid one, only to be thrown into one of the others. We no longer even know whether these watchmen are guiding us towards another destination, nor even if a destination remains promised or determined.[16]

Here we begin to touch on his concern: Where is this thinking destined? Can the thought—and, like negative theology, this can never be reduced to a "thought" or contained within a process of "thinking" as it involves an encounter with or experience of the impossible—that disrupts the very meaning of "community" retain its name without losing itself? These two terms—*teleiopoesis* and "X without X"—form a kind of an axis within Derrida's text. They serve to maintain a distance from both Nietzsche's sons and the very word "community," but this distance cannot be read as an act of repudiation. Rather, like a distance between friends, it is intimate, troubled, apprehensive, and hesitant. These terms do not form an indictment; they articulate a concern, perhaps even a suspicion. Let us consider each term more extensively and explore the contours of this troubled proximity.

Derrida introduces teleiopoesis in the second chapter of *Politics of Friendship*. With this single word he refers to or formalizes an entire logic that runs through Nietzsche's text. As he states,

Teleiopoiós qualifies, in a great number of contexts and semantic orders, that which *renders* absolute, perfect, completed, accomplished, finished, that which *brings* to an end. But permit us to play too with the other *tele*, the one that speaks to distance and the far-removed, for what is indeed in question here is a poetics of distance at one remove, and of an absolute acceleration in the spanning of space by the very structure of the sentence (it begins at the end, it is initiated with the signature of the other). *Rendering, making, transforming, producing, creating*—this is what counts; but, given that this happens only in the auto-tele-affection of the said sentence, in so far that it implies or incorporates its reader, one would—precisely to be complete— have to speak of *auto-teleiopoetics*.[17]

Teleiopoetics operates on both time and space. It concerns that which is distant (*tele-*) and the end, fulfillment, or completion (*telos*). As it operates— at least in part—as a performative, its effect is dependent upon the presentation of a speaker that is situated within a "now." This "now" is not historical; it is exceptional, it is a time out of joint. It remains open within the text. Its distance is thus an intimate one in the sense that it can be crossed. Any reader who receives the message and responds may also enter the "now." It is, in short, a poetics of immanent displacement: it is said, issued, or addressed from a "now" that is, paradoxically, before its time. As such, it has much in common with the prophetic register; its structure is messianic, it is the speech of the forerunner or precursor, of the one who interrupts historical time—from a position both *within* and *outside*—by naming that which is not yet.[18] But, unlike prophetic speech, its source is not the absolute. Rather, it is signed, in advance, by those that it names: "We Europeans of the day after tomorrow."[19] Teleiopoetics incorporates the reader: "we are born, sworn, jealous friends of *solitude*, of our own deepest, most midnight, most midday solitude—such a type of man are we, we free spirits! and perhaps *you* too are something of the same type, you coming men? you *new* philosophers?"[20]

This short selection of Nietzsche's text exemplifies "what counts" about teleiopoesis: it circumscribes, marks out, and defines the place of those yet to come. It hails its readers—at an impossible distance—as friends, and more, they are related, bound by blood as *untimely* brothers. The hospitality of the text is thus narrow: only the few are welcome, only those with eyes to see and ears to hear may take their seats and share in this solitude. Are these friends of solitude—these brothers who are both here and yet to come— "democratic"? Nietzsche's text is openly hostile to both "democratic taste" and "modern ideas," but what is the target of this hostility? Is it democracy in general—as an idea or possibility—or is it what has been presented as democracy? Are these brothers iconoclasts preparing the way for the possibility of a democracy yet to come, or have they come to close that door? This question is—as Derrida notes—left "suspended" by the "perhaps."[21] The purpose of their affiliation is not yet clear. For now they are solitary watchmen awaiting the arrival of that which has already begun. The risk is that they are—in the end—a fraternal order, and thus closed off to the possibility of democracy.

As we have already noted the logical—or rather a-logical—formula "X without X" refers to a number of impossible syntagms that appear in the work of Bataille, Blanchot, and Nancy. The formula covers both the self-cancelling repetition (i.e., community without community, relation without relation, etc.) and the annulling predication of the subject (i.e., inoperative, unavowable, etc.). But what is the point of this tactical manoeuvre? What function or role does this "X without X" play? Is it an attempt to undermine, dislodge, or disrupt the apparent meaning of "community"? Is the intent to perform a kind of Heideggerian *Destruktion* of the concept of "community"? If so, can the repetition be the introduction of a kind of ontic-ontological distinction? Is this self-annihilating collision of subjects and predicates an attempt to find some way of referring to the ineffable, ecstatic experience of *being-in-common*? Of course, there is a danger in even attempting to answer these questions, as each is operating on the assumption that each of Nietzsche's "sons" is employing this tactic in the same way. At this point we can say that Derrida ascribes a commonality to these "untenable syntagms and arguments."[22] And so, we can begin to approach the general function—and it is a question of function and not meaning—of the "X without X" by relating it to teleiopoesis. As Derrida states, "Teleiopoesis makes the arrivants come—or rather, allows them to come—by withdrawing; it produces an event, sinking into the darkness of a friendship which is not yet."[23]

Teleiopoesis *makes the arrivants come*—they are "perhaps" marked off, prefigured, circumscribed—and by doing so it interrupts historical time. Its performative force—the *in-* or *con-*vocation of those friends, philosophers, and brothers that are not yet—both opens up and leaves open an untimely "now" within the text. This "now" welcomes in those who respond to the call, it welcomes the "friends of solitude" to partake in a singular community. Returning to Derrida: "At the end of the teleiopoetic sentence you, readers, may have already become, nevertheless, the cosignatories of the addresses addressed to you, providing, at least, that you have heard it, which you are invited to do to the best of your ability—which thus remains your absolutely and irreplaceably singular responsibility."[24]

If teleiopoesis is the general temporal logic of the address, "X without X" is the "now" that the "friends of solitude" share. The "X without X" remains—as the shared point of disaggregation—at the end of the teleiopoetic sentence. It is the shared place of waiting. The problem, according to Derrida, is that the arrivants are made or produced: it is both an *auto-teleiopoetics* and auto-tele-affection.[25] That is to say, it is a call addressed to and sent from the *autós* in an attempt to feel or get a sense of its *self*. This is the risk of the "X without X": the patrimony that Nietzsche leaves to his "sons." But this does not mean they accept this inheritance. Those who take up the call and give themselves over to the responsibility, and indeed the risk, of thinking through the meaning of community are not simply seeking a way out. As Derrida states, they are

> always emitting mad and impossible pleas, almost speechless warnings, words that consume themselves in a dark light, such as these typical and recurrent syntagms: "relation without relation," community without community ("the community of those without community"), "inoperative" community, "unavowable" communism or community, and all the "X without X" whose list is, by definition, endless, finite in its infinitude.[26]

These warnings paradoxically draw on the resources of signification in an attempt to direct us beyond its bounds. The danger is that "[s]uch a political history or philosophy would deck itself out in "realism" just in time to fall short of the thing—and to repeat, repeat, and repeat again, with neither consciousness nor memory of its compulsive droning."[27]

This loss of consciousness and memory is the risk associated with the "X without X." By setting signification against itself a void is exposed, but this void can also serve as the foundation of yet another closed or "fraternal" community. Derrida's concern is that Nietzsche's sons are—to borrow the imagery of Andrei Platonov—digging a "foundation pit." That is, the attempt to uncover or unwork the meaning of "community"—to dig down to the point at which the *common* is constitutively open—ends with the return of the fraternal order.

NANCY AND *LA COMMUNAUTÉ DÉSŒUVRÉE*

Nancy's *La Communauté désœuvrée* first appeared as an article in the 1983 spring issue of *Aléa*. It was written as an invited response to the topic "community, number," which was formulated by the editor Jean-Christophe Bailly. As Nancy notes, "It so happened that when Bailly suggested this topic, I was finishing a year-long course dedicated to Bataille considered from a political angle. I was researching, very precisely, the possibility of a hitherto unheard-of resource that would avoid fascism and communism as much as democratic or republican individualism."[28]

The context of the article is significant. It begins as a response to the relationship between community and the question of number—that is, it *begins* with the problem of number, the "more than one" or *plus d'un* that Derrida puts it to it in *Politics of Friendship*—but the approach that it takes to this relationship finds its starting point in Bataille. Nancy uses Bataille's work as the point of entry, and for good reason: there is a sense of urgency in Bataille's work, an exigency of community. He takes the question of community to its limits—most clearly in his pre-war writings—in an attempt to both disrupt the nostalgic call for community that animated the discourse of fascism and avoid the empty universalism of communism. Nancy thus set out to retrace the trajectory of Bataille's work in an effort to find the resources to respond to the exigency summarized in Bailly's expression "community, number." What he finds in Bataille's work during the course of the seminar leaves him dissatisfied: "Bataille had not made it possible for me to touch on a new and unprecedented politics. On the contrary, in many respects he had made political possibility as such even more remote."[29]

While this sense of dissatisfaction is palpable in *La Communauté désœuvrée*, Nancy does not simply abandon his search. He does not return to Bataille's text to simply collect, label, and catalogue its conceptual contents for posterity. Nor is he acting as some form of philosophical auditor moving through the text in order to flatly determine what is living and what is dead. Rather, Nancy reads Bataille by taking a step back within the text. The aim is to attend to the text, to follow its course with care, in an effort to catch a glimpse of unexplored paths or points from which the trajectory of the work might be reimagined otherwise. This practice is evident in both the initial article and the revised version that appeared in 1986 as the lead essay of a book bearing the same title. In the book Nancy extends his reading of Bataille in relation to Heidegger in two additional essays, "Myth Interrupted" and "Literary Communism." The English translation of the text was issued in 1991 and contains two further essays, "Shattered Love" and "Of Divine Places." The additional essays serve to highlight the transition in Nancy's work that leads from "community" to the more general (and Heideggerian) formulations of "being-together," "being-in-common," and "being-with."[30] While our primary focus will be on "The Inoperative Community" we will also touch on a series of corresponding texts in an effort to provide an outline of the trajectory of Nancy's work on "community."

Bailly's expression "community, number" provides us with a key point of reference for reading Nancy's essay. It highlights the conceptual tension that the essay sets out to explore. This tension characterizes the relationship between community and society (*Gemeinschaft* and *Gesellschaft*) and, as Nancy argues, the amphibology of the concept of community. The former tension serves as a kind of contextual backdrop for the text. In that, it is the division between community and society—or, to shift to the form of Bailly's expression, community/number—that signals the end or closure of what Nancy refers to generally as "(Western) philosophy's political programs," which, in his estimation, "ended up giving us only various programs for the realization of an *essence* of community."[31] As Nancy states,

The acute awareness, which is our own, of the closure of these programs governs the movement of this book. We often call this "the end of ideology," and we silently and insidiously add "the end of political options" in order to substitute the consensus of a single program that we call "democracy." And we fail to notice that this is how one loses sight of community as such, and of the political as the place of its exposition.[32]

Here we find that the experience or "acute awareness" of the division between community and society or, for that matter, community and democracy, provides a shared context. This "acute awareness" of the end—of both "ideology" and "political options"—is "our own."

This signals the transition to the latter tension (i.e., that which exists within the meaning of community). The meaning of the word "community" is divided between *communion* and *being-in-common*. The former is characterized by a mode of essentialism that defines community as the possession of a common being or substance. It is a logic of absolute immanence, which Nancy sees as exemplified in both the role of *Gemeinschaft* in Nazi ideology and the concept of *deus communis* in Christianity.[33] On the other hand the latter is characterized by the very impossibility of immanence. Like negative theology it expresses a common—or to use one of Nancy's key terms "shared"— relationship with the transcendence that is characterized by the absence of god (*deus absconditus*). Unlike negative theology there is no mysticism, no theology:

> The discourse of the "death of God" also misses the point that the "divine" is what it is (if it "is") only inasmuch as it is removed from immanence, or withdrawn from it—within it, one might say, yet withdrawn from it. And this, moreover, occurs in the very precise sense that it is not because there is a "divine" that its share would be subtracted from immanence, but on the contrary, it is only to the extent that immanence itself, here or there (but is it localizable? Is it not rather this that localizes, that spaces?), is subtracted from immanence that there can be something like the "divine."[34]

Here community is found in the *experience* of being-in-common or being-with. It is a community of shared separation—the "*with*" or "*in*"—and not common being. Nancy will employ a number of terms and expressions to convey this latter mode of community: from compearance (*comparution*), sharing (*partage*), spacing (*espacement*), the political (*le politique*) and unworking (*désoeuvrement*, a term he borrows from Blanchot) to complicated expressions such as "You (are/and/is) (entirely other than) I" ("*Toi [e(s)t] [tout autre que] moi*") and "You shares me" ("*Toi partage moi*").[35] This collection of terms and expressions disrupts the meaning of "community" by highlighting its syntax—that is, its arrangement, the rules that govern its shared separation or spacing. As Nancy states, "community is, in a sense, resistance itself: namely resistance to immanence."[36] This resistance can be read as Nancy's response to "community, number." Like syntax it sets the course of both modes of being-with (i.e., community and communion). Our aim will be to provide an outline for this "resistance" by providing the reader with a more thorough examination of the distinction between communion and community.

COMMUNION

In Nancy's work the term "communion" refers to a specific figuration of community. Figuration here can be understood both as a specific shape or figure (i.e., an idea of the "truth" or "essence" of the common) and as the practice of shaping or figuring the "common" with others over time (i.e., to *con*-figure). With regard to the former, "communion" is predicated on what Nancy will refer to as the philosophy of "absolute immanence."[37] Its logic is one of communal fusion and as such it understands the ontological separation implied in *being-in-common* or *being-with* as a temporary limitation to the "actual" or "true" "*essence* of community." This entails a specific way of framing or distributing historical time. The existent or present "community"—which is characterized by separation—is interpreted as a falling away from the "truth" of "community" (i.e., communion). As Nancy states,

> The lost, or broken, community can be exemplified in all kinds of ways, by all kinds of paradigms: the natural family, the Athenian city, the Roman Republic, the first Christian community, corporations, communes, or brotherhoods—always it is a matter of a lost age in which community was woven of tight, harmonious, and infrangible bonds and in which above all it played back to itself, through its institutions, its rituals, and its symbols, the representation, indeed the living offering, of its own immanent unity, intimacy, and autonomy.[38]

As a result "community" is positioned as both past and future: it is that-which-once-was and, with work, it is that-which-may-be-again. This positioning of the present as a time of loss structures affect in a particular manner. If we can say that the question of the "common" (or rather the fact that the "common" *is* in question) brings with it a feeling of unease or anxiety, then beginning with the *loss* of community effectively explains, orders, and thus orients this affect. The anxiety of the present becomes nostalgia, which in turn provides a motivational orientation or trajectory towards the promise of the future return of the "true" community. "Communion" is thus a movement, a trajectory, that aims towards the end. This "end" can go by a variety of names—for instance, the end of history or of man—but what is the nature of its labour? What does this movement work on? Returning to Nancy:

> A community presupposed as having to be one *of human beings* presupposes that it effect, or that it must effect, as such and integrally, its own essence, which is itself the accomplishment of the essence of humanness.... Consequently, economic ties, technological operations, and political fusion (into a *body* or under a *leader*) represent or rather present, expose, and realize this essence necessarily in themselves. Essence is set to work in them; through them, it becomes their own work. This is what we have called "totalitarianism," but it might be better named "immanentism," as long as we do not restrict the term to designating certain types of societies or regimes but rather see in it the general horizon of our time, encompassing both democracies and their fragile juridical parapets.[39]

The object of work is thus "man" and the process or action of work is "politics." The problem here lies in the *presupposition* that Nancy points out. As he puts it, "it is *man*, taken absolutely, considered as the immanent being par excellence, that constitutes the stumbling block to a thinking of community."[40] In effect, once the basic ontological precept of "communion" is accepted, the *question* of the "common" becomes the *promise* of "communion." Or, to rephrase, the question of the political—captured so clearly in Bailly's expression "community, number"—becomes the promise of politics.

How does this *presupposition* affect the trajectory of "communion"? This is a deceptively simple question. Referring to Beckett's *Waiting for Godot* we can find an example of the problematic. Act I of the play opens with a simple account of the setting: "A country road. A tree. Evening."[41] The road cuts across space in the single dimension of length. As neither its beginning nor its end are given, it is for all intents and purposes infinite. The tree provides a determinable point beside the road. Vladimir and Estragon do not move along the road, rather, they wait sleeping in the ditch near the tree. They are beside linear time, oriented to it, but not moving within it. There is no progress. A period of time is specified, in that we are informed that it is "evening." This specification belongs, at least in part, to the messianic register that recurs throughout the course of the play. It is late and the end approaches, but does not arrive. Act II reinforces this by effectively repeating it: "Next day. Same time. Same place."[42]

The logic of "communion"—taken to the point of its own undoing—is mirrored in this spatiotemporal structure. The trajectory of "communion" is presented as linear and, in a sense, it is. Time is divided up into past, present, and future, but the very idea of movement through time is tied to the progressive realization of the very thing that it *presupposes*. This *presupposition*—whether formulated as the essence of "man" or that of "community"—is set outside of time. It is both the origin and the destination. Thus, time is a space between two points that are, in fact, one and the same. It is, or at least it should be, a kind of self-cancelling interval or segment within a process of self-mediation.[43] And yet from within this interval, there is no way to measure progress and therefore no way to actually distinguish between moving and sitting still. The linear trajectory of "communion" is, like Beckett's "country road," an abstraction. It is removed from the actual experience of time. Vladimir and Estragon do not travel the road—they do not move forward or experience time as a quantifiable progression towards a goal—they wait beside it. Their experience of time is one of endless duration, and yet they remain beside the road.

"Communion" is held together by a combination of a "promise" and a "project." It founds itself—and in this it is both *auto-nomos* and *auto-telic*—by proclaiming the essence of "man," but this can only be done on the basis of its current absence. As Nancy states, "What this community has "lost"—the immanence and the intimacy of a communion—is lost only in the sense that such a "loss" is constitutive of 'community' itself."[44] This proclaimed "loss" is in fact an act of exclusion. He expands on this in his essay "*La Comparution*/The Compearance": "*Community excludes its own foundation*—because it wants to disbar *the concealing of the ground* which is its essence: the *in-*common, the between-us of the compearance."[45]

The foundation is excluded or disbarred—*actively forgotten*—because were it remembered, the proclamation of the "essence of man" would be just that, a *proclamation* and as such it would be open to contestation. As a result "communion" is driven forward to seek the final proof of its claim. It is driven towards *that-which-is-promised*. As the etymology of the term "promise" [*prō-mittere*], it must send forward or defer the return of this "lost" immanence. But the promise in and of itself is not sufficient; there must be movement towards the return. This is the "project" [*prō-jectum*] of "communion." The end of the "project" is thrown out, or rather, forward in advance of the "now." Its activity or work is presented as progressive, and is thus set alongside the dimension of the line. While this activity is generally expressed in a wide array of verbs—*to realize, to fulfill, to uncover*, et cetera—none of them capture its paradoxical quality.[46] This particular quality can be seen in Marx and Engels' claim that what the bourgeoisie *produces* "above all, is its own grave-diggers."[47] In a very similar manner "communion" *un*works itself. It is bound to do so by the very tenets of its logic.

This logic is exemplified in every element of "communion," from its foundational claim to its trajectory and the very mode of its movement. As Nancy states, this logic is that "of being as ab-solute, as perfectly detached, distinct, and closed: being without relation."[48] The problem with this logic is that it contradicts itself. Returning to Nancy: "A simple and redoubtable logic will always imply that within its very separation the absolute encloses, if we can say this, more than what is simply separated."[49]

In a certain sense, this "simple and redoubtable logic" is reflected in the idiomatic phrase "to bite off more than one can chew." The generally accepted meaning of this phrase is precautionary. This precaution applies both to the economic relationship between ends and means and to desire. This being so, it can be divided into two related precautions:

1 One should not take on more than one is able to do.
2 One should restrain one's desire in relation to one's means.

The logic of the absolute transgresses this precaution. It attempts to enclose everything within itself, but in so doing there is (always already) a remainder that it cannot account for. Says Nancy:

> the closure must not only close around a territory (while still remaining exposed, at its outer edge, to another territory, with which it thereby communicates), but also, in order to complete the absoluteness of its separation, around the enclosure itself. The absolute must be the absolute of its own absoluteness, or not be at all. In other words: to be absolutely alone, it is not enough to be so; I must also be alone being alone—and this is of course contradictory. The logic of the absolute violates the absolute. It implicates it in a relation that it refuses and precludes by its essence. This relation tears and forces open, from within and from without at the same time, and from an outside that is nothing other than the rejection of an impossible interiority, the "without relation" from which the absolute would constitute itself.[50]

This "implication" of a relation *with* the more, the extra, or remainder (Derrida's *plus'd une* or Bailly's "community, number") is inescapable. Each attempt to conceal, expel, disbar, or in some way expunge this implication simply *un*works itself.

In this respect it echoes the futility of the murder. Understood as a logistical or technical problem, killing is quite simple. There is no shortage of means that one may use to end the life of another. The real problem of murder lies in evading responsibility. Does this act *annihilate* the other or does it in fact multiply, or more precisely *multi-ply*, them?[51] That is, does it *increase* the "implication"? On this point Nancy and Levinas coincide. Consider this passage from *Totality and Infinity*: "The movement of annihilation in murder is therefore a purely relative annihilation, a passage to the limit of a negation attempted within the world. In fact it leads us towards an order of which we can say nothing, not even being, antithesis of the impossible nothingness."[52] Nancy briefly touches on this subject in *Corpus*: "Anyone who murders a body, relentlessly attacking the obvious, cannot know, or wishes not to know, that he only renders the 'subject'—this *hoc*—more clear, more unmercifully clear with each blow."[53]

The act of murder simply repeats and multiplies the resistance of the other.[54] It is the combination of this multiplication of the other—the innumerable traces of evidence both real and imagined—and the call to responsibility that set the itinerary of the murderer. The fear of being discovered and punished brings the murderer to become a fugitive. This *multiplication* also applies to the very logic of "communion." Derrida expands on the connection between the absolute (One) and murder in *Archive Fever*:

> As soon as there is the One, there is murder, wounding, traumatism. *L'Un se garde de l'autre*. The One guards against/keeps some of the other. It protects *itself* from the other, but, in the movement of this jealous violence, it comprises in itself, thus guarding it, the self-otherness or self-difference (the difference within oneself) which makes it One. The "One differing, deferring from itself." The One as the Other. At once, at the same time, but in a same time that is out of joint, the One forgets to remember itself to itself, it keeps and erases the archive of this injustice that it is. Of this violence that it does. *L'Un se fait violence*. The One makes itself violence. It violates and does violence to itself but it also institutes itself as violence. It becomes what it is, the very violence—that it does to itself. Self-determination as violence. *L'Un se garde de l'autre pour se faire violence* (*because* it makes itself violence and *so as* to make itself violence).[55]

As Nancy holds in *Being Singular Plural* this desire to somehow "fix the origin, or *to give the origin to itself*, once and for all, and in one place for all … is a desire for murder."[56] And yet, it is a desire that no particular act of murder could fulfill. As Nancy puts it, it is a desire

> not only [for] murder but also for an increase of cruelty and horror, which is like the tendency toward the intensification of murder, carving up, relentlessness, meticulous execution, the joy of agony. Or it is the massacre, the mass grave, massive and technological execution, the bookkeeping of the camps. It is always a matter of expediting the transformation of the other into the Other or making the Other appear in the place of the other, and, therefore, a matter of identifying the Other and the origin itself.[57]

It is an impossible desire (i.e., the desire for "communion") whose very impossibility drives it to the point of madness. By attempting to annul the other—and taking this annulling on as its *work*—"communion" simply draws attention to what it is driven to forget—namely, that its *promise*, that which it seeks to realize or achieve, is not *given to it* but rather self-proclaimed. And, as such, it is responsible—both as a collectivity and as individuals—for each and every action that it undertook to realize this *absolute end*. The cohesion of "communion" is the cohesion of a conspiracy: its work is to evade its implication *to-* or *with-* others, but this evasion simply multiplies the implication. As Nancy points out:

> This is why political or collective enterprises dominated by a will to absolute immanence have as their truth the truth of death. Immanence, communal fusion, contains no other logic than that of the suicide of the community that is governed by it. Thus the logic of Nazi Germany was not only that of the extermination of the other, of the subhuman deemed exterior to the communion of blood and soil, but also effectively, the logic of sacrifice aimed at all of those in the "Aryan" community who did not satisfy the criteria of *pure* immanence, so much so that—it being obviously impossible to set a limit on such criteria—the suicide of the German nation itself might have represented a plausible extrapolation of the process: moreover, it would not be false to say that this really took place, with regard to certain aspects of the spiritual reality of this nation.[58]

At the end of the grand projects of "communion"—with all of their promises of fusion and absolution—there is the sudden realization that the "implication" that it sought to evade has marked it from the beginning. In this its perceived *progress to* the absolute becomes a *flight from* responsibility. Each step away that it has taken has served to do nothing but multiply its ultimate implication *to-* and *with-* the other. This implication becomes the persecution that, "tears and forces open, from within and from without at the same time."[59] This is why and how "communion" *un*works itself. But what does it leave behind?

COMMUNITY

In the preface to *The Inoperative Community*, Nancy retrospectively puts forward a provisional guiding principle for his analysis of community:

> community does not consist in the transcendence (nor in the transcendental) of a being supposedly immanent to community. It consists on the contrary in the immanence of a "transcendence"—that of finite existence as such, which is to say, of its "exposition." Exposition, precisely, is not a "being" that one can "sup-pose" (like a sub-stance) to be in community. Community is presuppositionless: this is why it is haunted by such ambiguous ideas as foundation and sovereignty, which are at once ideas of what would be completely suppositionless and ideas of what would always be presupposed. But community cannot be presupposed. It is only exposed.[60]

Here we find that "community" is the inverse of "communion." Whereas the latter is, as we have seen, characterized by the "transcendence of a being" that *is*—or rather, is *always already* in the process of becoming—"immanent to community." The former is the immanence of a "transcendence." We must pause at this point and carefully consider this principle. At first glance it might easily be mistaken for a reference to apophatic experience, and thus be read as an expression borrowed from the tradition of negative theology. And yet, by simultaneously suspending "transcendence" in quotation marks and using the indefinite article ("*un*") in place of the definite ("*le*"), Nancy introduces a distance in the text that effectively staves off this interpretation. This use of punctuation *sets off* "transcendence" within the sentence thereby marking it as both separate from the text and open to qualification. The qualification immediately follows the dash: the "transcendence" that Nancy is referring to in this case is that of "finite existence." Thus, qualified "transcendence" becomes synonymous with "exposition." This implies that unlike "communion," that which *goes beyond* or *exceeds* the limit of the present is *not* a common being or substance (i.e., it is not an absence that can be filled). Community is, as Nancy says, *presuppositionless*. There is no transcendent "substance" or "essence" that could serve as a navigation point to orient us beyond the confines of the now. As such, community does not exist within the linear time of the second coming. It does not travel the road. Rather, like Vladimir and Estragon, it remains waiting beside it. As Nancy states: "community, far from being what society has crushed or lost, is *what happens to us*—question, waiting, event, imperative—*in the wake of* society."[61]

It is *what happens to us*—what we "share"—in the *hic et nunc*. In *A Finite Thinking*, Nancy—in a clear reference to the temporal structure of "communion"—explicitly spells out the ethical consequences of this: "Since the here-and-now *is* finitude, the inappropriability of sense, every appropriation of the "here" by an "elsewhere," and of the "now" by an "afterward" (or by a "beforehand") is and does *evil*."[62] As a result, any "promise" that would bring us to see the "now" as the interim and the "here" as a "country road" is an act of expropriation, or rather, theft. And this theft deprives us—or "alienates," to use the term that Nancy both borrows from Marx and rethinks—of the space-time of the here-and-now.[63] It attempts to set time to the "logic of process and procedure," that is, to make time into work or, to use a term from Bataille's lexicon, "project."[64] Within this process community is—and can only be—*exposed as resistance*. But what does this mean?

Nancy readily admits that this is "not easy to think."[65] There is simply no easy or ready-made answer. Nancy's entire oeuvre can be read as an attempt to develop or expand upon this exact point. So how are we to approach this thinking of community? One possible solution would be to list the various terms and expressions that he uses to give sense to community and define them. While this might provide a degree of philosophical clarity, on its own it is simply an abstract exercise. It runs the risk of making a difficult text even more so. Since Nancy approaches community as *what happens to us*, we will attempt to follow his thinking by referring to a common or shared experience that can flesh out the text for the reader. We will begin with death.

According to Nancy, "community is revealed in the death of others."[66] The debt to Heidegger's *being-for* or *being-toward-death* is explicit, but there is a significant shift in focus. As Nancy puts it: "when it came to the question of community as such, the same Heidegger also went astray with his vision of a people and a destiny conceived at least in part as a subject, which proves no doubt that Dasein's 'being-toward-death' was never radically implicated in its being-with—in *Mitsein*—and that it is this implication that remains to be thought."[67]

It is not only the case that death is only "Dasein's ownmost possibility," nor is it that case that the only collective relation with death is evasion via the "tranquilization" that the "they" provides.[68] All of the functions that Heidegger assigns to the "they" (i.e., to "tranquilize," to "evade," to "console," etc.) are attempts to make the death of others work or at least to minimize its capacity to interrupt work. As he puts it, "the dying of Others is seen often enough as a social inconvenience, if not even a downright tactlessness, against which the public has to be guarded."[69] While this conservative reaction is no doubt possible (or perhaps even the most prevalent collective comportment towards the death of others), it is not the only one. According to Nancy, "community is calibrated on death as on that of which it is precisely impossible to *make a work*."[70] Here what is shared is not the work of "consoling," "evading," and "concealing" death, but the very impossibility of any consolation. Returning to Nancy: "Community occurs in order to acknowledge this impossibility, or more exactly—for there is neither function nor finality here—the impossibility of making a work out of death is inscribed and acknowledged as 'community.'"[71]

Death is not a communion. In its wake there is no fusion of "*egos* into an *Ego* or a higher *We*."[72] Contrary to the consoling refrain of public sacrifice (a "consolation" related to the one offered by Heidegger's "they"), the other does not die for something. This is the lie that builds monuments. These architectural objects are built in an anxious attempt to somehow reclaim death as a "sacrifice." The collection of statues and plaques that serve to mark the "sacrifice" of others only serve to efface their singularity, as the names written on them become little more than a statistical index of what once was. In this way the monument's promise of commemoration is much the same as the obliteration offered by mass graves. Both are failed attempts to conceal the impossibility of death. Quite simply, no "work" or "cause" is moved forward—via remembrance or forgetting—by death. As Nancy states,

> If community is revealed in the death of others it is because death itself is the true community of *I*'s that are not *egos*. It is not a communion that fuses the *egos* into an *Ego* or a higher *We*. It is the community of *others*. The genuine

community of mortal beings, or death as community, establishes their impossible communion. Community therefore occupies a singular place: it assumes the impossibility of community.[73]

This formulation is openly paradoxical: community *assumes* the impossibility of community. What can this mean? How can community *assume*—that is, to take up the obligation of or take over the responsibility for—its own impossibility?

In order to begin to answer this question, even in part, we will have to follow Nancy's reading of Bataille a bit more directly. After all, for Nancy it is Bataille who "has gone farthest into the crucial experience of the modern destiny of community."[74] His project confronts the nostalgia for a lost community by pushing its logic to the point of excess. While the basic logic of "communion" is one of displacement (i.e., negating the *here and now* via the promise of a *there and then*), it also requires a set of interim practices that enable it to maintain its internal cohesion. Bataille refers to this set of practices as "ascesis," "That an anaemic, taciturn particle of life, showing reluctance before the excesses of joy, *lacking freedom*, should attain—or should claim to attain—the extreme limit, is an illusion. One attains the extreme limit in the fullness of means: it demands fulfilled beings, ignoring no audacity. My principle against ascesis is that the extreme limit is accessible through excess, not through want."[75]

This is not simply a reversal of ascetic logic (i.e., from deprivation to excess). It raises the stakes of the game by playing the partial or limited mode of ascetic logic against its foundational principle (i.e., sacrifice). Returning to Bataille: "If ascesis is a sacrifice, it is only so *in a part* of itself which one loses with an eye to saving the other. But one should desire to lose oneself completely."[76]

By pushing sacrifice to the point of excess, Bataille forces a return to the *hic et nunc* without reserve. He terms this exposure "*l'expérience intérieure*" ("inner experience"). According to Nancy, the "content, truth, or ultimate lesson" of "inner experience" is articulated in the final sentence of the third volume of Bataille's *The Accursed Share*: "*la souveraineté n'est RIEN*" ("Sovereignty is NOTHING")."[77] Nancy unpacks this at length:

> "In" the "NOTHING" or in nothing—in sovereignty—being is "*outside itself*"; it is in an exteriority that is impossible to recapture, or perhaps we should say that it is *of* this exteriority, that it is of an outside that it cannot relate to *itself*, but with which it entertains an essential and incommensurable relation. This relation prescribes the place of the singular being. This is why the "inner experience" of which Bataille speaks is in no way "interior" or "subjective," but is indissociable from the experience of this relation to an incommensurable outside. Only community furnishes this relation its spacing, its rhythm.[78]

By shifting the stakes of sacrifice—from the part to the whole—Bataille effectively calls the bluff of "communion." Once everything is put on the line, there can be no more evasion or, as Bataille puts it, "putting off of existence to a later point."[79] This strategy is not without risk. It can be mistaken for yet another variation of theology *Via Negativa* (this was after all Sartre's position on Bataille). But, unlike negative theology, there is no reserve, no promise, and no eschatology. There is only the "sovereign" (i.e., unlimited) exposure to "NOTHING" (i.e., no "the" substance or essence). This is in no way a private experience: as Nancy reminds us "inner experience" is neither "interior" nor "subjective." Bataille is also emphatic on this point:

> Blanchot asked me: why not pursue my inner experience as if I were the *last man*? In a certain sense.... However, I know myself to be the reflection of the multitude and the sum of its anguish. On the other hand, if I were the last man, the anguish would be the most insane imaginable! I could in no way escape, I would remain before infinite annihilation thrown back into myself or yet still: empty, indifferent. But inner experience is conquest and as such *for others ... it is consciousness of others*.[80]

And in this *consciousness* the "subject" is thrown outside of itself ("it is laughable, in its own eyes laughable"), "making itself consciousness of others and, as the ancient chorus, the witness, the popularizer of drama, it loses itself in human communication; as subject it is thrown outside of itself, beyond itself; it ruins itself in an undefined throng of possible existences."[81] At this point there is a distinct rupture between Bataille's work and Nancy. As a result, we need to momentarily pause and reconsider Bataille's qualification of communication as being "human" communication.

Nancy takes issue with Bataille's claim that "inner experience" is "human" communication:

> Community means, consequently, that there is no singular being without another singular being, and that there is therefore what might be called in a rather in appropriate idiom, an originary or ontological "sociality" that in its principle extends far beyond the simple theme of man as a social being (the *zoon politikon* is secondary to this community). For on the one hand, it is not obvious that the community of singularities is limited to "man" and excludes, for example, the "animal."[82]

The approach that Nancy takes to Bataille on this point in many ways mirrors Heidegger's response to Sartre's *Existentialism Is a Humanism*. And, like that response, the question of humanism is symptomatic of a more general problem, namely, the status of "subjectivity." According to Nancy there is a paradoxical limitation within Bataille's thought: he is "magnetically" drawn to a thinking of community, but the path that he takes is governed by the sovereignty of a "subject."[83] Nancy is not suggesting that this paradox goes unnoticed by Bataille. There is a kind of tortured and repeated tension between "inner experience" as being *passive* and *for others* and it being a kind of auto-affection via the other as the instrument or medium of self-knowing. It is this latter possibility that leads Bataille to the spectacle of human sacrifice and the secret society known as *Acéphale*. Consider this selection from the notes appended to *Inner Experience*:

> the only true sacrifice is human sacrifice. For the victim, whom the sacrificial knife puts into death's power, is there for me. In him, I was able to perceive myself destroyed by the rage to destroy, or, at least, when I was afraid to look too closely, I felt myself to be in solidarity with the existence which fell before me into Nothingness. If I myself were dead, if I myself had been destroyed, my anguish would not have gone further than the knife. I would not have been able to recognize myself open to the winds of the outside since all knowledge would be dissolved in me as soon as my heart would have ceased to beat. In order that in me this existence given to men cease to be unprofitably closed and communicate, it was necessary that another die before me. And not only before me but before others in all things similar to me and, like me, adherents through anguish to the annihilation which takes place, and yet, like me, protected from a blow savagely directed towards the victim.[84]

While it might be said that death is also at the centre of this community, the difference between Nancy's *Inoperative Community* and this particular version of Bataille are significant. Here the other is presented as the medium through which the "I"—and the others that are "similar"—are both bound (i.e., in a shared "anguish") and, in some sense, released. A form of "community" is found in and through the death of the sacrificial victim. They experience the fear of death at a safe distance, and as a result they are able to engage in the fantasy of self-annihilation (the resonance with Kant's analytic of the sublime is striking). Unlike Nancy's elliptical thinking of community as being-together or being-with, there is a distinct circularity here. In this example the self goes to the limit via the other in order to know the limit and to return to itself with this knowledge. It is ironically similar to the kind of spiritual profiteering that Bataille finds in the preface to Hegel's *Phenomenology*. While Bataille doubtlessly indulged in the temptations of fraternity (i.e., the closed community), he also hesitated (consider for instance his reading of Gilles de Rais or the Marquis de Sade). Returning to the notes from *Inner Experience*:

> This text is not finished: what should have emerged from what follows is that the necessity of sacrifice should not be understood in a literal sense [*Crossed out:* it is a question of the mystical complicity with the death of one's fellow being and not of really renewing the savage practice. Cruelty and anguish

are married in this way] but as the expression of the nature of things which more ancient men found in their rites. It is a question of complicity with death and only *that which is* revealing itself in anguish to the mind, not of acts to accomplish.[85]

While this shift from the actual practice of sacrifice to the figurative reenactment of it within the mind remains deeply problematic (i.e., the act itself is displaced, but—again in a move echoing Kant's third critique—the subject remains in place as a spectator able to spiritually profit from the thought of terror and sacrifice), it does serve to indicate the tension on this point in Bataille's work.[86]

Now, returning to our question, for community to *assume* its own impossibility it must bring itself to the point of this impossibility. That is, it must expose itself to an outside that is not absolutely determinable. This exposure is not the setting of a final boundary or limit to community that could in some way form a *hortus conclusus*. This exposure—or, to use another Nancean term, "exposition"—cannot be set as boundary that is, or can ever be, a "there" in opposition to a "here." Nor can it be seen as the ultimate fusion of self and other in *parousia*. As a result, community is neither limited nor absolute.[87] What is held in "common" cannot be circumscribed as either transcendent (i.e., the absent presence of the absolute) or ontological (i.e., a "common" being that would be strictly determinable within time and space). The thinking of community is a neither negative theology or an ontology.[88] Rather, for Nancy community is a spacing (*espacement*) that does not establish a determinate or determinable distance. There is no final place or locus—no ultimate gathering point—only the shared (*partage*) separation of finitude. This is not to say that there are no *determination*s—such a refusal would doubtlessly confine this thinking to the very negative theology that it so explicitly refuses—but, to borrow a Nancean formulation, there is no "the" determination. That is, there is no final or complete determination that would enable this "exposition" to be circular (i.e., for it to be auto-affective). There are determinations—or "figurations"—but there is no return of sense to the self as itself. This being so, there is no "communion" of *being* with *essence*—or rather, essence does not touch itself though being—rather, there is "communication"—not in the sense of the exchange of information, but as the co-appearing (*com-paraît*) of finitude.

At this point we begin to approach the paradox expressed in formulations such as the "community of those without community"; finitude *co-appears* (*com-paraît*), it *shares* (*partage*), *spaces* (*espacement*), and is *exposed*. Even taken at face value, it is clear that the terms listed suggest surfaces, limits, or boundaries that are in contact. In this they do not meld or fuse into a single undifferentiated mass; rather, by touching, they communicate a shared distance. There is in this way a distinct ontological dimension to it; but, as we noted above, it is not an ontology, or rather it is not a closed ontology. That is, it is not the kind of ontology that would enable one to determine or completely fix—or dialectically sublate—the meaning of finitude and thus close it off from the transcendent. Rather, as for Heidegger, the aim is to think the difference between being and existence (Heidegger's "ontic-ontological difference"). But Nancy's thinking is far from a simple repetition. He traverses the course set by Heidegger from a very different angle. We can find a prime example of this difference in his essay "Originary Ethics":

> "Originary ethics" is a more appropriate name for "fundamental ontology." Ethics *is* what is fundamental about ontology. Nonetheless, we cannot simply substitute one name for the other without losing sight of the following essential point: ethos isn't external to or superimposed upon being; it is not added to it, does not happen to it, does not give it rules that come from elsewhere. Rather, being *is*—because it is in no sense a being—what ek-sists beings, what ex-poses them to making sense.[89]

In the move from "fundamental ontology" to "originary ethics," Nancy does not simply attempt to clarify what Heidegger was in some way doing all along. The very initial position of the thinking that addresses the "meaning of being" is shifted.

For Nancy—unlike Heidegger—this thinking does not begin from the position of a there-being (*Dasein*) in the singular. Instead Nancy will hold that there is no there-being—no *spacing*—without being-with or being-together.[90] As Nancy states in his essay *Elliptical Sense*,

> In these circumstances, the opposition or complementarity between the transcendental (as the withdrawal of the origin) and the ontological (as the resource at the origin) loses all pertinence. What becomes necessary is another kind of ontology altogether, or else a completely different transcendental; or, perhaps, nothing of the sort, but an ellipsis of the two. Neither the retirement of being nor its givenness, but presence itself, being itself *qua* being, exposed as a trace or as a tracing, withdrawing presence, but retracing this withdrawal, presenting the withdrawal as what it most properly is: the nonpresentable.[91]

Nancy's thinking of community is neither ontological nor transcendental, rather, it attempts to hold itself at the their shared limit. Finitude *co-appears* and in this appearance it neither solidifies nor vanishes. The ellipsis—understood as "the other in the return to the self"—is not a temporary or supplemental placeholder for the circle (or for that matter the Hegelian "circle of circles").[92] In co-appearance—as the *being-with* of community—what appears is not a common substance that could finally close the circuit and allow the subject to know *itself-as-it-is-in-itself* through another. There is rather a touching: "A singular being appears, as finitude itself: at the end (or at the beginning) with the contact of the skin (or the heart) of another singular being, at the confines of the same singularity that is, as such, always *other*, always shared, always exposed."[93]

Through this contact—or, to use a term Nancy borrows from Bataille, communication—the limit is both delimited (i.e., there is no fusion of the self and other) and unlimited (i.e., this distinction cannot be absolutely determined as either internal or external). Returning to Nancy: "What is exposed in compearance is the following, and we must learn to read it in all its possible combinations: 'you (are/and/is) (entirely other than) I' (*'toi [e(s)t] [tout autre que] moi'*). Or again, more simply: you shares me (*'toi partage moi'*)."[94]

What *is* communicated? This is an already deceptive formulation. Both the interrogative pronoun ("what") and the copula ("is") suggest the presence of an "x," a particular thing or being that might close the circuit of the sentence with the response "x is x" or "x is y," et cetera. And yet, this expectation is precisely what is disrupted. What is touched upon at this point is not (and for that matter is never) what is expected. What is touched on here, at the limit, is that there is no "x"—at least not in such a way that one could seize hold of or grasp and by doing so somehow know it and thereby know oneself (*gnōthi seauton*). This is, after all, the auto-affective desire that drives the "what is x" of "first philosophy." What is communicated—what is contacted (*contāctus*) or touched—is the impossibility of grasping. And yet it is not nothing, not simply thin air; it is rather a *resistance*. That is, this touching does not enable one to establish a boundary or limit that would in some way contain or seal off the other. To touch is always already to be touched; it is an auto-hetero-affect that "tears and forces open, from within and from without at the same time."[95] As Nancy states, "The relation (community) is, if it *is*, nothing other than what it undoes, in its very principle—and at its closure or on its limit—the autarchy of absolute immanence."[96]

This movement—of communication, of touching—does not complete a circuit. It is a going out from the self that does not return as the same (an ellipsis of sense). What is "common" or "shared" is this exposure or exposition at the limit. It is the exposure of the impossibility of a common substance or essence and thus of a circle (i.e., the *solipsis* or *ouroboros*). Returning to Nancy:

> We cannot not compear. Only the fascist masses tend to annihilate community in the delirium of an incarnated communion. Symmetrically, the concentration camp—and the extermination camp, the camp of exterminating concentration—is in essence the will to destroy community. But in even the camp itself, undoubtedly, community never entirely ceases to resist this will. Community is, in a sense, resistance itself: namely, resistance to immanence.

Consequently, community is transcendence: but "transcendence," which no longer has any "sacred" meaning, signifying precisely a resistance to immanence (resistance to the communion of everyone or to the exclusive passion of one or several: to all the forms and all the violences of subjectivity).[97]

This does not mean that once communication has taken place community is somehow secure or established. There is no community without risk, no exposure without the possibility of a turning away. The self can attempt to deny the limit. It can cast its gaze beyond the "now" and orient itself to a point that exists beyond all limits. It can, if it chooses, wait alongside the "country road," but what it cannot do is escape *being-with* (it cannot *not* compear). Even if it sets itself to work against this *touch* and against the *other* by moving to *blows*, *torture*, and *death*, it simply exposes itself at the limit that was there all along.

Left at this point, it might seem that "community"—and its extended constellation of concepts and syntagms—is dependent upon a kind of "philosophy of presence"—that is, that "communication" and the "community of those without community" requires the sensible physical *presence* of others *hic et nunc*. As a consequence, such a community would see writing as a temporary or supplemental mode of communication. But this is not the case. Compearance cannot be reduced to "appearance" or "phenomena" (as such a reduction would return us to the onto-theology of a common substance or essence).[98] On the contrary, Nancy states that compearance (as "the experience of community as communication") "implies writing."[99] In fact, for Nancy, community compears in "literary communication": "'literature' does not designate here what this word ordinarily indicates. What is in fact involved is the following: that there is an *inscription* of the communitarian exposition, and that this exposition, as such, can *only* be inscribed, or can be offered only by way of an inscription."[100]

Writing is a response to the experience of being-in-common. It *figures* or bears the role of *figuration*, that is, it is an activity that attempts to give expression to the impossibility of *being-in-common*. This does not mean that "writing" is somehow without *risk*. Writing can be used to exclude another, but in order to exclude it must designate, name, and identify.[101] These figures—whether those of "hate speech" or less direct forms of colonial romanticism and its various *bon(s) sauvage(s)*—set out to figure the distances and boundaries that would establish a *cordon sanitaire*. But it is a project that they can never be done with. Each *figure* threatens to breach the line and contaminate the enclosure. The apparent solidity of these figures—the very solidity that simultaneously justifies their exclusion from "humanity" and elevates or empowers those that "figure" them to serve as judges—is dependent upon a logic of perpetual difference and displacement (i.e., *différance*).

The excluded *figure* forms the limit or boundary of the *true* or *pure* "human," but the surety of this knowledge (its ground or basis) is situated simultaneously as origin and end. Within the here and now contact with (i.e., touching, compearance, *being-in-common, being-with*) a *figure* of exclusion is resisted at all costs—exclusion establishes lines that must not be crossed or even touched—and yet contact is its obsession. It constantly and obsessively implicates itself with the other. The writing of "communion" is thus bound by a paradox: all of its raging at and against the limit (i.e., "there is no limit," "the limit is temporary," etc.) does little but to multiply its relation to the limit. "Literary communism" is not the attempted exclusion of the limit, but its exposition. As Nancy states, "what is shared is the unworking of works."[102] The program or itinerary of this sharing-out of the common forms the very principle of Bataille's *Inner Experience*: "to emerge through project from the realm of project."[103] The other side of project—its culmination or *eschaton*—is expressed in Bataille's ecstatic proclamation: "Sovereignty is NOTHING."[104] It is neither an experience of the positive-immanent (i.e., a revealed substance or essence) nor the transcendent-negative (i.e., negative theology or Hegel's "bad" infinity). It is not *all or nothing*; rather, it is the problem of existence in its undecidable ontic-ontological presentation. The problem of community is thus not *figuration*—as to deny figuration would simply return us to negative theology or to Hegel's "absolute freedom"—but rather

> How to exclude without fixing (*figurer*)? and how to fix without excluding? Exclusion without fixing is to legitimate (*faire droit*) the absence of grounding, or of presupposition, to legitimate being together. Fixing without excluding is to uphold the lines of exteriority, the two sides of the same edge. If "politics" is "management," as political economists pretend it to be, then it is the management of this unmanageable edge. For ontological, not moral, reasons, this management cannot be assimilation: no Leviathan's belly awaits.[105]

To engage with this problem, that is to address it, not as a curious externality that can be held at a distance, but as the problem of shared existence—a problem that implicates all and leaves none untouched—is to be engaged in the "political":

> "Political" would mean a community ordering itself to the unworking of its communication, or destined to this unworking: a community consciously undergoing the experience of its sharing. To attain such a signification of the "political" does not depend, or in any case not simply, on what is called a "political will." It implies being already engaged in the community, that is to say, undergoing, in whatever manner, the experience of community as communication: it implies writing. We must not stop writing, or letting the singular outline of our being-in-common expose itself.[106] (*Inoperative Community*, 41)

Now, if the "community of those without community" is "political," in this sense, is it democratic (and if so how or in what sense is it democratic?) or is it a fraternal order? Or is this *thinking* of "community" not reducible to either (i.e., the question is not whether "community" is either "democratic" or "fraternal"), but rather a thinking of the relation between them?

RISK, TACTICS, AND LINES OF COMMUNICATION: FRATERNITY AND DEMOCRACY

Now, given the ground we have covered, how are we to make sense of this division between Derrida and Nancy? Is it possible to somehow map Derrida's concerns in relation to Nancy's text? And furthermore, once the trajectories of these concerns are plotted, do they form lines of contention or of communication? One thing is clear from the outset: whatever procedure one employs, the parameters or boundaries of this "map" are contingent. No matter how many times one arranges and rearranges their texts or how methodically one searches each single page, the ultimate selection of themes, concepts, sentences, and words will be neither final nor complete. This does not mean that this map or even the process of mapping is in some way pointless; rather, it means that the text is not a stockroom that one can simply enter and begin cataloguing the inventory. It is not bounded or contained in the same manner. The text is a territory whose boundaries are open to contestation. This being so, the process of mapping is always exploratory in nature, and the map or maps formed are provisional or rough. They open up possible lines of approach to the text, and chart its contours from the perspective of the lines they follow. This precautionary note is not given to somehow exonerate the cartographer from responsibility for the map (i.e., the map is provisional and thus the reader must "use at your own risk"— *caveat emptor*). But, to reiterate, this "map" and these lines do not form a final index or registry—this is not a *settling of accounts*—rather they are an invitation to revisit the texts, to see them again from another angle and in a different light.

Setting that to one side, we can now return to the task at hand. As we have already noted, Derrida's concerns can be divided into two general (but related) types that we can, for the sake of convenience, refer to as fraternity (i.e., *teleiopoesis*) and disorientation (i.e., "X without X"). Now that we have covered Nancy's *La Communauté désœuvrée* and the distinction between "communion" and "community," we can move to Nancy's responses to Derrida's concerns. These responses are distributed thorough Nancy's work (following the 1983 publication of *La Communauté désœuvrée* in *Aléa*) and, in the typical French manner, implicit. That is, the responses do not take the form of "Derrida states X and my response to this is Y." Rather, they tend to occur around specific concepts and themes and/or the various constellations they may form. For instance, some of Nancy's more explicit responses to the relationship between fraternity and community occur in two short essays, "Around the Notion of Literary Communism" and "The Confronted Community." The former—first published as "*Autour de la notion de commaunauté littéraire*" in the May 1995 issue of *Tumultes*— takes the form of a response to a set of questions posed by Philippe Mesnard. In the closing section of this text, Nancy states,

> I am well aware of the difficulty—indeed, the opacity—of my attempted response or of my preludes to a real response. I have wanted to say here, above all else, that the project I have sketched (in *The Inoperative Community* and in one section of "*Compearance*") in order to indicate in "literature" the truth of "politics" now appears to me to require serious revision and amendment. This does not seem to me to invalidate my initial analyses concerning the "essence" of being-in-common. Nevertheless, this project does approach something that must be denounced: the renewal of a myth of community (a renewal contrary to my intended theme, being-in-common).[107]

Two points stand out here. First, Nancy's project is by no means static (a fact that Derrida—and anyone familiar with Nancy's texts—is well aware of), and second, that he is aware of the possibility that his approach could lead to a return of the myth of community. According to Nancy this possibility—the possibility of a return to fraternity—is directly contrary to the theme of being-in-common. He continues,

> What I have tried to say is this: there is, or there has been, a double project or fiction of politics in literature and of literature in politics. This double projection has been taken as the truth of both, of the one by way of the other and of the one in the other. This is, in a way, a truth (illusion) common to Romanticism and communism—basically, fascism, if we want to see in this apotropaic term an irresistible temptation toward the completion of community as signification (and thus, a refusal to confront being-in-common as the element of unachievable sense).[108]

Holding here a moment: this "double projection" of the politics in literature and literature in politics forms two sides of the same image. The first side is "positive" and can be referred to either as "fascism" or "communion." It presents a complete image of the "people." With this image the theological-political is both "secularized" and "immanentized." The second side is negative and transcendent. It is the formless-form of "democracy." With this "double projection" the terms of Bailly's phrase "community, number" are effectively and artificially separated: there is the positivity of "community" and the negativity of "number." The projected "truth"—which is, as Nancy stipulates, an "illusion"—is the hand-in-glove combination of *the* "people" with *the* form of government. This static "totality"—this fusion or closure of the gap that places the heterogeneous terms "community" and "number" in common—is the fixation of political theology. To close this gap (or, as Nancy—borrowing a term from Merleau-Ponty—will refer to it, the "chaismus") is to reach the end. It answers the question of "first" philosophy (Aristotle's "What is X?") and thus meets its command to "know thyself" (*gnōthi seauton* or *nosce te ipsum*). With this the circle closes. There is no more exposure, no more impossibility, and therefore no responsibility and no freedom. As Nancy states, this illusion is (perhaps) fraternity: "And perhaps fraternity names the illusion that this chiasmus is being resolved—either that or it indicates something, the one to the other. Freedom is in a way the chiasma of the one and the other. (Fraternity perhaps names the illusory resolution of this chiasma—or perhaps it indicates something still unsuspected). But this still remains to be thought."[109]

The position of fraternity here is, to say the least, curious. On the one hand it is attached to the closure of the "chiasma," and consequently abandoned to "communion" and "myth." But, at the same time, it is also suspended by the "perhaps." What is unclear here is the very status of "fraternity": Is it the logic of fusion or does it hold within itself the possibility of thinking of the figure or bond? And returning, at least in part, to Derrida's concern in *The Politics of Friendship*, if there is something that remains to be thought in *fraternity* how can it be separated from a thinking of or between *brothers*?

In *The Sense of the World*—originally published as *Le sens de monde* in 1993—there is a more extended treatment of "fraternity." The treatment—or response, as the case may be—takes place in the closing section of the chapter entitled "Politics II" (which, is subtitled "(K)not. Tying. Seizure of Speech"). Before turning to it we should first establish the general problematic of this section of the text. Nancy begins this subsection by setting out the problems associated with the choice between the "subject" and the "citizen":

> It is not possible to pose the problem in terms of the choice between subject and citizen if this choice only balances between the appropriative violence of the subject and the abstract spatiality of citizenship. Or between supraidentity and subidentity (the Aryan-Jewish couple, according to the Nazi myth). Between absolutely satiated sense and sense absolutely emptied out. Between desire (full of its lack) and truth (empty of its fullness). For this would no longer be a choice. In the final analysis, in both cases, it would be the same postulation of self-sufficiency.[110]

Once again there is the splitting of "community" (subject, satiated sense, desire) and "number" (citizen, sense absolutely emptied out, truth). As should be obvious by this point, Nancy sees this as a false dichotomy. This separation is part of the program of self-sufficiency: Presenting "community" and "number" as mutually exclusive categories makes a messianic program necessary. That is, the problem of existence—of *being-with*—becomes impossible in a very specific manner. It becomes a problem that can only be thought of in terms of resolution—a sword-in-the-stone or all-or-nothing problem—and, as such, one that should be abandoned. The proper orientation to the world thus becomes the inward retreat of the "beautiful soul": here the world is simply written off as beyond salvation (a position exemplified in the Christian concept of *valle lacrimarum* or "vale of tears" and numerous other quietisms). The contradiction being—as Hegel's analysis in the *Phenomenology* clearly demonstrates—that the "pure" morality this position lays claim to is a product of its own refusal to act, and that refusal is in and of itself an action for which it is responsible.[111] Once the stage—and it is a *stage* that this all-or-nothing problem presents us with, that is, an *opening* or *place* reserved for the entrance of *the* sovereign—is set in this manner all that is left to do is to wait for him to arrive. The waiting ends when *the* sovereign takes the stage and resolves the problem (i.e., as in the Arthurian legend only the "true" king can retrieve the sword).[112] Nancy does not approach "community" and "number" as an either/or selection between mutually exclusive categories; rather, he is attempting to think their connection or communication (and not their fusion). That is, he is attempting to think through a politics of "dependence or interdependence, of heteronomy or heterology."[113] As Nancy states, "What we are seeking—or what, as one says, "is seeking us"—is thus a politics of the tie as such, rather than of its untying [*dénouement*] into a space or substance."[114]

Holding here a moment, we can see that what Nancy is referring to as a politics of the tie is not the *dénouement* (i.e., not only is it not a resolution or "untying," but it is not *the final* resolution) of politics into a space (i.e., the open space of "number" and the negative theology of "democracy") or a substance (i.e., the complete subject of "community" and the fascism of "communion"). As a result, the politics of the tie is "incommensurable with the ligature of the fasces."[115] Returning to the text: "It is less the tie that binds than the tie that reties, less the tie that encloses than the tie that makes up a network."[116]

The "tie" is thus neither final nor complete: it is neither "blood" nor "soil." It is contingent not necessary. Consequently, this "tie" cannot be assumed. It is *in question* in each instance, and thus it is never absolved of its accountability to others. And yet, in a move that appears to be at the very least confusing if not outright contradictory, Nancy will relate this "tie" to a term that is by *definition* closed, namely, to "fraternity."

So where does "fraternity" fit into this politics of the "tie"? The answer to this is also somewhat curious. Nancy utilizes the tripartite motto of France (*liberté, égalité, fraternité*) as a reference point for his rethinking of the relation between politics and community. It is not that he simply takes these terms at face value in some hopeless attempt to draw upon the rhetorical force of the revolution; rather, he takes the risk (this tendency to take risks is, as we will shortly see, a characteristic that Derrida both admires and is wary of) of radically reinterpreting these terms.[117] Returning to *The Sense of the World*, Nancy outlines two "traits" that this politics manifests. The first is as follows: "Every *one* as such subverts in fact the virtual closure or totalization of the network (in the subjective or in the civic mode). Every *one* displaces or disarranges sovereignty and community. Thus, it is a matter here of an intransigent politics of *justice* defined, above all, by an absolute unconditional "equaliberty" of "everyone" as tying of the (k)not of sense (that is, as *existence*)."[118]

This "trait" is politics: the coupling of "liberty" and "equality" opens the question of measure. If either term of "equaliberty" is separated from the other, then either everyone becomes interchangeable (i.e., numerical equivalence) or the liberty of some comes at the cost of the subjugation of others (i.e., the closed community that "displaces" others at its boundaries). Maintaining this coupling is, as Nancy notes, a matter of "an intransigent politics of *justice*." This point is driven home in his brief essay—first published in 2000—*Is Everything Political?*

> The words *equality* and *freedom* are but problematic names, nonsaturated by signification, under which it is a matter of keeping open (dare one say wide open?) the exigency of *not* accomplishing an essence or an end of the incommensurable, and *yet*, and *precisely*, of sustaining its (im)possibility: the exigency to regulate power—the force that must sustain this nonorganic unity—according to an incommensurable "justice."[119]

Left at this point this politics of the "tie" could be expressed with Derrida's phrase "every other is completely other" ["*tout autre est tout autre*"].[120] And yet, Nancy maintains that in and of itself this "trait" is incomplete, as one could read in this nothing but the conventional appeal for formal equality (i.e., the discourse of universal "rights" and "freedoms"). It is a consideration of "number" without "community" or "spacing" without "figuring." As such, it *risks* losing the very sense of singularity (i.e., that it is an issue of *existence* and not the empty freedom of formal equality). It thus requires an "additional element":

> This politics thus requires an additional element, beyond justice, liberty, and equality. One could perhaps [*Note:* once again it is suspended by the "perhaps"] call this additional element "fraternity" if it were possible to conceive of fraternity without father or mother, anterior rather than posterior to all law and common substance. Or if it were possible to conceive of "fraternity" *as* Law and *as* substance: incommensurable, nonderivable.[121]

The challenge here is explicit: politics requires more than "spacing" and "number." Something must take place, but—in order to retain the sense of politics—it must take place in such a way that it does not close off or, in some sense, completely take up space. The additional element might perhaps be called "fraternity," but it would not be fraternal. That is, it would not be an exclusively relational term (i.e., one that only has meaning by excluding the "father," "mother," "sister," etc.). Nor would it be a strictly "human" term (being-in-common is *not* a "humanism"). As Nancy states in *Being Singular Plural*, "'fraternity' is supposed to be the solution to equality (or to 'equiliberty' ['égaliberté']) by evoking or invoking a 'generic identity.' What is lacking there is exactly the common origin of the common."[122]

The question we are then left with is: What remains of "fraternity" once it is stripped of the very significations that tie it to a "common origin"? Nancy is clearly aware of the risks of this term (hence the "perhaps"), but he also does not want to discard it. Rather than retract it, he ups the stakes. But why? One possibility is that, unlike friendship, "fraternity" is not a voluntary relation. It is a paradoxical bond, in that it can be neither undone (i.e., no "final solution" can sever it) nor completed (i.e., known as it is in and of itself). In this sense the connection with "community"—as *being-with, being-together, being-in-common*—is clear. Community is *neither* a voluntary relation nor a hypothesis: it is "posited as a given, as a fact: our first given."[123] The challenge here is to think "fraternity" without "fraternalism." But is this possible?

This challenge, or perhaps, what is at stake in this challenge—the very *impossibility* of its stakes—brings us back to Derrida's concerns. That is, it brings us to the point at which both concerns (i.e., fraternity or the return of fraternalism and the risk of disorientation) coincide. Derrida articulates this point in the closing chapters of *On Touching—Jean-Luc Nancy*:

> Nancy doesn't say much about "betting," it seems to me (but I may be wrong in this), yet I perceive him as a thinker of the bet and a player—or rather like a bettor, a desperate bettor, that is: he never stops stalking, committing, committing himself, and doing anything to calculate some *hyperbolic* odds with *exactitude* as well as exaggeration. He does this without any expectations, counting neither on the gains of some Pascalian "wager" nor on any salvation.[124]

The logic of this "bet" or practice of "betting" is not that of investment (i.e., a logic that would minimize exposure in relation to the possibility of profit). It is neither economic nor sacrificial, as there is neither the assurance nor even the promise of anything beyond the *risk* itself. Nowhere is this more apparent than in his treatment of "fraternity" (i.e., that "extra element"—which, might perhaps be termed "community"—that brings sense to the spacing of "number"). It is the question of the quality (*quidditās*) of the "common." Not in isolation (not as "the" thing *in-itself* or *for-itself*), but relation with quantity (*quantitās*). "Fraternity"—as the logic of *prīmōgenitūra* and *paterfamilias*—touches upon the stakes of the "common." It offers forward claims to blood and soil that would form the very bonds (or ligature) of the *fasces*. Its sets—or rather it attempts to set—the meaning of the "common" by binding them to it in substance and/or essence. Like the "noble lie" (*gennaion pseudos*) in Plato's *Republic* it presents the foundations for a logic that binds the "many" to the "one." But, it is also a *risk*. A *risk* that is constantly being calculated, managed, and deferred.

It is (perhaps) this *risky* use of language that brings Derrida to outline his "fraternal" concerns in a footnote to the second chapter of *Politics of Friendship*:

> There is still perhaps some brotherhood in Bataille, Blanchot and Nancy, and I wonder, in the innermost recesses of my admiring friendship, if it does not deserve a little loosening up, and if it should still guide the thinking of community, be it a community without community, or a brotherhood without brotherhood.... I am also thinking—without being too sure what to think—about all the assembled "brothers," all the men "gathered into fraternities," in *The Inoperative Community*.... Must not the interruption of the mythical scene also, by some supplement to the question concerning what transpires "before the law," at the mythical moment of the father's murder (from Freud to Kafka), reach and affect the figure of the brothers?[125]

Despite the shift in register (i.e., from the *teleiopoesis* of Nietzsche and sons to Freud and Kafka),[126] the concern here is also the possibility of a return to fraternal order with its logic of *prīmōgenitūra* and *paterfamilias*. Nancy responds directly to this question in *The Sense of the World*: "And if it is necessary to put it in these terms: without "Father" (or "Mother"), yet not at the sacrificial price of a 'murder of the Father'—but, rather, in the dissolution of the Figure of the Father-already-Dead and his Thanatocracy. This would be the law of the Law, its very coming."[127]

While the entire paragraph can be read as an indirect response to Derrida's concerns, Nancy addresses a direct response following the (perhaps) exasperated "and if it is necessary to put it in these terms."[128] Nancy interrupts the chain of sacrificial inheritance by cutting it off at the root. It is not that the body of the father is murdered and spiritually shared out by the sons, but that the very *figure* of the Father-already-Dead (i.e., his *corpus mysticum*) is dissolved. What remains is not the ghostly void of *negative theology*, but a "fraternity" stripped of both its affiliations (paternity and maternity). It is not a bond of blood or soil, but of *being-in-common*. This "additional element" is both incommensurable (i.e., it cannot be measured, or rather the measure of it cannot be absolutely or finally set) and nonderivable (i.e., it is singular and thus one cannot use another standard to set its measure). How is it possible to conceive of this "fraternity" *as* Law and *as* Substance? Perhaps this means that both Law and Substance are *constitutively open*, that is, both are "incommensurable" and "nonderivable." This does not mean that Ivan Karamazov's infamous claim that in a world without God all is permitted stands; rather, it means that all laws and all claims to substance (any claims to define the substance or essence of the people or *demos*) are open to the possibility of contention. It means that no lawmakers are without responsibility for the measures that they set. It also means—as Nancy suggests in the footnote to this very selection—"that the "lie" introduces ipso facto, and more surely than truth, the dimension of community."[129] It means that "fraternity"—as the filial bond of blood and soil—is fictional.

The grounds of "fraternity" (the very basis of its cohesion) are fictional. And once this fiction is in play, politics itself becomes governed by the logic of the fiction that gives it form. Every event—every encounter with what lies beyond the bounds of fiction—must be woven into the logic of the lie. And if the event cannot be woven into the lie, it becomes the exception that calls the rule into question (i.e., the origin of both the rule and the authority to make it are opened to contestation). To escape these constraints, the "One"—whether formulated as "substance" or "subject"—would have to be able to *absolutely* determine itself. As Nancy states in his essay *In Praise of the Melee*,

> a pure identity would not only be inert, empty, colorless, and flavorless (words which describe many of those who uphold pure identities): it would be an absurdity. A pure identity annuls itself, cannot identify itself. It is solely identical to an itself that is identical to itself, and that thus goes around in a circle and never attains existence. Was there, for example, anyone pure enough to be worthy of the name "Aryan"? We know how this question could lead a real Nazi, a Nazi who identified absolutely with his cause or with his thing, to sterilization or even to suicide.[130]

If it could set its own bounds—that is, *know itself absolutely*—then it could be *sovereign* and, as such, beyond question. But the "many"—as the *plus d'un* or law of number— always exposes the "one," drawing it out of itself and into question. In order to retain its position it must set itself apart—it prepares a "high seat" [*thrónos*]—and claims that the "many" is, in fact, "one" (the onto-theological alchemy expressed in *E pluribus unum*).[131] It can govern from this position, but its authority is that of a representative, substitute, or placeholder. No matter how tightly it binds the many to itself—no matter how closed the "brotherhood" becomes—it cannot close itself off; it cannot be "without relation."[132] Despite all of its promises and denials, it is and always remains -*with*, and it is this relation that "undoes, in its very principle—and at its closure or on its limit—the autarchy of absolute immanence."[133] By taking on "fraternity" Nancy traces its path towards its own limit. His strategy is to, in effect, increase the stakes of "fraternity" and thereby call its bluff. By doing so he switches the time scale for payment from "later" to "now."

The logic of "fraternity" ultimately undoes itself.[134] But, if this is the case then, again, why retain—even if this retention is suspended by the "perhaps" or the logic of "X without X"—the name? After all, as he notes in "The Confronted Community"—an essay written in 2001—he does gradually drift away from "community":

> Little by little I have preferred replacing it with the awkward expressions *being-together, being-in-common*, and finally *being-with*. There were reasons for these shifts and for resigning myself to this awkwardness, at least temporarily. I could see from all sides the dangers aroused by the use of the word "community": its resonance fully invincible and even bloated with substance and interiority; its reference inevitably Christian (as in spiritual, fraternal, communal community); or more broadly religious (as in Jewish community, community of prayer, community of believers, or *"umma"*), as it is used to support an array of so-called "ethnicities." All this could only be a warning. It was clear that the emphasis placed on this necessary but still insufficiently clarified concept was at least, at this time, on par with the revival of communitarian trends that could be fascistic.[135]

Nancy did not unwittingly stumble upon these dangers; he engaged with the concept of "community" precisely because of them. But why replace the word with these "awkward" expressions? Nancy continues: "I therefore preferred to concentrate my work around the 'with': almost indistinguishable from the *co-* of community, yet it carries with it a clearer indication of the spacing at the heart of proximity and intimacy. 'With' is plain and neutral: neither communion nor atomization; just the sharing/dividing [*partage*] of a place, at the most, contact: a being-together without assemblage."[136]

This gradual replacement is thus not a withdrawal or step back from "community": it is a step left suspended (or, as Blanchot would put it, *Le Pas au-delà*, which can be translated as both "the not-beyond" and "the step beyond" depending on whether the *pas* is used as an adverb or a noun) at the limits of "community." That is, instead of taking the cautious route of avoiding the risks of "community" altogether, Nancy follows the course of these risks to the point at which they rupture (i.e., to the point of fascism with its ethnic cleansing and final solutions). There is, much like Heidegger's so-called "turn" [*Kehre*], a shift from a more descriptive project of tracing out the stakes of the "common" and following its various trajectories to the more prescriptive project. For Nancy this latter project takes the forms of thinking through the politics of the *co-, with-,* or *tie* (i.e., the analysis of *Mitdasein* that

Heidegger leaves "suspended" in *Being and Time*). The thinking of "community"—with its host of fraternal connotations—is *not* a project of resurrection. But it also cannot prevent the *risk* of a return to brotherhood. This *risk* is ontological. The fact that there is no master key that might somehow end or close ontic-ontological difference entails that there is no end to *risk*. There is always the possibility of "fraternity"—this *risk* is a necessary component of both freedom and responsibility—but it is a possibility governed by a paradoxical logic (the logic of the absolute). While its aim is set on solving the problem of existence—simultaneously fulfilling the charge of philosophy [*gnōthi seauton*] and answering its first question [*to ti ên einai, to ti esti, ti esti*]—and therefore being able to be the ground of its own authority (i.e., to be absolute and thus beyond question), within the *hic et nunc* it can do nothing but promise a solution while continuing to act as if this solution were already in place.

The trajectory of "fraternity" is thus—despite its "mystical" claims—neither circular nor linear. It is not the former because it does not—and indeed cannot—complete the auto-affective loop of self-knowing (i.e., it cannot sense itself sensing itself and only itself) that would grant it the Archimedean point that it requires if it is to issue *a* law as *the* law. It is not the latter because despite all of its promises and reassurances there is no progress, no movement towards the end (i.e., the point at which the grounds of its authority would be manifest to all). Rather, its trajectory is elliptical: it goes out, but it does not return or at least it does not return to itself unchanged. With its very first step—to *name* itself as sovereign and *bind* itself to itself by ties of "blood and soil"—it undoes itself. It does so because, as Nancy put it, it implicates itself in "a relation that it refuses and precludes by its essence."[137] This exclusion, or rather this attempt to exclude, existence is, for Nancy, a *free renunciation of freedom* or, more simply, "evil."[138] It is *unfree* in that its claim to autonomy is grounded by a logic of displacement (i.e., in the *always already* not-yet), but it is accountable for its actions within the "now." It is this accountability that it attempts to shut out. It only has two possible responses to those that challenge its authority:

1 Defer the question by referring to either the beginning or the end of time.
2 Silence the other by marking it as a traitor, criminal, or enemy and thus making use of the sovereign exception (the centre of the fasces is, after all, the axe that symbolizes the power of execution).

This being so, the cohesion of brotherhood is that of a conspiracy (i.e., to set the figure of existence as a specific "essence" or "substance") and its trajectory is that of the murderer (i.e., it can neither prove its claim nor ground its authority in the *here and now*, so it must constantly move towards the *not-yet*). And yet, if "fraternity" (understood as a closed figure of the "common") is *evil*, why retain the name?[139] Why call—or even suggest the possibility of "perhaps" calling—that additional element "fraternity"? And furthermore how are we to make sense of a "fraternity" "without father or mother, anterior rather than posterior to all law and common substance"?[140]

Perhaps the answer is quite simply that Nancy sees this *risk* as a responsibility. While "fraternity" carries with it all the dangers of closure or communion, it is also a *free* action. By staking his bet on "fraternity," Nancy commits himself to following its course. This "bet," as Derrida notes, is not a measured investment. Nancy does not take "fraternity" at its word. While it constantly gestures towards unseen points in an attempt to form a coherent line, he, like a certain Hegel, sees the shadow of a freedom whose "actualization can only be the fury of destruction."[141] And so by staking his bet in the here and now he effectively demands (again in line with a certain Hegel) *Hic Rhodus, hic salta*.[142] This means that he seeks out what "fraternity" means apart from all its promises or paternal claims (i.e., its "mystical foundations"). By betting, he drives at making "fraternity" jump *hic et nunc*. This "desperate betting" is a responsibility, precisely because we cannot—like Pilate or some other version of the "beautiful soul"—simply wash our hands and thereby remove ourselves from the situation. If we simply abandon "fraternity" to silence, that is, if we set it to one side and pursue only *freedom* and *equality*, we would simply set the stage for its return by offering nothing but a cold and empty stage (i.e., the measureless void of "number" without "community"). Just as we cannot think freedom without evil, we cannot think democracy or community without "fraternity." In thinking this "additional element," Nancy is committing himself to a thinking of sense and response or, as he puts it, to the politics of the tie (as the *-with* or *co-* of "community").

As he states in his essay "*Responding to Existence*,"

> Sense, then, has the same structure as responsibility: it is engagement, oath. *Spondere* is to engage by a ritualized oath. To one's *sponsio*, the other's *responsio* responds. The response is first of all a re-engagement—an engagement in return for what engaged us or what engaged itself for us: the world, existence, others. It is a mutual pledge to truthfulness without which neither speech nor expression [*regard*] would be possible.[143]

He continues later in the same paragraph: "What we usually call a 'response' is a solution; here, though, it is a matter of the referral or the return [*renvoi*] of the promise of the engagement. Sense is the engagement between several beings, and truth always, inevitably, lies in this between or in this with."[144]

"Fraternity" (as *communion* or *evil*) constitutes an attempt to override this exchange by binding itself with an oath that lacks both parties. By removing or displacing both the one who issues the oath (i.e., the Absolute) and the one who accepts it (i.e., the "spirit" or "soul"), it becomes unquestionable. It acquires jurisdiction (the right to both make and enforce law) by displacing the very logic of responsibility (i.e., both the "who" and the "when" of responsibility are infinitely deferred). But this "fiction" undoes itself by having to act in the here and now. If one does not accept its "fictional" justifications and calls the bluff of sovereign power—by "criminal" acts or "treasonous" questions—they are confronted the foundations of law itself, namely the executioner's stage. But by imposing death one does not simply close the issue. There is no mystical revelation in the death of the other, no moment that might somehow complete the circle or the line and thereby ground sovereign power. Death only serves to mark out an ellipsis. With the execution only one party remains standing, and therefore only one can be held accountable past that point. Quite simply, with each execution sovereign power multiplies its own implication *to* or *with* others. By following "fraternity" down to the pit and the gallows it inevitably constructs (the centre of the fasces is itself an instrument of death),[145] we find its own impossibility. When confronted by the emptiness of the execution—the death that, as Hegel notes, has no more significance than "cutting off a head of cabbage or swallowing a mouthful of water"—all of the mythical bonds and promises of "fraternity" evaporate, leaving only the senseless butchering of "numbers."[146] At this point—once the "fiction" is no longer accepted as a valid claim to power—as Hegel rightly observes, "*being suspected* ... takes the place, or has the significance and effect, of *being guilty*."[147] When the game is up and the stakes are all called in, the "true" equality of this "fraternal" bond is the *law of suspects*: anyone can end up as a "number" to be buried in the mass graves.

And yet, still, why call this shared impossibility "fraternity"? Can we think fraternity while stripping it of all of its blood and soil? Without father, mother, sister, or brothers? This is Nancy's challenge. While Derrida (perhaps) agrees that "[p]erhaps this risk must be assumed in order to keep the question of the "who" from being politically enframed by the schema of being-common or being-in-common, even when it is neutralized, in a question of identity (individual, subjective, ethnic, national, state, etc.)."[148]

He both remains concerned with and troubled by all of this talk of "fraternity." He is not exactly "sure what to think" of "community without community" or indeed of "brotherhood without brotherhood."[149] Nancy does not aim to settle this issue. Quite the contrary: he consciously wants to unsettle it. "Fraternity" does indeed mark Nancy's tendency to gamble with impossible odds. (After all, what sense can "fraternity" have without brothers? Nancy's answer is deceptively simple: "*existence*" or more precisely "*ek-sistence*.") Perhaps, in the end, the difference between them is tactical. Derrida adopts a more cautious and circumspect tack overall, while Nancy is constantly raising the stakes. But this is not simply a game for either of them. There is a sleepless vigilance to this thinking about "fraternity" and "friendship." And it is this vigilance that—for all their "fraternal" differences[150]—he shares with Derrida. Both maintain that there is no end to the *risk* of what we call "democracy." Returning to Nancy's essay "*Responding to Existence*":

> It is often said that philosophy only poses questions. I would say that today it has to think only of the response: not a response-solution or a response-verdict, but a co-respondence. In such a co-respondence—which defines our co-responsibility—there must be something that does not close the exchange but, on the contrary, institutes and relaunches it. There must be voices, timbres, and singular modes. These voices are in themselves, in their co-respondence, the creation of sense. Democratic responsibility is responsibility for such a creation. But immediately and from the outset, this means that democracy itself is not something given, an available sense. It is responsible precisely for what is not given: the *demos*, the people, the ones with the others.[151]

Democracy is not simply one *form* of government among others. It is "not something given." As such, it cannot be the object of a question. There is no "democratic" property: no *essence* or *substance* that might somehow be theoretically determined. This does not mean "democracy" is *impossible* and should thereby be consigned to the realm of myth and fantasy. Rather, it means that it "is 'only' the *putting into question of an affirmation*."[152] It can only be known through its practice, and this practice is radically open to the question of "democracy." It is, in Nancy's terms, a *spacing*: it makes room for "numbers." But, if we stop at this point and simply maintain that democracy is indeterminate (an openness or spacing), we expose ourselves to the *risk* of reserving this space.[153] In other words, the openness of democracy must not be confused with the void of negative theology. It is not an empty space or *sanctum sanctorum* reserved for "One" that is *yet-to-come* (i.e., a space whose very emptiness is used to defer both freedom and responsibility).[154] Rather, it is a spacing that must be open to figures and to the process of figuring.[155] The *demos*—as *being-with* or *in-common*—must always be in question, but it must also be in play *hic et nunc*. This is the position or place of "fraternity" for Nancy. What remains of "fraternity" (always suspended by "perhaps" and without "fraternalism") is a connection or a tie that is both "incommensurable" and "nonderivable."[156] This does not put Derrida and Nancy on opposing sides of a line (between, say, some form of pre-ontological notion of "being" and "transcendence"), but places them in communication at the limit. What remains to be thought—and what must not stop being thought—is how to take responsibility for freedom without the *fasces* of exception or the *void* of messianism.

Section II

WRITING AND RESISTANCE

If the political is not dissolved in the sociotechnical element of forces and needs (in which, in effect, it seems to be dissolving under our eyes), it must inscribe the sharing of community. The outline of singularity would be "political"—as would be the outline of its communication and its ecstasy. "Political" would mean a community ordering itself to the unworking of its communication, or destined to the unworking: a community consciously undergoing the experience of sharing. To attain such a signification of the "political" does not depend, or in any case not simply, on what is called a "political will." It implies already being engaged in the community, that is to say, undergoing, in whatever manner, the experience of community as communication: it implies writing.
—Jean-Luc Nancy, *The Inoperative Community*

Chapter 2

KEEPING TIME BENEATH A CANOPY OF SKINS
Reading at the Limits of Sense and Sign(s) in Augustine and Bataille

Who but you, O God, have made for us a solid firmament of authority over us in your divine scripture? For "the heaven will fold up like a book" (Isaiah 34:4), and now "like a skin it is stretched out" (Psalms 103:2). Your divine scripture has more sublime authority since the death of the mortal authors through whom you provided it for us. You know, Lord, you know how you clothed human beings with skins when by sin they became mortal (Genesis 3:21). So you have stretched out the firmament of your book "like a skin," that is your words which are not mutually discordant, and which you have placed over us by the ministry of mortal men. Indeed, by the very fact of their death the solid authority of your utterances published by them is in a sublime way "stretched out" over everything inferior.
—St. Augustine, *Confessions*

I write for one, who, entering into my book, would fall as into a hole, who would never again get out.
—Bataille, *Inner Experience*

AT FIRST GLANCE IT MIGHT seem as if our subject matter could not be more dissimilar. To read one of the most important figures in the development of Western Christianity in conjunction with the author who entitled a major portion of his project the *La Somme atheologique* (reversing, of course, Aquinas's *Summa Theologica*) might seem, at least to some readers, inappropriate if not perverse. But despite the admittedly vast differences that divide these texts, they share a basic structuring principle: each is written as a response to an experience that exceeds sense (understood as both meaning and orientation). In Augustine's *Confessions* there is the experience of conversion, his struggle to recapture his memory of God's presence, and to understand the "hidden meaning" that exists behind the semblance of temporal existence. In Bataille's text, we find what he refers to as "inner experience"—which is, as Derrida notes, neither an "experience" nor "inner"—and its fundamental relationship with both "communication" and "community."[1] Each text takes its bearings from an impossible excess, and each is written as a response to an ecstatic experience; yet they articulate this response in very different ways. Our task is to attend to these differences by paying close attention to how each text utilizes writing to first solicit and then reorient its reader.

The orientation each text generates can perhaps be thought of as a "philosophy of history" as defined by Löwith in his *Meaning in History*. That is, each might be understood as "an interpretation of universal history in accordance with a principle by which historical events and successions are unified and directed towards an ultimate meaning."[2] While this applies rather directly to Augustine, its application to Bataille is, as we will see later on, much less direct and much more complicated. In fact, as our analysis progresses it will become clear that Bataille's "inner experience" and the historico-political orientation he develops from it aims at interrupting—understood as internally rupturing the onto-chronological continuity of—Augustine's project. By tracing the relationship between experience and each text's philosophy of history, we can begin to reconsider the historical and ethical dimensions of both Augustine and Bataille. Our concern is how each orientation relates to the question of community. In this context we can begin to relate these orientations to one another on a political stage, and thus show the political consequences of how each addresses the gap between sense and sign.

The stark contrast between the two epigraphs to this chapter sets the stage for our inquiry. In each we are presented with a text that operates on both the space and time of its reader. In the first we are immediately confronted with the problem of authorship. Augustine's text is addressed to God, and by addressing God Augustine occupies a liminal space within the text. He is both the author of the *Confessions* and a reader of the scriptures he recites within his text. Yet, if we take Augustine seriously, we cannot simply solve the question of authorship by dividing the citations from the body of the text, because he believes that any "truth" within his text is the product of God speaking through him. He recollects, he gathers, arranges—this is, after all the very activity of thought [*cogito*] according to Augustine—but he does not speak; he is spoken to and through.[3] Lyotard captures the ambiguity of the question of authorship in the *Confessions* in his unfinished work *La Confession d'Augustin*:

> The suspicion dawns, approaching closer and closer, but very rapidly, that the you, you the silent one, pulls all the strings of the confessive sentence, "carries" all its valences, occupies all the strategic positions, holds them to defend them against any invading conquest. The two poles of the address—addressee and addresser—are both yours, as well as the two poles of meaning—referent and signification.[4]

Returning to the epigraph, we find that the author openly takes on the role of the reader and situates himself within a space between scripture and his own skin. This author-reader takes shelter within the scriptural text. The text is stretched over the horizon as a second skin that, at one and the same time, holds back and promises the ultimate *parousia* of the author, and with it the end of both the text and the skin it shelters. In many ways this selection provides a condensed summary of Augustine's philosophy of history. The present is not as it should be, it is incomplete, and time itself is a sign of this displacement. The confessant reads through the dispersion and distention of time, he looks to the eternal Word of the scripture for both shelter and reassurance of his eventual release. This release might be thought of as the shift from the diachrony of language—its historical arc or dispersion in time—to the absolute synchrony that exists above the firmament (the "skin" that covers the mortal sky). As Augustine states in Book XIII,

> There are, I believe, other waters above this firmament, immortal and kept from earthy corruption. Let them praise your name (Ps. 148:2–5). Let the peoples above the heavens, your angels, praise you. They have no need to look up to this firmament and to read so as to know your word. They ever "see your face" (Matt. 18:10) and there, without syllables requiring time to pronounce, they read what your eternal will intends. They read, they choose, they love. They ever read, and what they read never passes away. By choosing and loving they read the immutability of your design. Their codex is never closed, nor is their book ever folded shut. For you yourself are a book to them and you are "for eternity." (Ps. 47:15)[5]

The reader-author works in time and with language in an effort to get beyond both. He struggles to get beyond writing, beyond the dispersion of the sign, to a reading outside of both time and the text. The present of the reader-author is caught between memory and expectation. The experience of the present, of the now, is one of waiting and delay: "But now 'my years pass in groans' (Ps. 30:11) and you, Lord, are my consolation. You are my eternal Father, but I am scattered in times whose order I do not understand. The storms of incoherent events tear to pieces my thoughts, the inmost entrails of my soul, until that day when, purified and molten by the fire of your love, I flow together to merge into you."[6]

If we pause at this point and attempt to characterize—in an admittedly provisional fashion—the temporal orientation of the subject in Augustine's *Confessions*, we can conclude that it is eschatological. The "now" of this orientation is always a "not yet" and, as a result, the subject interprets the entirety of its experience (both present and past) in relation to the "not yet." This subject is, as we will see later on, cryptological. For this subject the gap between sense and the sign is an indication of an absent presence. As such, its activity is cognition understood in the sense of gathering up and arranging mental content in an effort to discover its "secret meaning." This characterization is by no means radical—this is, after all, the prototype of Christian eschatological onto-chronology—but it is important to keep in mind in the context of our current analysis. It leaves us with a series of rather troubling questions concerning the place of the sign. That is, what is the difference between the sign being read *over* or *through* and what the reader takes to be its "true" or "essential" meaning? If we understand the project of the author-reader as one of the recovery and recollection of "absolute" meaning from the dispersion of lived experience, what is the by-product or remainder of this process? What is the cost of the author-reader's salvation? We will return to this line of inquiry later on.

In the second quote the author openly declares his intentions to the reader. This second text is not constructed to shelter its reader between its pages; rather, it invites the reader to fall through it. We might argue—paraphrasing Bataille's own formulation—that the constitutive principle of this second text is to set the sign against sense and by doing so emerge through writing from the realm of writing.[7] The time-space of this fall through the text is as immediate as it is without orientation. The reader is invited to the "now" of what Bataille refers to as "inner experience." According to Bataille this "now" is neither isolation nor communion (i.e., between the self and God), but communication. It is not "communication" as generally understood (the transmission of sense through the medium of the sign), but the communication of the un-mediateable insufficiency that divides sense from signification. This being so, in a fragmentary note Bataille defines "inner experience" as the movement in which "man contests himself in his entirety."[8] This contestation derails the historical project of ultimate meaning by simultaneously communicating the irreparable non-sense of meaning and non-signification of language within the now. As Bataille states, "The goal of present activity is the unknown future. The dice are thrown with a view to the beyond of individual being—to what doesn't exist yet. This action exceeds the individuals being's limits."[9] By exceeding these limits the individual exposes itself to a present without a possible future, it throws the dice and risks itself absolutely: "'Communication' cannot proceed from one full and intact individual to another. It requires individuals whose separate existence in themselves is risked, placed at the limit of death and nothingness; the moral summit is the moment of risk taking, it is a being suspended in the beyond of oneself, at the limit of nothingness."[10]

This "communication" requires a community of those who live it precisely because it does not originate as a voluntary action from within the subject; rather, like the sensation of an effect, it comes from outside the subject.[11] Within his text the sign does not simply convey or carry meaning, rather, the sign exposes its inextricable entanglement with sense. He employs the resources of signification against sense. The result is a sliding effect in which the *différance* between the sign and sense is communicated. In contrast to Augustine's crypto-eschatology, the gap between sign and sense is not projected into a future in which it is recoverable; rather, this gap *is* the hole the reader falls through. To quote Derrida, "Bataille's atheology is also an a-teleology and an aneschatology."[12] Its temporality is the "now" without reserve: the "now" of the messianic without the "not yet" of messianism.

Now that we have a basic sketch of the contrast between these two texts, we can begin to chart our course through them. But first we must recognize that, given the fact that we are addressing concepts connected to the very heart of each of their respective projects, our course through these texts will in many ways be provisional rather than exhaustive. This does not excuse us from providing the reader with as much detail and precision as possible; rather, it serves to emphasize the responsibility we have in acting as readers of these texts. Acknowledging the sheer expanse of the terrain we will be traversing does not excuse us from cutting a path that any attentive reader could follow.

With this in mind we will begin by taking up the question of reading in the *Confessions*. While this may seem like a rather puzzling choice for an entry point, we should keep in mind that the question of how to read the Word is a central concern of Augustine's, due to both his desire to respond to the Manichean criticisms of key Christian texts and his general project of reading the "truth" of the Word in the world.[13] Even the conversion experience in Milan consisted in Augustine's hearing a child's voice repeating "*Tolle lege, tolle lege*" ("Pick up and read, pick up and read") and interpreting it as a divine command to pick up the book and read.[14] We will move on to a consideration of writing in Bataille's work. This line of will of course closely parallel Derrida's "*De l'économie restreinte à l'économie générale: Un hegelianisme sans reserve*" [From a Restricted to a General Economy: A Hegelianism without Reserve]. Once we have these two courses in place we will proceed to a more general consideration of the implication of each for the reader in terms of both temporality and community.

READING BETWEEN TWO SKINS: EXEGESIS AND CONVERSION

In Book VII, Augustine remarks on Ambrose's habit of reading in silence: "When he was reading, his eyes ran over the page and his heart perceived the sense, but his voice and tongue were silent."[15]

This observation might be understood as Augustine simply expressing his surprise upon encountering a manner of reading that was uncommon during his time, but there is a peculiar quality to this observation. If it were simply an expression of surprise it would seem odd to shift from observation of a practice (i.e., "When he was reading ... his voice and tongue were silent") to the attribution of a specific ability ("his heart perceived the sense"). This technique of silent reading privileges inner reflection—as opposed to dialogue—as a means of accessing the "truth" of the text and, as such, it is connected to Ambrose's principle of exegesis: "And I was delighted to hear Ambrose in his sermons to the people saying, as if he were most carefully enunciating a principle of exegesis: 'The letter kills, the spirit gives life' (2 Cor. 3:6). Those texts which, taken literally, seemed to contain perverse teaching he would expound spiritually, removing the mystical veil."[16]

Here the technique of silent reading finds its guiding principle; the letter of the text both contains and conceals the "true" spiritual meaning of the text. Augustine expresses his initial hesitation to accept this claim to a "secret meaning" behind the literal content of the text by stating that he feared a "precipitate plunge" [*timens praecipitium*]. The precipice that opens up before him at this point is passed over rather quickly within the *Confessions*. If we pause here and consider this precipice outside of the metaphysical apparatus he utilizes to avoid it, we find a kind of blind spot within the text. Ambrose's exegetical principle operates by contesting what we could refer to as common or literal signification. By contesting the commonly accepted meanings of terms, this principle opens up the space between the sign and its meaning or sense. This space interrupts the process of signification and exposes the subject to the very precipice of polysemy. In other words, by contesting the capacity of the sign to convey meaning there is no way of securing its "proper" sense. Thus, on its own, this principle of exegesis—much like Socratic *Elenchus*—operates by breaking down the commonly accepted meanings of words to the point of aporia.[17]

In order to avoid the precipice of the aporia, he retrospectively interprets his fear and hesitation as a manifestation of the conflict between his "two wills."[18] His carnal will clings to the apparent qualities of the letter, while his spiritual will longs to accept this principle and read beyond the limitations of the letter. He claims that had he been able to convert himself at this point and accept this principle fully, he "could have been healed."[19] By being healed his "mind's eye thus purified would have been directed in some degree towards your truth which abides for ever and is indefectible."[20] With this interpretation in place the precipice that initially caused him to fear becomes a "narrow opening" within the text.[21] That is, it becomes a project—understood as both a verb (*pro-iacere*: to throw forth) and a noun (a scheme, purpose, objective, etc.)—in which sense is oriented both by and towards that which both exceeds and thereby ultimately abolishes sense. The *telos* or *eschaton* of this project is to be in God's presence: Augustine provides a series of divine qualities that range from light, love, the highest beauty, the highest good, to the unchangeable substance [*Deus lux, Deus Dilectio, Deus summa pulchritude, Deus summum bonum, Deus incommutabilis substantia*]. With this *telos* in place, Augustine is able to orient his project and generate a rank-ordering of values that is, as Heidegger notes, of Greek origin and ultimately stems from Plato.[22]

Augustine thus manages to avoid this aporia by internalizing the division that the exegetical principle presupposes. It was not that *he* doubted the "truth" of this principle, that *he* feared the aporetic confusion of polysemy; rather, it was his attachment to his physical senses that prevented him from accepting this principle and reading beyond the limits of the letter. He internalizes this division between the letter and the spirit by folding in upon himself. His body assumes the role of the letter—it is extended, dispersed, a burden [*Molestia*] that brings him endless temptation [*Tentatio*]—and his soul is that trace of the divine that orients him beyond the limits of the letter. As a result of this reconfiguration, which Augustine will refer to as his "conversion," the aporia is no longer a precipice that confronts him (a "now" from which the future is impossible/unthinkable); it is an absence present within him (an orientation towards a "now" that is "not yet").[23] This enables him to begin to make sense of the world in a new way. The *absence-that-is-present-within-him* orients him towards the *presence-that-is-yet-to-come*. Lyotard comments on the consequences of this project: "The past is what is no longer, the future is what is not yet, and the now has no other being than the becoming past of the future. The chase after the future through the past that drives and troubles the *Confessions* is only *possible* if, in the evanescence of these times, something withholds, is maintained immutable."[24]

The source of authority that guarantees the stability of meaning is (and must remain) beyond doubt. If this authority is not evident to us, it must be because we are either unable or unwilling to turn (i.e., convert) our minds towards the spiritual "truth" that exists beyond the letter. He effectively claims, "Do not fear *there is* absolute meaning," and yet when he is asked to define it he can only apologetically state, "I cannot read it fully as of yet, but I am trying." In short, in and through this exegetical principle "meaning" is saved by the combined operation of difference (it is not "x") and deferral (it is "not yet").[25] The cost of this deferral is that the letter—here standing for the *world* of temporal things—must be continually sacrificed. Returning to Lyotard:

> The trance of life is this transitivity of finite being. Its literal meaning is non-time, for the "letter" is in itself nonbeing. The plot of confessive narrative is only possible if the event doubles up with another meaning, called "allegorical" by exegesis, if the *opera*, things as they are given, also constitute a *signa*. It is conversion, then—since it gives us the ability to read signs in works, to read a little of divine writing in the writing of the bios—that justifies confession as a journey that goes backward so as to move forward.[26]

Augustine's project maintains its sense of progress by living Ambrose's exegetical principle: it gets beyond the "letter" by *reading beyond* its limits. What he gains is an orientation and a sense of time: he must search within himself for the presence that corresponds to the absence within him, but this search occurs in a "now" that is (always already) not yet present to itself.

The Experience of Conversion and the Vision(s)

Despite the fact that the entire text is related from the perspective of one who has already converted Augustine provides us with a recounting of the actual process by which he enters the "narrow opening." In the garden his past speaks: "'How long, how long is it to be? 'Tomorrow, tomorrow.' 'Why not now? Why not an end to my impure life this very hour?'"[27]

As his "past" speaks he hears a child's voice from a nearby house chanting, "*Tolle lege, tolle lege*" ("Pick up and read, pick up and read"). "At once my countenance changed, and I began to think intently whether there might be some sort of children's game in which such a chant is used. But I could not remember having heard of one. I checked the flood of tears and stood up. I interpreted it solely as a divine command to me to open the book and read the first chapter I might find."[28]

He hurries back to where Alypius is sitting and picks up the book of the apostle, opens it and silently reads Romans 13:13–14: "Not in riots and drunken parties, not in eroticism and indecencies, not in strife and rivalry, but put on the Lord Jesus Christ and make no provision for the flesh in its lusts."[29]

Upon reading this he neither wishes nor needs to read further: he is converted and is no longer troubled by the shadows of doubt. It is useful to recount this in the context of Ambrose's exegetical principle, as it is through his conversion that Augustine fully accepts and applies it as a way of reading not only the "letter" of scripture but also the world itself. By reading the world as the letter he is able to momentarily ascend beyond the letter to the Word. The vision at Ostia recounts the lived practice of this principle taken to its limit.

While conversing with his mother about the "quality of life the eternal life of the saints will have" Augustine approaches the limit of thought:

> The conversation led us towards the conclusion that the pleasure of the bodily senses, however delightful in the radiant light of this physical world, is seen by comparison with the life of eternity to be not even worth considering. Our minds were lifted up by an ardent affection towards eternal being itself. Step by step we climbed beyond all corporeal objects and the heaven itself, where sun, moon, and stars shed light on the earth. We ascended even further by internal reflection and dialogues and wonder at your works, and we entered into our own minds.[30]

Pausing at this point and focusing on the planes of movement, we see that the motion begins with a consideration and rejection of the external world of sense. This rejection introduces a move away from the world that is simultaneously upward (it is an "ascent" up the gradient of "being") and inward (the furthest point of the ascent causes them to enter their own minds). The movement begins with language and progresses via language towards the silence of thought. Augustine continues,

> We moved up and beyond them so as to attain to the region of inexhaustible abundance where you feed Israel eternally with truth for food. There life is the wisdom by which all creatures come into being, both things which were and which will be. Furthermore, in this wisdom there is no past and future, but only being, since it is eternal. For to exist in the past or the future is no property of the eternal.[31]

This "region of inexhaustible abundance" [*regionem ubertatis indeficientis*] is presented as the *telos* of the movement. Augustine provides us with the attributes of this "region" (i.e., it is eternal, and, to borrow Heidegger's terminology, it is the source of the Being of beings), but he does not experience this region fully. "And while we talked and panted after it, we touched it in some small degree by a moment of total concentration of the heart. And we sighed and left behind us "the firstfruits of the Spirit" (Rom. 8:23) bound to that higher world, as we returned to the noise of our human speech where a sentence has both a beginning and an ending."[32]

The final stage of the ascent is ecstatic (understood in the etymological sense of *ek-stásis*, i.e., out of or beyond place) and thus can only be described in affective terms ("panted after it" [*inhiamus illi*], "touched it" [*attingimus*], "by a moment of total concentration of the heart" [*eam modice toto ictu cordis*]).[33] As a result, affective terms are used to qualify the experience of encountering this eternal "region" and the return from this hiatus is presented as a fall back into time-bound language. From this experience a path is marked out:

> If to anyone the tumult of the flesh has fallen silent, if the images of earth, water, and air are quiescent, if the heavens themselves are shut out and the very soul itself is making no sound and is surpassing itself by no longer thinking about itself, if all dreams and visions in the imagination are excluded, if all language and every sign and everything transitory is silent—for if anyone could hear them, this is what all of them would be saying, "We did not make ourselves, we were made by him who abides for eternity" (Ps. 79:3, 5)—if after this declaration they were to keep silence, having directed our ears to him that made them, then he alone would speak not through them but through himself.[34]

This movement from the tumult of the phenomenal world towards silence is a movement towards a speech that exceeds speech. Continuing:

> We would hear his word, not through the tongue of the flesh, nor through the voice of an angel, nor through the sound of thunder, nor through the obscurity of a symbolic utterance. Him who in these things we love we would hear in person without their mediation. That is how it was when at that moment we extended our reach and in a flash of mental energy attained the eternal wisdom which abides beyond all things.[35]

To hear this "speech"—the "speech" that silently conditions the possibility of beings—we would have to listen (without hearing) to a voice that has no sound (no extension in time or space).

The Practice of Reading the Word through the Letter

Augustine elaborates on the paradoxical limitations of language in relation to the Word in Book XI. Considering the relationship between the Word and creation, Augustine asks, "But how did you speak? Surely not in the way a voice came out of the cloud saying, 'This is my beloved Son' (Matt. 17:5). That voice is past and done with: it began and is ended. The syllables sounded and have passed away, the second after the first, the third after the second, and so on until, after all the others, the last one came, and after the last silence followed."[36]

If this were true, the Word would be conditioned by time, and this would imply it is not immutable. In that case there would be no way to secure a passage beyond the limits of the letter—no "narrow opening" to pass through—and Augustine is returned (despite never leaving) to the precipice of polysemy. Consequently, he continues to provide us with a theory of mediation: "Therefore it is clear and evident that the utterance came through the movement of some created thing, serving your eternal will but itself temporal."[37]

The Word (as both eternal and immutable) is thus transmitted through the movement of some created thing, which is both mortal and changeable. This theory of communication has at least three basic requirements: (1) the signal must not be contaminated by the process of transmission (i.e., it must be possible to *completely* divide the message from the medium that carries it); (2) the signal must be receivable (i.e., there must be someone who can receive, decipher, and communicate the message); (3) there must be a way of distinguishing the "true" message from a false or corrupted message. Augustine continues,

> And these your words, made for temporal succession, were reported by the external ear to the judicious mind whose internal ear is disposed to hear your

eternal word. But that mind would compare these words, sounding in time, with your eternal word in silence, and say: "It is very different, the difference is enormous. The sounds are far inferior to me, and have no being, because they are fleeting and transient. But the word of my God is superior to me and abides for ever." (Isa. 40:8)[38]

In this difference (i.e., the difference between words and the Word) Augustine senses a problem, namely, if the Word is communicated through words does this mean that the Word cannot be without words? While Hegel accepts this proposition and constructs his system around it, Augustine does not.

> You call us, therefore, to understand the Word, God who is with you God (John 1:1). That word is spoken eternally, and by it all things are uttered eternally. It is not the case that what was being said comes to an end, and something else is said, so that everything is uttered in a succession without a conclusion, but everything is said in the simultaneity of eternity."[39]

According to this formulation, the Word is pure and unending sound: a voice speaking without succession or duration. As such, the Word is the "now" of *incommutabilis substantia*: the "now" that Augustine orients himself towards. It is the Word that the angels read; they read a codex "without syllables requiring time to pronounce."[40]

In Book XIII Augustine asks God why Genesis relates the process of creation in a successive manner:

> To this you replied to me, since you are my God and speak with a loud voice in the inner ear to your servant, and broke my deafness with the cry: "O man, what my scripture says, I say. Yet scripture speaks in time-conditioned language, and time does not touch my Word, existing with me in an equal eternity. So I see those things which through my Spirit you see, just as I also say the things which through my Spirit you say. Accordingly, while your vision of them is temporally determined, my seeing is not temporal, just as you speak of these things in temporal terms but I do not speak in the successiveness of time."[41]

Now that we have the qualities of the Word secured (eternal, immutable, speech without end), we still have the problem of transmission (movement from the Word to words) and reception (from words to the Word).

The transmission from Word to words is the process of creation. Being falls into multiplicity, and in doing so it is distended (Augustine defines time as distention in Book XI.xxvi), stretched out between form and formlessness:[42] "One thing grows out of another, and so, by your blessing, God, things are multiplied. You have relieved the tedium for mortal senses by the fact that what is one thing for our understanding can be symbolized and expressed in many ways by physical movements."[43]

And again: "only in signs given corporeal expression and in intellectual concepts do we find an increasing and a multiplying which illustrates how one thing can be expressed in several ways and how one formulation can bear many meanings. Signs given corporeal expression are the creatures generated form the waters, necessary because of our deep involvement in the flesh."[44]

Despite this dispersion of Being into time, there remains a "narrow opening" that leads back to eternal truth. This "narrow opening" or "secret meaning" is, in our terms, the transmission and it remains (in varying degrees) in all beings. It speaks through beings, but this voice can only be heard by the "internal ear" of the mind. It is through this "inner" hearing that one can determine can discern the "truth."

> May I hear and understand how in the beginning you made heaven and earth (Gen. 1:1). Moses wrote this. He wrote this and went his way, passing out of this world from you to you. He is not now before me, but if he were, I would clasp him and ask him and through you beg him to explain to me the creation. I would concentrate my bodily ears to hear the sounds breaking forth from his mouth.... Yet how would I know whether or not he was telling the truth? If I did know this, I could not be sure of it from him. Within me, within the lodging of my thinking, there would speak a truth which is neither Hebrew nor Greek nor Latin nor any barbarian tongue and which uses neither mouth nor tongue as instruments and utters no audible syllables. It would say: "What he is saying is true."[45]

Augustine expands upon this point later on:

> in the gospel the Word speaks through the flesh, and this sounded externally in human ears, so that it should be believed and sought inwardly, founding the eternal truth where the Master who alone is good (Matt. 19:16) teaches all his disciplines. There, Lord, I hear your voice speaking to me, for one who teaches us speaks to us, but one who does not teach us, even though he may speak, does not speak to us. Who is our teacher except the reliable truth? Even when we are instructed through some mutable creature, we are led to reliable truth when we are learning truly by standing still and listening to him.[46]

In order to perceive the "secret meaning" speaking *through* beings, one must "stand still" and "listen." This listening is not attending to what is said by others—it is neither dialogue nor conversation—but, a listening without hearing or hearing without listening. However one wishes to formulate it, what is heard is not the *saying* (the act of speaking), but the *said* (meaning). This "listening" is not an attending to another that speaks to me, it is a reading in and through silence, a silencing of the ceaseless buzzing world. In short, it is a listening through or over others in an effort to hear the Word. Conversion can thus be characterized as a *turning-away-from-time-within-time*: the convert turns his or her attention away from beings to attend to the Being of beings. In attending, it "stands still" and "listens" for a "truth" it *knows* must be there. But what is the nature of this knowledge? That is, what guarantees that the convert is receiving the "true" transmission? Finally, how is this activity (receiving the transmission/"standing still") lived?

With regard to how the activity of "standing still" is lived, we can turn to Book XI. In Chapter XXVIII of this book, Augustine uses of the analogy of reciting a psalm to explain the experience of time.

> Suppose I am about to recite a psalm which I know. Before I begin, my expectation is directed towards the whole. But when I have begun, the verses from it which I take into the past become the object of my memory. The life of this act of mine is stretched two ways, into my memory because of the words I have already said and into my expectation because of those which I am about to say. But my attention is on what is present: by that the future is transferred into the past. As the action advances further and further, the shorter the expectation and the longer the memory, until all expectation is consumed, the entire action is finished, and it has passed into the memory.[47]

This can be read as a phenomenology of the confessant. He recollects and rearranges his memories in an effort to find the notes that he has sung. Memories "have to be brought together (*cogenda*) so as to be capable of being known; that means they have to be gathered (*colligenda*) from their dispersed state."[48] This is the very activity of thought: "To bring together (*cogo*) and to cogitate (*cogito*) are words related as *ago* (I do) and *agito* (agitate) or *facio* (I make) to *factito* (I make frequently)."[49] Once these notes are deciphered—extricated from the silent, unfathomable depths of the "huge cavern" or "vast hall" known as "memory"—they provide the confessant with the rhyme scheme of the psalm.[50] With this held within memory, the confessant can read the notes within the present. This "now" is the point by which the future is transferred into the psalm. The future is the expectation that the rhyme scheme projects and thus it is not unexpected. Rather, "What occurs in the psalm as a whole occurs in its particular pieces and its individual syllables. The same is true of a longer action in which perhaps that psalm is a part. It is also valid of the entire life of an individual person, where all actions are parts of a whole, and the total history of 'the sons of men' (Ps. 30:20) where all human lives are but parts."[51]

The parts of the psalm—from "particular pieces" to "individual syllables"—correspond to the "truth" of the whole. So as the confessant "stands still" and sounds out the song (that it, at one and the same time, *is* and *is not yet*) its future is assured by the progression of the song. "A person singing or listening to a song he knows well suffers a distention or stretching in feeling and in sense perception from the expectation of future sounds and the memory of past sound."[52]

The rhyme scheme of the song measures and marks the progression of time towards an end that it has anticipated. In the act of confession the confessant attempts to instrumentalize itself. By singing a song that is not its own—discovering it within by *anamnesis*—the confessant gives *time* to the surrounding world. The song is the Word that temporizes the world. The confessant "stands still"—re-collects and re-composes the syllables—and thereby claims the passive moral agency (the agency of the medium) in relation to the song. The song marks and measures the world. By "standing still" and reading, the confessant draws the noise of language towards the silent song that the "inner ear" attends to. It sings for the benefit of "others"—for the "ears of believing sons of men"—to draw them with language away from language. It calls out for others to join in the song that they (always already) are. There is a community of singers dedicated to the coming silence. Yet none of the singers can determine the line that divides the "song" from "sound" (cf. Augustine's discussion of kinds of priority in Book XII.xxix). This is the anxiety that drives their song; they desire the final silence, they sing towards it, and yet within the present of their song they can only witness its movement.

In other words if we refuse Augustine's claim to go beyond the question of meaning (i.e., of polysemy) via the practice of "standing still" and the experience of the divine, we can question the nature of his knowledge. From this perspective we can state that the epistemological claim that drives song (that the "truth" or "essence" of the phenomenal can be "read") cannot determine precise ontological distinctions (i.e., what is the line that divides the "letter" from the "spirit" or the "body" from the "soul"). As a result, if we interrupt the "song" of the confessant and demand evidence to support the metaphysical or onto-theological claims it articulates, all it can offer are a mixture of affective statements pertaining to the "feeling" of the "truth," interrogatives ("Don't you feel the truth?"), and promises (the truth is "not yet"). The orientation and meaning it claims—the sense that enables it to escape the precipice of polysemy—to receive by "reading" the world is never complete, and thus is never beyond doubt. The restlessness of *Confessions* is a product of this claim to absolute meaning: the confessant *cannot* stop giving voice to the song. The confessant must sing until the end of time itself; if it were to fall silent and the world remained in place, it would be returned to the very precipice it sought to escape.

At this point we can return to the epistemological question we posed earlier on (i.e., What is the nature of the knowledge that orients the confessant?).[53] If we pose this question from the outside—that is, without accepting the metaphysical apparatus (immutable substance, the "truth" of his experience of the divine) that enables the confessant to make "sense" of the world—the answer is affective. The confessant "feels" the "truth" of his or her perceptions. The motivation that drives this is the desire for absolute truth: "May I know you, who know me. May I "know as I also am known" (I Cor. 12:12)."[54] The desire to *"know-as-I-am-known"* is the desire for communion, that is, it is the desire to occupy, at one and the same time, the position of both the addressee and the addresser.[55] The signs that the confessant claims to read behind the phenomenal world are interpreted as indicators or signs that lead beyond the world to the ultimate fusion with the Absolute. The *Confessions* is bound by the logic of the superlative. Everything is oriented to and by an immutable but imperceptible point. The act of reading moves towards the end of writing, language strives towards its own obliteration, the song marks out the time of its silence by pointing towards the eternal present of the Absolute.[56] Without the "truth" promised by the repetition of the song, the perception of time changes; the past, my memory, is no longer a treasury or storehouse, but, much like Borges's "Library of Babel," an infinite library without an index. The future is open and not assured. I may expect just as I may compose my memories into a past that I claim as my own, but both are subject to the unforeseeable disaster. The present is no longer simply the movement of the future into the past (as it was with the song) but a moment in which the "I" that I claim to be is called into question. Augustine senses the precipice of the present—the frontier that divides thought from the unthinkable—he approaches the abyss, he fears falling into it and losing all orientation. In order to avoid this, he "stands still" and begins to sing a song—the song that marks and measures time by reading through or over beings—that will silence the world. Those who join in his song and enter his community all bear within their song a silence that is "not yet." Lyotard captures the world of this community: "The book in the form of the firmament filters the formidable presence of the author. Chased out of the paradise of your intimacy, we are left for memory by you the collection of your works, the world, a text of which we form as much a part as its readers. Decipherable decipherers, in the library of shadows."[57] They read the world in order to gain entry into the library of angels: "Books without letter, unwritten scripture, the library of the angels is, in truth, empty."[58]

The troubling question that remains is: What is read-over, or indeed read-out, and read-out without end, in order for the song to continue? This will draw us towards the "a" of *différance* and the question of ethics; but for now we will turn our attention to Bataille.

A Speech That Maintains Silence: From Sliding Words to Community

There is silence in Bataille's writing, but unlike in Augustine this silence is not the silence of reading or "standing still" or even the promised silence of *incommutabilis substantia*. Rather, Bataille's writing "communicates" silence. At this point we are confronted by a deceptively simple question: How can silence be communicated? If we take the term "communication" to mean the process by which meaning is transmitted by means of signs, the answer seems obvious. All that is required for us to communicate silence is to simply say or write the word "silence." The problem is that "silence" refers to an action or state that its very communication violates. In *Inner Experience* Bataille uses "silence" as an example of a "slipping" word: "I will give only one example of a 'slipping' *word*. I say *word*: it could just as well be the sentence into which one inserts the word, but I limit myself to the word *silence*. It is already, as I have said, the abolition of the sound which the word is; among all words it is the most perverse, or the most poetic: it is a token of its own death."[59]

In effect, by communicating the word "silence" we highlight the inadequation of the sign and its sense. Bataille's writing is the communication of this inadequation. This sets it immediately apart from Augustine's cryptomantic exegesis.[60] In that, the inadequation is not interpreted as a "sign" (understood in its mantic or prophetic sense) of a meaning *yet-to-come*. With this distinction kept in mind, the question then becomes how does Bataille communicate silence? And furthermore, how is this connected with "inner experience"?

To address the first part of our question, we will have to refer back to Bataille's example of the "slipping" word and ask what the example serves to illustrate. Bataille stating that he will give "only one example" makes it immediately clear that he does not see this "slipping" quality as a unique feature of one particular word. The example serves to highlight a universal property of signification. This being so, "silence" (as inadequation between the sign and its referent) is a common property of all communication. In his *Course in General Linguistics*, Saussure will take this to be the first principle governing the linguistic sign: the connection between the sign and referent is arbitrary.[61] There is no *inner connection* between a sign and what it refers to. In this sense all discourse communicates "silence," but Bataille seizes upon this principle and writes towards it.

> The sand into which we bury ourselves in order not to see, is formed of words, and contestation, having to make use of them, causes one to think—if I pass from one image to another different one—of the stuck, struggling man whose efforts sink him for certain: and it is true that words, their labyrinths, the exhausting immensity of their "possibles," in short their treachery, have

something of quicksand about them. We would not get out of this sand, without some sort of cord which is extended to us. Although words drain almost all life from within us—there is almost not a single sprig of this life which the bustling host of these ants (words) hasn't seized, dragged, accumulated without respite—there subsists in us a silent, elusive, ungraspable part. In the region of words, of discourse, this part is neglected.[62]

Here Bataille presents the constitutive silence of the sign as labyrinthine. If we were to attempt to follow the innumerable semantic possibilities of each word, we would become hopelessly lost. The more we struggle after meaning—the meaning that would complete us and fill that "silent, elusive, ungraspable part"—the faster we sink. Instead of struggling against this sinking, Bataille writes towards it. He arranges terms in such a way that they expose their constitutive inadequacy. Thus, the image of the "struggling man" sinking is replaced with a sudden and precipitous fall. This writing operates by strategically exposing the silence of language as silence without reserve (i.e., not the silence of expectation).

As Derrida notes, Bataille's project functions by employing two forms of writing:

1 In one whole group of texts, the sovereign renunciation of recognition enjoins the erasure of the written text. For example, the erasure of poetic writing as minor writing.
2 But there is a sovereign form of writing, which on the contrary, must interrupt the servile complicity of speech and meaning.[63]

In the first, the fall into silence is indicated by the "erasure of the written text." This form gestures towards the "extreme limit" (the fall into "inner experience") by exposing the impossibility of signification. To quote Bataille,

> One can know nothing of man which has not taken the form of a sentence, and the infatuation for poetry, on the other hand makes of untranslatable strings of words a summit. The extreme limit is elsewhere.... Should some sort of expression give evidence of it: the extreme limit is distinct from it. It is never literature. If poetry expresses it, the extreme limit is distinct from it: to the point of not being poetic, for if poetry has it as an object, it doesn't reach it. When the extreme limit is there, the means which serve to attain it are no longer there.[64]

The second is the project of contesting signification in and by writing. As Derrida states,

> *This*—major—writing will be called *writing* because it *exceeds* the *logos* (of meaning, lordship, presence etc.). Within this writing—the one sought by

Bataille—the *same* concepts, apparently unchanged in themselves, will be subject to a mutation of meaning, or rather will be struck by (even though they are apparently indifferent), the loss of sense toward which they slide, thereby ruining themselves immeasurably.[65]

In this mode, "I write in order to annihilate the play of subordinate operations within myself."[66] These two forms (referred to as minor and major respectively) function together to operationalize the principle of inner experience: "to emerge through project from the realm of project."[67] Bataille expands on this principle, "Inner experience is led by discursive reason. Reason alone has the power to undo its work, to hurl down what it has built up."[68] This being the case, we could see the major form as the work of unworking signification by and through writing and minor form as the written gesture towards the experience of non-knowledge.

The experience of non-knowledge ("inner experience") must be distinguished from the mantic experience of Augustine. There are similarities; in each the inadequacy of speech leads to an ecstatic experience and this experience cannot be signified. But the inadequacy of speech is different in the two cases. For Augustine, the inadequacy of speech (and indeed all beings) functions (function) as essential traces of the Absolute. These traces give the convert a specific trajectory (the conversation "ascends" via a consideration of beings to move into the mind). The "experience" itself is internal (within the mind) and atemporal (an instant). It is an experience of communion (unmediated fusion with the Absolute). The result of the "vision" is to reinforce the trajectory of the convert (away from the time of beings/words and towards timelessness of Being/silence). In order to follow this trajectory, the convert has to continually mark, measure, and negate beings. This practice of judgment and separation is how the convert "reads" the world, finds the traces of Being in beings. The gaze of the convert is divided in two: the eyes of the body and the "inner vision" of cognition. The orientation is maintained by a constant negation of beings (i.e., the body of the convert and the objects of its desire). It *reads-out* beings in order to experience Being: if one were to ask how the judgments the convert makes are justified, the only possible answer is affective ("I feel the truth") and messianic ("the truth is yet to come"). There is no responsibility, no possibility of contestation, because the confessant claims that it is a vessel, a conduit, or medium of another that is *not-yet*. The only possible form of *being-with-others* is the community of the "same" (e.g., the many-membered body). Each member partakes in and thereby affirms the *reading-out* of temporal things in order to commune with the Absolute. The ultimate aim is fusion with Being in absolute immanence, but the path to this end is the endless repetition of the negation of beings. By reading-out (i.e., by silencing) the difference between beings and Being, each member is able to attend to the silent promise of the *Being-that-is-yet-to-come*.

For Bataille, the inadequacy of speech *is not and cannot be* a "sign" of an equivalence that is *yet-to-come*. Bataille's writing—in both its major and its minor form—articulates writing towards this inadequacy *as* inadequacy. By "communicating" this inadequacy, it unworks an entire mode of existing in the world. This "mode" is the mode of project:

> "Action" is utterly dependent upon project. And what is serious, is that discursive thought is itself engaged in the mode of existence of project. Discursive thought is evinced by an individual engaged in action: it takes place within him beginning with his projects, on the level of reflexion upon projects. Project is not only the mode of existence implied by action, necessary to action—it is a way of being in paradoxical time: *it is the putting off of existence to a later point.*[69]

"Project" as a mode of *being-in-the-world* is paradoxical because the subject takes the present as a point of action in which it can make progress towards its intended goal. This being so, the intentional state that characterizes this paradoxical way of being is expectation. While the term "project" can refer to the projects of particular subjects (everyday plans and goals), in this context the project referred to is the universal project of reason (the search for absolute knowledge). The itinerary of this project is that of absolute idealism. Within this project language functions as the means to know and to act upon the world. In order for this project to make progress, language must be a neutral (or, at the very least, neutralizable) means to gather, arrange, and transmit meaning. Quite simply, there must be a way past the precipice of polysemy, a way of deriving the essential truth of things. Bataille characterizes this itinerary as evasion and draws our attention to the stakes of this paradoxical way of being: "What is strange is that in evading experience, one doesn't see the responsibility which one has assumed."[70]

The problem he draws our attention to is that by "reading" the "truth" of the phenomenal world a series of judgments and actions are made that can only be justified from the perspective of the end. The subject who enacts the "truth" that it perceives behind phenomenal reality as the natural "law" can only do so by deferring the responsibility for its judgments to the Absolute that is *yet-to-come*. This subject cannot see the responsibility it assumes, because its intentional state is that of expectation (i.e., in Augustine the language of disgust that targets both his body and women as the objects of his desire is justified by metaphysical arguments that cannot be immediately justified). Bataille interrupts the itinerary of this project from within by using language to "communicate" the irresolvable inadequacy of the sign to the referent. He exposes the fundamental contingency of language, and thus contaminates the entire storehouse of accumulated knowledge. The "truth" that Augustine gathers and arranges by "standing still"—the "truth" of *incommutabilis substantia* that would consummate itself by *sounding-out* language itself—is interrupted by the very principles that govern its communication (i.e., the arbitrary nature of the sign and its linear temporality). This interruption is a contestation of a way of being in time. It contests the deferred responsibility of the confessant by contesting the very nature of communication. It is no longer the transmission of transcendental essence via the neutral medium of the sign, but a contingent (and thus contestable) nomination that is delivered *with* and *for others*. "Inner experience" is the sudden and precipitous fall from the itinerary of project into the present without reserve or orientation. As Bataille defines it, "inner experience" is "the opposite of action."[71] Which is not to say that it un-acts or un-does what has been done in the sense of revising past acts, but it undoes or unworks the epistemological and metaphysical context that makes our past actions make sense. It is the experience (not in the sense of an internal state or of the mental content derived thereof, as this "experience" destabilizes the distinction between internal and external) of non-knowledge that exposes me without reserve to *being-with-others*.

Two Modes of "Community"/Two Modes of Temporality

Now that we have a basic grasp of the communication of silence and its connection with "inner experience," we can approach the question of community. Bataille introduces the following principle: "there cannot be knowledge without a community of seekers, nor inner experience without a community of those who live it."[72] He goes on to stipulate that "Community is to be understood in a different sense from Church or from order."[73]

The distinction between these two modes of community rests on two distinct models of communication. In the community-of-order, communication is the transmission of a message via a neutral medium; that is, it operates under the presumption of absolute meaning. While it acknowledges that the sign is different from its referent, it maintains that this difference is methodologically bridgeable. The method it develops is designed to override the arbitrary nature of the sign and absolutely stabilize meaning. While the precise form of this method varies, in general it is cryptomantic (i.e., the secret of absolute meaning is given in mantic experiences). It thus overrides the principles that govern language by teleologically suspending them. Under this suspension the silence of language is read as the promise of a meaning *yet-to-come*. In this way a community is organized around a "secret" whose "truth" is *yet-to-come*. Its members are members because they recognize and affirm their essential sameness. The freedom that the community-of-order offers its members is the freedom from freedom. That is, identifying their will with the project, their actions gain a determined form. This method is able to provide a fixed set of natural laws, but these laws can only be justified via messianism. The danger here (in this evasion of freedom) is, as Bataille points out, "one doesn't see the responsibility which one has assumed."[74] The paradoxical temporality of this community-of-order can only be maintained in and by the illusion of progress. The problem is that by projecting the source of justification and responsibility into the future, one forms a positive feedback loop: each output (decision/action) returns to the system as an input (sign/promise). There is thus an accelerative tendency in the community-of-order: the demand for the end can and will only grow over time.[75] This is precisely why Nancy states that communal fusion and immanence have "no other logic than that of the suicide of the community that is governed by it."[76]

In the community of "inner experience" communication is the communication of *difference as difference*. It is the communication of the impossibility of "absolute truth." This communication can be understood as messianic in the sense that it arrives in a now without any *yet-to-come*, but it is not messianism, in that it does not hold its final meaning in reserve and govern the now under to the promise of the *yet-to-come*. In a certain respect the change this communication brings is akin to the one Benjamin (who heard it from Gershom Scholem) recounts: "The Hassidim tell a story about the world to come that says everything there will be just as it is here. Just as our room is now, so it will be in the world to come; where our baby sleeps now, there too it will sleep in the other world. And the clothes we wear in this world, those too we will wear there. Everything will be as it is now, just a little different."[77]

Here the "little" difference would be the interruption of paradoxical time (i.e., Augustine's "standing still" or Bataille's "evading experience"). Everything remains the same in terms of the material world precisely because it was never anything else (there were no "signs" of the Absolute). The change this interruption brings is that "one [now *sees*] the responsibility which one has assumed: none can overwhelm more: it is *inexpiable sin*."[78] "Inner experience" is culpability without limitation because there is no absolute to pronounce judgment and set the measure of the offence.[79] In an instant the past events that have been carefully gathered and arranged into a series suddenly fall apart, and like Benjamin's angel of history I see "one single catastrophe which keeps piling wreckage upon wreckage"; but unlike the angel I am not on the margins of this catastrophe.[80] I am at its midst and I am to blame. The experience of this is, in Bataille's terms, *angoisse*: "Non-knowledge is ANGUISH before all else. In anguish, there appears a nudity which puts one into ecstasy. But ecstasy itself (nudity, communication) is elusive if anguish is elusive. Thus ecstasy only remains possible in the anguish of ecstasy, in this sense, that it cannot be the satisfaction of *grasped knowledge*."[81]

This "ecstasy" is not the silent internal flight of Augustine's mantic vision:

> The subject—weariness of itself, necessity of proceeding to the extreme limit—seeks ecstasy, it is true: never does it have the will for its ecstasy. There exists an irreducible discord between the subject seeking ecstasy and the ecstasy itself. However, the subject knows ecstasy and senses it: not as a voluntary direction coming from itself, but like the sensation of an effect coming from the outside.[82]

Bataille reinforces this point very clearly: "inner experience is conquest and as such *for others* ... it is *consciousness of others.*"[83] This community is, as Bataille refers to it, "the community of those without community."[84] The law of this community is the absence of *the* law, that is, it is the law of *being-with-others* without the "sign" of the *yet-to-come*. In this mode of existence the now is the now of being called into question, of being contested, and responsible. In this sense one could revise Ivan Karamazov's infamous and terrifying formulation—"If God is dead, all is permitted" by replacing the consequent: "If God is dead, all is contestable."[85]

This leaves us with a serious question concerning the nature of this community-of-those-without-community, namely: What is it that the members of this community hold in common? As this questions draws us from Bataille to a series of other thinkers and texts, it exceeds the scope of our current analysis; but, that said, it does require some provisional commentary here. If we can see how the community-of-order is a community of sameness maintained by paradoxical temporality of the project, what binds the members of community that Bataille speaks of? According to Nancy, "The relation (the community) is, if it is, nothing other than what undoes, in its very principle—and at its closure or on its limit—the autarchy of absolute immanence."[86]

Nancy clarifies this point later on:

> It is not a communion that fuses the *egos* into an *Ego* or a higher *We*. It is the community of *others*. The genuine community of mortal beings, or death as community, establishes their impossible communion. Community therefore occupies a singular place: it assumes the impossibility of its own immanence, the impossibility of a communitarian being in the form of a subject. In a certain sense community acknowledges and inscribes—this is its peculiar gesture—the impossibility of community.[87]

Nancy will refer to this "peculiar gesture" as the *co-appearance* or *com-pearance* [*com-paraît*] of finitude. This *com-pearance* is universal in a sense that extends beyond either the "species-being" of Marx or Aristotle's "*zoon politikon*," in that it is the *being-with* of finitude. Returning to Nancy:

In order to designate this singular mode of appearing, this specific phenomenality, which is no doubt more originary than any other (for it could be that the world appears to the community, not to the individual), we would need to be able to say that finitude *co-appears* or *compears* (*com-paraît*) and can only *compear*: in this formulation we would need to hear that finitude always presents itself "together," hence severally; for finitude always presents itself in being-in-common and as this being itself, and it always presents itself at a *hearing* and before the judgment of the law of community, or, more originarily before the judgment of the community as law.[88]

It is this *compearance* that interrupts the paradoxical temporality of project and exposes us in a moment without reserve. In this moment what could not be seen from within project, what could not be seen precisely because project was predicated on *seeing through* it is the "letter." Not as the neutral medium of absolute sense, but as the silent spacing of communication. It appears "before the judgment of the community as law" in that it exposes the shared limit of that law. It is a resistance to the immanence of communion, but it is not a volitional resistance just as it is *not* a struggle for recognition. In a footnote, Nancy illustrates this resistance with a quotation from Robert Antelme's *L'espèce humaine* (*The Human Race*):

> The SS who view us all as one and the same cannot induce us to see ourselves that way. They cannot prevent us from choosing. On the contrary: here the need to choose is constant and immeasurably greater. The more transformed we become, the farther we retreat from back home, the more the SS believe us reduced to the indistinctness and to the irresponsibility whereof we do present the appearance—the more distinctions our community does in fact contain, and the stricter those distinctions are. The inhabitant of the camps is not the abolition of these differences; on the contrary, he is their effective realization.[89]

He continues,

> Death is stronger than the SS. The SS cannot pursue the guy over the line into death. Yet again the SS are forced to hold up. It has reached its limit. There are moments when you could kill yourself just in order that the SS fetch up against this limit as it confronts the impassive object you'd have become, the dead body that has turned its back on them, that doesn't give a shit about their law.[90]

The utterly passive and silent resistance of the corpse exposes the shared limit of the law. To attempt to legislate, to found a community-of-order, whose laws extend beyond this limit by adopting the logic of messianism is to attempt to silence the question of death. To make the death of another have an absolutely fixed meaning, to end the very possibility of the question of death, is to live in absolute immanence of the *incommutabilis substantia*. To quote Blanchot: "To remain present in the proximity of another who by dying removes himself definitively, to take upon myself another's death as the only death that concerns me, this is what puts me beside myself, this is the only separation that can open me, in its very impossibility, to the Openness of a community."[91]

In order for death to cease to be experienced as a "separation"—that is, in order for the community-of-order to be complete—one would have to transcend the limitations of what Benjamin refers to as "mythical" violence. Only "divine" violence, the violence that is "lethal without spilling blood," can fulfill the desire of the community-of-order, only it can bring absolute immanence.[92] It is "divine" violence that Augustine both longs for—"my years pass in groans ... until the day when, purified and molten by the fire of your love, I flow together to merge into you"—and is constantly denied.[93] Without the violence that transcends violence (the violence of the silent and silencing voice of God), the corpse remains a silent testament to the limits of the law and to the "community of those without community."

REVIEWING THE COURSE

Given both the convoluted and the expansive nature of the material we have covered up to this point, it may be useful to address a series of questions in a more direct fashion. The hope here is that by posing a short series of questions we can provide a concise summary of the similarities and differences that draw Augustine and Bataille into a troubled form of proximity.

1 What is the relation between the sign and the referent?
    a For Augustine, there is an indicative trace of the essence of the referent concealed within the sign. The "truth" of the connection between the sign and the referent is *incommutabilis substantia*. While this "truth" is not readily apparent in the present, it can be experienced when the correct exegetical method is put into practice. The process of conversion is a *turning towards* the "truth" that is *yet-to-come*. By *turning* the confessant is able to read the inadequacy of the sign as an apparent limitation. The doubled sensory apparatus of the confessant (i.e., the senses of the body are rejected as the source of error and replaced by a series of "inner" senses) overwhelms this apparent limitation and is able to see the gap between the sign and the referent as a promise of the "now" that is *yet-to-come* (the complete now in which fallen

language is replaced by a communion that knows neither difference or time).
b For Bataille, the connection between the sign and the referent is arbitrary. The disjunction between them is evidenced by the word "silence." There is no experience of an *incommutabilis substantia* to stabilize the slide of meaning towards the precipice of polysemy (or, in Bataille's terms, towards nonknowledge). Bataille seizes upon this principle and writes in an effort to communicate this inadequacy. To "communicate" it is not to somehow bridge the gap between the sign and the referent and secure absolute meaning; rather, "communication" in his terms is to communicate the inadequacy as inadequacy. In other terms he writes the *trace as trace*.

2 How does this relation shape their philosophy of history?
a For Augustine, the "truth" is always already different from its present state and to come, which is to say deferred. This being so, temporality is conceived from the perspective of this "truth." Time is a distention, a falling away from the eternal present of *Deus incommutabilis substantia*. In the eternal present there is no difference between essence and existence. There is only the pure and silent communion of God and the angels. In time existence is divided from its true essence, and this division brings with it the *timens praecipitium* that there is no absolute meaning, no Archimedean point to anchor meaning to, and thus nothing to prevent one from falling into the abyss of polysemy. The finite present is thus *not-as-it-should-be*; its "truth" is *yet-to-come*. Time is suffered by the confessant; it is a vale of tears, because it is experienced as separation from the absolute truth of *incommutabilis substantia*. It is linear in that each temporal mode (past, present, future) is oriented by (i.e., the "truth" of each moment both within memory and in the lived present is a "sign" that points towards the Absolute) and towards the *yet-to-come*.
b For Bataille, the only truth is the impossibility of absolute truth. His understanding of temporality is thus centred on the moment. The "now" is not that of expectation but of *timens praecipitium* without the possibility of evasion. To experience the impossibility of absolute truth is to return to the very precipice that Augustine thinks he has left behind. Bataille's struggle is to *live the impossibility of meaning*. To live this impossibility is to live in a present with others; that is, it is to share, to "communicate," this impossibility. The past is no

longer an oriented line or series of meaningful "signs" that one collects in an effort to bridge the gap that divides essence and existence; rather, it is the site of unending contestation. The future is a *to-come* without the possibility of expectation. The present is also a suffering, but it is not the suffering of a transitory state, but rather a suffering for and with others in the face of death.

3   How does this structure their model of community?
   a   The community possible within the Augustinian model of "sense" is the community-of-order, in which members recognize and affirm their essential sameness. The offer of membership is universal, but conditional. The member must accept the "truth" of *incommutabilis substantia* as its own and it must live this "truth" as its law. The law has the benefit of being remarkably stable and of promising a way beyond the *timens praecipitium* of death. The freedom it offers is, in a paradoxical sense, the freedom from freedom. As a result of its commitment to *incommutabilis substantia* the confessant cannot assume responsibility for its speech: it can take responsibility for actions under the law that his or her speech articulates, but it cannot take responsibility for the law itself. For example, Augustine can and does assume responsibility for his actions and intentional states (he is even troubled by the content of his non-intentional states) in relation to the objects of his desire, but he cannot assume responsibility for the law that categorizes these objects. The confessant can gather and arrange the "truth" and with this it can articulate the "law," but this "law" is not its own. This structure has a positive feedback problem, in that every action (out-put) is justified by its status as a "sign" and is thus taken back into the system (in-put). The suffering of time that accompanies this mode of existence is a suffering unto death.
   b   Bataille's struggle to live the impossibility of meaning is the community-of-those-without-community. This paradoxical repetition of predicates that suspends while crossing out (i.e., "x without x") can be seen as an attempt to "communicate" the inadequacy of the sign "community." While the term suggests the very "common unity" that grounds the community-of-order, the repetition brings with it the question that the term on its own serves to conceal: What, or rather how, is "common-unity" lived? More specifically, how is it lived *now*? As a result, it does not pertain only to those excluded from

the community, but forces the question into the midst of community itself: "How do you live in your common-unity?" Not "How will you live your common unity?" but "How do you live it now?" In a sense it forces the community-of-order to define the meaning of community. The response is that community as it is now is incomplete, but its "true" common-unity is *yet-to-come*. The meaning of the term *community* is thus salvaged from the ruin of tautology by messianism. The "community-of-those-without-community" steers meaning directly into the impossibility of the tautological in an effort to force the question of community into the now without the *yet-to-come*. It asks how "common unity" is lived in the impossibility of meaning. This being so, it is not the unity of essence that binds the members of the community-of-order, but shared singularity (and as a result the question of inclusion is no longer bound to the limits of the "subject," the "individual," or the "human").

Chapter 3

THE WAY OUT IS THROUGH
Sade's Novel and the Crime of Writing

> A paradox underlies his behaviour. De Sade speaks, but he is the mouthpiece of a silent life, of utter and inevitably speechless solitude.
> —Georges Bataille, *Erotism: Death and Sensuality*

WITHIN THE SADEAN OEUVRE *Reflections on the Novel* (*Idée sur les romans*) holds a relatively small, if not outright obscure, position. This seemingly conventional discursive essay was published in the 8th Brumaire of the Republic (1800) as the introductory text to his four-volume work *Les Crimes de l'amour*. In it Sade attempts to answer three interrelated questions:

1 What is the kind of literary work called a novel?
2 Amongst what people did the novel originate, and what are the most famous examples that history has to offer?
3 And, finally, what are the rules one must follow in order to succeed in perfecting the art of novel writing?[1]

The essay thus serves as both a genealogy of European fiction and a reduction of the "novel" to a set of axiomatic guidelines.[2] That is to say, the essay shifts from a discursive archeology of the "novel" to a programmatic formula for writing. If we read this essay as an introduction to the Sadean project as a whole, it is possible to see the project as a process of discursive refinement, that is, as a process that operates directly on the signifier through the instrumentalization of a specific discursive form. In short, we begin to see Sade not as an *author* but as a *writer*. As Roland Barthes argues, "Being a writer and not a realistic author Sade always chooses the discourse over the referent; he always sides with *semiosis* rather than *mimesis*: what he "represents" is constantly being deformed by the meaning, and it is on the level of the meaning, not of the referent, that we should read him."[3]

But if this is indeed the case, what is guiding Sade's semiosis? Is there a method to his discursive operations? Is there a "dark" mimesis guiding his use of the sign? According to Georges Bataille, Sade is "the mouthpiece of a silent life."[4] His writing is paradoxical in that he struggles to use the sign to end the possibility of speech. Thus, the "dark" mimesis beneath Sade's semiosis is total negation. And yet, this still leaves us with the question of how Sade writes.

My focus in this chapter is on Sade's use of writing both in terms of an overarching strategy and a continual process of tactical adjustment. In terms of the former, Sade organizes his text as a means of disseminating a mode of materialism that draws heavily on the work of several of his contemporaries (La Mettrie, Rousseau, Condillac, d'Holbach, Diderot, Helvétius, etc.).[5] Like them he holds that nature is the source of truth and that this truth can be known via the senses, but unlike them his project is committed to the end of "saying everything."[6] As Marcel Hénaff notes,

> The Sadean paradox is precisely to attempt a systematic description of what can be defined outside the system. And yet, to founder in an exhaustive inventory is to resign oneself to the unsaid, to renounce the possibility of really saying everything. This worry about missing an element, about leaving a blank space, unleashes an entire mechanism of repetition: redoing the same scenes, the same treatises, the same arguments. We observe in fact, a veritably obsessional type of conjuring ritual, with its compulsion to backtrack and to verify that nothing whatsoever had been neglected, that nothing was forgotten. All this to control subsequent traces, plans, and outcomes. In short, it is a question of obtaining a complete repertory, a saturation *without remainder*, so that the *too much* can enter into the *all*.[7]

The end is thus not to simply expose the truth of nature's law; rather, Sade operates directly on the signifier in an effort to commit the absolute crime. In an essay entitled "Sade's Reason" Maurice Blanchot observes that

> If crime is the spirit of Nature, there can be no crime against nature, and, consequently, no crime is possible. Sade asserts this, sometimes with great satisfaction, sometimes with fiery rage. Denying the possibility of crime allows him to deny morality, God, and all human values, but the denial of crime also entails relinquishing the spirit of negation, admitting that this spirit itself could be usurped. He vigorously opposes this conclusion, which leads him to gradually remove all reality from Nature.[8]

According to Blanchot, Sade moves from Nature to the principle of energy and sovereignty. He wants to be absolutely exempt from the law of nature, to be complete by transgressing all law. Blanchot continues:

Sade completely understood that man's energetic sovereignty, to the extent that man acquires this sovereignty by identifying with the spirit of negation, is a paradoxical state. The complete man, completely affirmed, is also completely destroyed. He is the man of all passions and he is unfeeling. He began by destroying himself, first insofar as he was man, then as God, and then as Nature, and thus he became the Unique. Now he can do everything, for the negation in him overthrew everything. To account for its formation, Sade resorts to a highly coherent concept which he gives the classical name of "apathy." Apathy is the spirit of negation applied to the man who has chosen to be sovereign. It is, in a certain way, the cause and the principle of energy.[9]

In order to go beyond all law he must go to the very end of signification. The tactics are thus experimental. The text can be seen as an extension of this paradoxical logic of energetics. Each repetition, each shift in its organization, is a tentative step towards completing a semiotic circuit. The aim of this process is to go beyond the limited or conditional negation of "crime" to "pure negation."[10]

My line of inquiry begins with the principles of the perfect novel, or rather the tentative principles for the perfection of the novel: one must remember it is an (always already) incomplete work. Thus, I will begin by focusing on the principles outlined in *Reflections on the Novel*. Sade admits that the perfect novel, the novel that would "say everything," has not been written. In fact, the principles that will lead to its perfection are still in a developmental stage, still being refined. Despite this, its time draws near. As Sade exclaims, "'tis only by advancing that any art moves nearer to perfection; the goal can only be reached by successive attempts."[11]

In order to address the systemic discursive progression of the Sadean text, we must ask what the purpose of this process of textual purification is, that is, what is its end goal, its *telos*. Why must this specific discursive form be refined? What makes the "novel" unique among the literary arts? Or more specifically, why does Sade choose the discursive form he refers to as the "novel"?

For Sade, the purpose of the "novel" is to "seize" nature by acting as "the faithful mirror" of "the heart of man."[12] Its function is thus to provide an authentic representation, a representation that through its sheer degree of verisimilitude would draw nature, in its totality, into the discursive field. Sade's privileging of the "heart" is interesting here, as it is that through which nature (in its totality) may be "seized"; it is the point from which the silent, hidden law of nature may be accessed. Yet, we must ask, why is the heart the privileged organ of discourse? By privileging the heart Sade effectively bypasses the authority of the ear (the privileged organ of scholasticism) and with it the law of the book. Sade thus appeals directly to the authority of sensuous experience.[13] This is a very Rousseauian move: "whatever God wishes a man to do he does not cause it to be told to him by another man, but he says it to him himself, he writes it in the depths of his heart."[14] Like Rousseau, Sade appeals to a "natural writing" that "is immediately united to the voice and to breath."[15] "There is however a sacred organ whose intimate murmur used to resound in us before the voices of error or of education made themselves heard; but this other voice, which reminds us of our bondage to the elements, constrains us only to that which favors the harmonious accord of these elements."[16]

The novelist does not receive his instructions in a grammatological form—the law of nature is inscribed pneumatologically.[17] That is, it has been inscribed into the living rhythm of body as a "burning need," as pleasure. We should remember here that Sade's definition of pleasure does not exclude pain. That is, it is not a hedonistic form of pleasure, but rather a system predicated on maximizing neural excitation: "For what is pleasure? Simply this: that which occurs when voluptuous atoms, or atoms emanated from voluptuous objects, clash hard with and fire the electrical particles circulating in the hollows of our nerve fibers."[18] This neurological, or rather, neurogrammatical inscription can only be deciphered through an experiential exploration of every fold of the heart; the heart that Sade describes as "Nature's veritable labyrinth."[19] The novelist thus charts this labyrinth by following the inner voice of nature (the single thread of purity):

> the novelist is the child of Nature, that she has created him to be her painter; if he does not become his mother's lover the moment she gives birth to him, let him never write, for we shall never read him. But if he feels that burning need to portray everything, if, with fear and trembling he probes into the bosom of Nature, in search of his art and for models to discover, if he possess the fever of talent and enthusiasm of genius, let him follow the hand that leads him; once having divined man, he will paint him.[20]

The novelist, following the hand of nature and adhering to the principles she has inscribed within his heart, aims at producing a work of such authenticity that it would be in effect a seamless representation. In short, a perfect novel would no longer be a representation; rather, it would be the "faithful mirror" through which man would know himself-as-he-is-in-himself. If the purpose of philosophy is to understand "man" as he is in himself, then, Sade exclaims, the novel is "as essential as the knowledge of history."[21] History's ability to represent "man" is distinctly limited: "For the etching needle of history only depicts man when he reveals himself publicly, and then 'tis no longer he: ambition, pride cover his brow with a mask which portrays for us naught but these two passions, and not the man."[22]

The novel is unique precisely because it is capable of exposing man in his totality, that is, as he is when he drops his mask. It is the vocation, the calling, of the novelist to penetrate beyond this mask and "paint" a complete image of man "from within."²³ The "perfect" novel is thus one that says everything, that obliterates the gap between the signifier and the signified.

The Sadean project can thus be read as directly engaging in what Derrida refers to as "the metaphysics of the proper": the aim of the project is the total effacement of writing from the logos.²⁴ As the title of this chapter suggests, Sade's aim is transcendental; he is searching for an exit from the labyrinth of language through the practice of writing. This aim is the dark heart that animates the Sadean system; it is that which drives reason to the point of disarticulation. This affliction without source, or irrationality that resides just beyond the apparent surface of reason, is, as Blanchot argues, "Sade's primary and main peculiarity."²⁵ The result of this peculiarity at the heart of the Sadean system is that everything is written, weighed, balanced, and measured in accordance with reason and yet everything remains at "the mercy of something unsaid," everything "obeys the movement of a still hidden force" that remains "buried within the obscurity of unreflective thought and unformulatable moments."²⁶

My interest here is in the relationship between this "hidden force" and writing. To formulate it as a question, I would simply ask: What is the role of *différance* in the Sadean system of writing? Is the accelerative logic of energetic sovereignty with its alternation between apathy and expenditure predicated upon a perverse reformulation of the *différance* of signification? This reformulation would effectively attempt to set signification against itself. It would do so by interpreting the silent "a" *différance*, the space, or spacing that is open within signification, as both a barrier and a resource. It is a barrier in that it prevents everything from being said. With it, the unsaid always remains within the said, as a condition of the very possibility of saying. And yet, paradoxically, it is precisely what remains unsaid that fuels Sade's writing. From *aporia* to *autrui* and *àvenir*, the "a" of *différance* is an openness, a silent hospitality, or *chora*, within the process of signification that resists the philosophical desire for an absolutely determinate meaning or absolutely delimitable context. This being so, how does Sade's writing deal with this resistance?

In his essay entitled *Différance* Derrida puts the enigma of *différance* in the context of Freud's *Beyond the Pleasure Principle* and the paradoxical logic of the death drive.²⁷ Accordingly, my question can also be expressed in psychoanalytic terms: Namely, if we accept Lacan's diagnosis and proclaim Sade "perverse" in the psychoanalytic sense—a diagnostic category founded on a reading of the Sadean text—how is this perversion encoded in the text? If the pervert is the "subject that knows," the subject "who goes as far as he can along the path of jouissance," then what of his perverse system of writing?²⁸ That is, is this "perverse" writing predicated upon a way of deciphering and thus ending the play of discourse? That is, if Sade's novel is in fact a technical attempt to chart, stake out, and finally obliterate the trace, how does it proceed? It is interesting to note that, according to Lacan, Sade locates himself as the object of the invocatory drive—as the voice box of the Other—yet he writes, or rather transcribes, the voice that speaks through him.[29] To reiterate, my focus is on how this voice (the voice of the Other) affects the structure of Sade's writing, how its demands constantly systematize and organize the text in an effort to form a total, or terminal transcription, that is, to form a text that literally "says everything."

In sum, my interest is in how the death drive is written out. In order to address these questions, we must begin questioning the nature of the novelist's access to the law of nature in the Sadean text. That is, we must begin by examining the "natural language" that guides the novelist.

THE BURNING NEED TO PORTRAY: THE NEUROGRAMMATICAL INSCRIPTION OF THE LAW OF NATURE

> The violent throbbings it causes us to feel, either at the idea or upon the execution of the crime cruelty suggests to us, are invincible proof that we are born to serve as blind instruments to the kingdoms' laws as well as to Nature's, and that once we lend ourselves to do their bidding, voluptuousness invades us through every pore.[30]
>
> —D. A. F. de Sade, *Juliette*

The economy, or rather *an*economy (*an-* in both the privative and positional sense—an economy of lack or want and that circulates against, towards, and in return for a constant absence) of Sadean writing is predicated on both preserving and amplifying the sensuous inner voice of nature through a programmatic instrumentalization of the silent "a" of *différance* or the *gramme*. As I have argued, the Sadean text can be read as a systemic attempt to obliterate the *gramme*; but for Sade this obliteration would be the realization of its proper function: the complete conduction of the inner voice without degradation, distortion, or noise. The *gramme* is the material substrate through which this miraculous transformation of vocative energetics is to take place. If a full transmission were to be achieved, the element would be absolutely consumed in the process of the reaction, leaving only pure, inviolable energy.

The Sadean program of writing is a neurogrammatical engineering that employs the novel as a capacitor, a storage mechanism that condenses and holds a neurovocative charge:

> Many of the extravagances you are about to see illustrated will doubtless displease you, yes, I am well aware of it, but there are amongst them a few which will warm you to the point of costing you some fuck, and that, reader, is all we ask of you; if we not said everything, analyzed everything, tax us not with partiality, for you cannot expect us to have guessed what suits you

best. Rather, it is up to you to take what you please and leave the rest alone, another reader will do the same, and little by little, everyone will find himself satisfied.[31]

The novel both stores and conducts the energy of the inner voice, but its conductive properties must be brought to a terminal point; to the point of committing "moral murder."

> *Clairwil:* I would like ... to find a crime which, even when I left off doing it, would go on having perpetual effect, in such a way that so long as I lived, at every hour of the day and as I lay sleeping at night, I would be constantly the cause of a particular disorder, and that this disorder might broaden to the point where it brought about a corruption so universal or a disturbance so formal that even after my life was over I would survive in the everlasting continuation of my wickedness.
>
> *Juliette:* For the fulfillment of your aims, my dear ... I know little else than what may be termed *moral murder*, which is arrived at by means of counsels, writings, or actions.[32]

This idealized goal (it is referred to as a terminus, a goal that may be "arrived at") is termed (provisionally, tentatively—it may *be*) "moral murder" precisely because within the law of the book these two categories are mutually exclusive: murder is the definitive transgression of morality. Thus, the transfusion of these two categories into one would require a pure writing, a writing that would absolutely overwhelm all possible objections by flooding into every pore of the reader, a writing that would convey the full amplitude of the neurogrammatical inscription of the inner voice of nature as law, as logos: "it is far less essential to inquire into the workings of Nature than to enjoy her and obey her laws; that these laws are as wise as they are simple; that they are written in the hearts of all men; and it is but necessary to interrogate that heart to discern its impulse."[33]

Sadean neurogrammatics is a procedure that sets out to realign the signifier with the signified. Connections are made and broken in accordance with their ability to convey sensuous current—the Sadean text is thus a dense array of grammatic circuitry. The voltage and amplitude of each connection must be meticulously wired, tested, and rewired in a constant attempt to attain a total transcription—a transmission without loss. The connection between the signifier and the signified is thus directly sensuous and the true writer seeks to properly align the one with the other by means of sensing the innate connection: "For what is pleasure? Simply this: that which occurs when voluptuous atoms, or atoms emanated from voluptuous objects, clash hard with and fire the electrical particles circulating in the hollows of our nerve fibers."[34]

The "voluptuous objects" speak directly to the neural fibres of the novelist; his vocation, his calling is to preserve and conduct the true sense of the word into the written form of the novel. In order to preserve the integrity of the signal, the novelist must absolutely reduce the effects of distortion and noise by reducing his inner charge to null state. Only then can it be properly measured and ordered.

> Therefore, that the pleasure be complete, the clash must be as violent as possible; but so delicate is the nature of this sensation that a mere nothing can spoil or nullify it; hence the soul must be prepared, tranquil, its serenity ensured by certain mental attitudes or certain physical postures, so that it lies as though in a calm and smiling vale; and then the imagination's fire must set the furnace of the senses alight. From this point onward give that imagination free reign, act at its every behest but, by making practical use of your philosophy and above all of the chill hardness of your heart and your lack of conscience, enable it to forge, to weave, to create new fantasies which, injecting energies into the voluptuous atoms, cause them to collide at greater speed and more potently with the molecules they are to make vibrate; these vibrations are your delight.[35]

If we imagine that the Sadean libertines as a series of prototypes, experimental conduits, designed to transmit the full amplitude of the natural current, we can shed some light on the logic by which they are systemically judged and executed. To resist the current, to trigger a discharge before the terminal threshold is reached, is fatal precisely because it hinders the progress of the final neurogrammatical alignment and thus Juliette (the embodiment of vice) survives a lightning strike with seeming ease while Justine (virtue) is absolutely consumed (cf. the end of Sade's *La Nouvelle Justine*).

The Sadean novelist, distinct from the libertine characters he portrays, is perhaps best understood as an engineer. He designs, tests, redesigns, and retests in a constant and progressive movement towards maximal efficiency; this requires him to attune himself to the inner voice of nature. He, like all men, is structured and governed by natural law; but he is gifted as well with a preternatural sensitivity. He must fashion himself into a vessel, a medium for the communication of the message that has been inscribed in him as a silent, sensuous current. This current is silent only in the sense that it is inaudible, which is not to say that it does not speak but rather that its speech is absolutely intimate and direct. The ideal novelist receives the full spectrum of this current and transfers it directly to the page without distortion, thus preserving the integrity of the signal. The successful one-to-one transfer of the current through the conduit would constitute the "perfect novel"—this "perfect novel" would seal the breach between the signifier and the signified.

In Platonic terms, it would complete the metaphysical circuit by fusing the sun and the eye. The medium (*gramme*) would be obliterated in the culmination of the process.

The imperfect novelist, the novelist that Sade advises with his provisional guidelines, strives to both preserve the integrity of the signal and to find the source of its greatest possible amplitude. By experimentally developing a series of principles to guide the process of writing, the novelist attempts to preserve the greatest possible amplitude within the text; the text serves as a capacitor, a reservoir of energy. Yet there is resistance in the system that occurs in the transfer from sensation to signifier. The written word is dangerously malleable; depending on the motives of the author it can serve as an instrument of either slavery or salvation, of inhibition or conduction. Sade: "Man is prey to two weaknesses, which derive from his existence and characterize it. Wheresoever on earth he dwells, man feels the need *to pray*, and *to love*: and herein lies the basis for all novels."[36]

The novel, as a written form, is also ambivalent.

> Let there be no doubt about it: it was in the countries which first recognized gods that the novel originated.... No sooner did man begin to suspect the existence of immortal beings than he endowed them with both actions and words.... Every people, therefore, has its gods, its demigods, its heroes, its true stories, and its fables; some part of it, as we have just seen, can have a solid basis in fact, as it pertains, to the heroes; all the rest is pure fantasy, incredible; it is all a work of pure invention, a novel, because the gods spoke only through the medium of men who, more or less interested in this ridiculous artifice, did not fail to make up the language of phantoms, from whatever they imagined would be most likely to seduce or terrify, and, consequently, from whatever was most incredible.[37]

The "true sense" of natural language has been perverted by the "ridiculous artifice" of men that sought to enslave others by pandering to their weaknesses and inventing the deceptive "language of phantoms." This perversion of the "true sense" of the neurogrammatics of Nature is only possible because of the dangerous ambivalence of writing. In order to recover this "true sense" the Sadean novelist must respect no boundary that attempts to inhibit the progress of his inquiry; he must excavate, delve, and cleanse the sedimentation of phantoms from the written word. The sensuous current must bypass any and all inferior conduits which interrupt, degrade, and distort the purity of the signal; it must bypass the written word through writing the "perfect novel."

CONTAGIOUS SPEECH: MURDER BY THE LETTER

since my arrival here my fuck has not once flowed because of the objects I find about me in this castle. Every time, I have discharged over what is not there, what is absent from its place, and so it is.[38]
—D. A. F. de Sade, *The 120 Days of Sodom*

The incompleteness of the system/text/novel is, paradoxically, integral to its continued functioning. Each barrier, each limitation, that inhibits the circulation of the current becomes a checkpoint, a site at which one may rationally measure the amplitude of the signal. "It is not in desire's consummation [that] happiness consists, but in the desire itself, in hurdling the obstacles placed before what one wishes."[39]

This point is echoed by Pierre Klossowski in his *Sade My Neighbor*:

> To get beyond the notion of evil, which is conditioned by the degree of reality accorded to the other, we have seen this mind exalt the ego to the limit. But the culmination of this exaltation was to be in the apathy in which, when the other is abolished, the ego is abolished at the same time, in which enjoyment is dissociated from destruction, and in which destruction is identified with desire in its pure form. In this way the Sadean mind reproduces in its reflection the perpetual motion of a Nature who creates but arouses obstacles for herself with those very creations and, for a moment, finds her freedom only in destroying her own work.[40]

The obstacle, that which inhibits the circulation of the current, is at once negated and necessary. It is necessary in that it is what transfers the current from one point to another and thus it is that through which the amplitude can be measured, yet this conductive property is always already insufficient for the task that it must fulfill. This principle of insufficiency is also a direct reflection of the ambivalence of any conductive medium—the medium can serve to short-circuit the circulation of the current and produce noise (random or irregular disturbances that are not part of the signal). This unwanted noise obscures the truth of the signal; this is the "language of phantoms" that the Sadean novelist must strike out. The progress of the novelist's project—the purification, or refinement, of the conductive properties of writing—is measured by the text's ability to sensually excite the reader and thus attune the reader to the true signal of nature. This attunement is both refined and spread via writing.

> Once this is accomplished, light your bedside lamp and write out a full description of the abomination which has just inflamed you, omitting nothing that could serve to aggravate its details; and then go to sleep thinking about them. Reread your notes the next day and, as you recommence your

operation, add everything your imagination, doubtless a bit weary by now of an idea which has already cost you some fuck, may suggest that could heighten its power to exacerbate. Now turn to the definitive shaping of this idea into a scheme and as you put the final touches on it, once again incorporate all fresh episodes, novelties, and ramifications that occur to you.[41]

Yet the limit, whether the limit be the body of the victim or the letter of the text, is always already insufficiently conductive, and thus the process must be repeated and intensified to a point beyond limitation:

> For it [pleasure] cannot possibly delect save when one outsteps every limit in one's quest; the proof thereof is that there must be a breaking of restraining rules before pleasure begins to be pleasure; go farther yet, break still another and the irritation becomes more violent, and necessarily so with each ascending step; and you do not really attain to the true goal wither these pleasure-takings point until the ferment of the senses has reached its extremest pitch, until you have got to the final limit of what our human faculties can endure, in such wise that your nerves are so prodigiously wrought upon that they are frayed as if to paralysis, smitten into a convulsion that resembles standstill and shocked insensibility.[42]

The aim of system is not economic, that is, it does not strive towards a constant or balanced state. The focus is on desire, on the current of the signal, on the exponential increase of its amplitude. When the system encounters resistance, it must accumulate a reservoir of energy so as to radically increase the intensity of its assault and thus increase the probability of overcoming its obstacle (apathy becomes the mechanism for maximum intensification by delaying/denying enjoyment).[43] The system thus appears circular as each transgressive expenditure of energy simultaneously obliterates and reconstitutes the obstacle—its success is a mere temporal displacement of the obstacle. The Sadean novelist resists the apparent circularity of the system by striving towards the "perfect novel." That is, the novel that would commit "moral murder" to writing. This perfect novel would conduct the full force of the signal, it would be pure neurogrammatical inscription—it would instantaneously universalize the "shocked insensibility" of the end (the true goal) of pleasure.

One must keep in mind that for Sade the greater the conductive properties of writing (its conductive properties being its ability to convey the neurological current of pleasure), the closer it is to the truth of the law of nature, the closer it is to sealing the breach between the signifier and signified—to communicating/committing "moral murder." This yearning for the total transcription—the final overcoming of the obstacle of the medium/writing/body—operates within the Sadean text under the name of "outrage."

> And far from thanking this illogical Nature for the slender freedom she allows us for accomplishing the desires she inspires in us, let us curse her from the bottom of our heart for so restricting the career which fulfills her aims; let us outrage her, let us abominate her for having left us so few wicked things to do, and then giving us such violent urges to commit crimes without measure or pause.[44]

Paradoxically, the novelist's "burning need to portray" commits him to following a path that cannot be followed—at least not to its end. As a result nature is denounced for demanding everything and providing so few means.

> There are but two or three crimes to perform in this world, and they, once done, there's no more to be said; all the rest is inferior, you cease any longer to feel. Ah, how many times, by God, have I not longed to be able to assail the sun, snatch it out of the universe, make a general darkness, or use that star to burn the world! Oh, that would be a crime, oh ye, and not a little misdemeanor such as are all the ones we perform who are limited in a whole year's time to metamorphosing a dozen creatures into lumps of clay.[45]

The result that he strives towards—a total verisimilitude, a "perfect novel"—is total destruction and as such it is outside what is said:

> I say original casting to facilitate the intelligence of my system, for, there never having been any creation and Nature being timeless, the first casting of a given being endures so long as that being's line survives; and would end were that line to be extinguished; the extinction of all beings would make room for the new castings Nature desires; to this end the one means is total destruction, and that is the result towards which crime strives.[46]

There is an exit from the cycle of the system, from the text—the novelist must serve the call of nature's law and fashion the key that will sate her desire (and thus his own); he must extinguish nature itself (after all, she "is at one and the same time the law and its destruction").[47] The possibility of the formation of such a key is encoded within the text of the body: "The soul—or, if you wish, the active principle that animates, moves, determines us—is nothing other than matter subtilized to a certain degree, by the means of which refinement it acquires the faculties that so amaze us."[48]

This key or transcendental signifier—the signifier that operates under perpetual erasure—is the object of the novelist's labours. Sade seeks a writing that obliterates all writing—a writing that banishes all phantoms. The system is a metaphysics of the proper—which is a deceptive term, as its propriety is totally improper, or rather inappropriable—precisely because its aim is to unbar the transcendental signifier and commit the total crime to writing; to commit and thereby communicate "moral murder" in writing.[49]

The progress of this process, the time of which is marked and measured by the spread of its contaminative writing, follows a particular track. "[T]he more we wish to be agitated, the more we desire to be moved violently, the more we must give rein to our imagination; we must bend it toward the inconceivable; our enjoyment will thereby be increased, made better for the track the intellect follows."[50]

The trajectory of the novel—the trajectory that leads to its perfection—is "bent towards the inconceivable" and it is this process of bending, refining, and shaping that comprises the labour of the novelist. The novelist follows "the hand that leads him" to follow the track of the intellect, the path of reason, the path of nature's law.[51] The "burning need to portray" has always been there, the truth of the neurological inscription of the law is always already present in each sensation, yet it is a buried truth, concealed beneath a host of phantoms, and thus its unveiling has a specific time.[52] The advent of the writing of "moral murder" is inevitable.

WHERE NO GUIDE HAS BROKEN GROUND: THE TIME OF THE PERFECT NOVEL

The "truth" that the Sadean novelist strives to portray, that is, the "truth" of the law of nature, has always already been present, yet its presence has been obscured. The role of the novelist is thus to excavate, to scrape away all of the confused sedimentation and uncover the truth. One might ask here why the novelist must excavate the "truth," or, more clearly, why the "truth" must be excavated—what has buried it? And further, why is the novelist the designated excavator? Why is his the privileged literary form—why is it the novel that can conduct the absolute "truth"? For Sade the historical advent of the novel and the process of sedimentation are coterminous:

> Let there be no doubt about it: **it was in the countries which first recognized gods that the novel originated**.... No sooner did man begin to suspect the existence of immortal beings than he endowed them with both actions and words.... Every people, therefore, has its gods, its demigods, its heroes, its true stories, and its fables; some part of it, as we have just seen, can have a solid basis in fact, as it pertains, to the heroes; all the rest is pure fantasy, incredible; **it is all a work of pure invention, a novel, because the gods spoke only through the medium of men who, more or less interested in this ridiculous artifice, did not fail to make up the *language of phantoms*, from whatever they imagined would be most likely to seduce or terrify, and, consequently, from whatever was most incredible.**[53]

The first novels were works of pure artifice, works that misattributed the voice of nature. They dislocated and detracted us from the source of "truth" by endowing imaginary "immortal beings" with speech. This is not to say that these novels contained absolutely no "truth"—for Sade God is the only pure lie and he cannot speak—but rather that the grain of truth they contained was hidden. History is the gradual discovery of this hidden grain; it is the progression from the contaminated "false" novel to the purified "perfect" novel.

> As minds grow increasingly corrupt, as a nation grows older, by virtue of the fact that Nature is increasingly studied and better analyzed, in order for prejudice to be increasingly eradicated, **all these things must be made more widely known**.... Doubtless we could not have advanced so far in those trying times of ignorance when, weighed down beneath the yoke of religion, whosoever valued the arts risked penalty of death for his efforts; when talent had as its reward the stakes of the Inquisition. **But in the state wherein we live today, let us always start from this principle.**[54]

Due to the state of knowledge in the current historical situation, it is now possible to imagine a perfect novel. The authority of the divine text is being openly challenged, and thus it is possible to begin to form the principles of a research program that will finally realign the written word with the truth of nature. That is, it is now possible to outline a program (a law that precedes writing and governs each inscription) that will, once and for all, seal the breach between the signifier and the signified. The task of the novelist is thus to trace out the origin of this hidden grain of truth that remained lost within the "language of phantoms."[55] Once the path of this grain, that is, its genealogical trajectory, has been discovered, the perfection of the novel is only a matter of time.

The novelist is best suited to the work of excavation because his medium is the most unlimited form of writing. While the historian is confined to "etching" the public face of man, the novelist's brush "portrays him from within ... seizes him when he drops this mask, and the description, which is far more interesting, is at the same time more faithful."[56] The novelist's discursive pallet is thus unlimited.

> the profound study of man's heart—Nature's veritable labyrinth—alone can inspire the novelist, whose work must make us see the man not only as he is, or as he purports to be—which is the duty of the historian—but as he is capable of being when subjected to the modifying influences of vice and the full impact of passion. Therefore we must know them all, we must employ every passion and vice, if we wish to labor in this field.[57]

The novelist is able to uncover the key to the "language of phantoms" and thus trace out the long obscured path of truth due to the nature of his vocation. His calling is to represent man as he truly is—only a true representation can transmit affect and thus arouse the reader's interest. The truth of the novelist's work can thus be gauged by the strength of the affect it communicates to the reader.

The novelist's aim must be truth if he is to provide the "faithful mirror" of man; this distinguishes the modern novelist from the first novelist.[58] The first novelist invents the "language of phantoms," while the modern novelist strives to dispel these phantoms, purifying language and enabling it to serve its proper representational function.[59] Thus, perhaps it is best to understand the distinction between the first novel and the modern novel as a continuum that extends from the corrupted "language of phantoms" to the purified neurogrammatical language of the "perfect novel." This continuum is possible precisely because the novel and by extension both fiction and writing in general are ambivalent; that is, they can convey either "truth" or "lies." Writing, as a work of "pure invention," is thus the entry point for original sin, the vehicle for the introduction of "lies." Here again we can draw parallels with Rousseau: "Everything is good as it comes from the hands of the Author of Nature; but everything degenerates in the hands of man."[60]

Sade and Rousseau agree that writing from the "hands of man" is impure. The Sadean novelist sidesteps this problem by disavowing his hand. That is, he is able to navigate his way through the "language of phantoms" and locate the truth precisely because his hand is not his own, but guided.[61] This is not to say the Sadean novelist is totally passive and thus immune to the malicious effects of the "language of phantoms," but rather that he directs all his discursive techniques towards learning how to be led by nature. In this sense the Sadean novelist makes no claim to authorship, at least in the traditional sense. He is not the origin of the truth of the text—he does not write from his own hand—rather, he is written through, the instrument of Nature's voice, and his skill is his ability to instrumentalize himself.

If the Sadean novelist is not an author—if he is more of an inventor, an engineer, or, as Sade will refer to him, a painter—why does Sade claim his work is new?

> No guide has broken ground for us in the other stories: plot, style, episodes—all are our own invention. It may be said that these are not what is best in our work. No matter; we have always believed, and we shall continue to believe, that 'tis better to invent, albeit poorly, than to translate or copy. The inventor can lay claim to talent or genius, and has not at least that much in his favor; what claim can the plagiarist make? I know of no baser profession, nor do I conceive of any avowal more humiliating than that which such men are obliged to make to themselves, namely, that they are totally lacking in wit, since they are obliged to borrow the wit of others.[62]

Sade's proprietary claim does not apply to the truth communicated through his text—that voice is not his own—rather, he lays claim over the spatial distribution of the signifier. The pattern of distribution is new: "Let us conclude with a positive reassurance that the stories we are presenting today are absolutely new and in no wise a mere reworking of already oft-told tales."[63]

The pattern of distribution, the arrangement of the text (plot, style, episode) is new, in the sense that it is unprecedented in the history of the novel. Sade designs discursive patterns that transmit the "truth" of Nature; and while other texts have managed to conduct this truth to a greater or lesser degree, his text exceeds them in the precision of its instrumentation. The Sadean text is closer to the origin of the signal. Within the text the distribution of signifiers approaches an optimal alignment with the truth of the signified, and thus the "language of phantoms," the noise that distorts the truth of the signal, has been reduced. But it is not yet eliminated. The absolute elimination of noise, the end of the "language of phantoms" can only be achieved in a "perfect novel," one that communicates, or rather transmits, the "truth" of Nature directly into the nervous system of the reader. Sade's work is preparatory, provisional—the outline of a novel that will be written.

WRITING IN NATURE'S HAND: THE LABYRINTH AND THE MONSTER-AUTHOR

The book never aspires to anything less than the retracing of what exceeds it.[64]
—Jean-Luc Nancy, "Exscription"

In *Reflections on the Novel* Sade set out to provisionally sketch the "rules one must follow in order to succeed in perfecting the art of the novel."[65] My question follows from this, or rather extends it by asking: Why must the novel be perfected, why must it be brought to completion? Sade answers this question in part:

> 'Tis therefore Nature that must be seized when one labors in the fields of fiction, 'tis the heart of man, the most remarkable of her works, and in no wise virtue, because virtue, however becoming, however necessary it may be, is yet but one of the many facets of this amazing heart, whereof the profound study is so necessary to the novelist, and **the novel, the faithful mirror of this heart, must perforce explore every fold.**[66]

The perfection of the novel is a descriptive project, a cartography of "Nature's veritable labyrinth."[67] This project, the Sadean project of writing, has a striking resemblance to that of the imprisoned priest in Borges's tale, *The Writing of God*. Tzinacan, the priest of the Pyramid of Qaholom, driven by both a hunger for vengeance and "the inevitability of doing something, of somehow filling time" struggles to decipher a message written by God into the flesh of the jaguar that resides in the adjacent cell.[68] The Word of God, the content contained within the cipher, is an absolute plenitude, a perfect word, a word that, if spoken, would instantaneously exhaust all language. The priest deciphers the text and discovers the formula that if spoken would make him omnipotent, yet he does not speak it; once the formula is glimpsed he forgets himself in silence.

Sade, imprisoned and craving vengeance, sets out to decipher the law of nature, the law that has been inscribed in the living labyrinth of his heart. This quest, undertaken in the name of the law, is a quest, or more clearly, an inquest into the nature of the letter, and further it is an inquest practised through writing. Sade writes under the dark compulsion of a silent force that supervises his inscriptions.[69] This force guides his hand towards the horizon of absolute knowledge. The hand not his own, the hand he disavows, effaces writing, strikes out the "language of phantoms," and purifies the logos by reappropriating difference. The process is gradual, laborious, yet it moves under the promise of a final retrieval of the trace in parousia.[70] Sade's key, his "invincible proof," is crime: "The violent throbbings it causes us to feel, either at the idea or upon the execution of the crime cruelty suggests to us, are invincible proof that we are born to serve as blind instruments to the kingdoms' laws as well as to Nature's, and that once we lend ourselves to do their bidding, voluptuousness invades us through every pore."[71]

Crime is Sade's entry point, his privileged point of access into the labyrinth of the heart. Under the skin of this signifier ("crime") he discovers the principle of *jouissance*, not pleasure in the constrained sense of agreeable sensation but rather the full spectrum of neural excitation. From this single principle Sade traces his way through the labyrinth of the heart, methodically unwriting the book, unmasking the language of phantoms, and leaving in its place pure unmitigated sensation. The procedure is imperfect and the precipitate of the reaction is impure, but the proof is invincible, and thus its perfection is inevitable.

Sade does not authorize this de-scription, this unwriting, of the book. He is merely the instrument through which it is de-scribed: "I am in her hands but a machine which she runs as she likes, and not one of my crimes does not serve her: the more she urges me to commit them, the more of them she needs; I should be a fool to disobey her."[72]

Sade's method, his procedure for committing "moral murder," is perversion to the letter. His writing is programmatic. That is, it follows a law that precedes the *gramme*, and thus he disavows[73] his claim of authorship; instead he is a conduit. As a conduit he is granted privileged access to the signal (he is able to see the signified under the skin of the signifier); his only possible aim is thus to maximize his capacity for transmission. Guided by the "invincible proof" of neurogrammatics he traces the way through the labyrinth. The completion of this process, the total description/unwriting/unravelling of the labyrinth can be thought of—via Austin—as a shift from perlocutionary to absolute illocutionary force. Sade's text succeeds in producing "certain consequential effects upon the feelings, thoughts, or actions of [his] audience," and these perlocutionary effects are meticulously catalogued and graded on their conductive properties; yet this is merely an impure byproduct of the final goal.[74] If he were to accomplish the goal he has been assigned, that is, if he were to perfect the novel and commit "moral murder" to writing, he would have formulated the "total speech act in the total speech situation."[75] He would have preformed his true function (he is, after all, answering the call of Nature as the privileged instrument of her speech) and given voice to the "unheard, inaudible, deafening speech" of the absolute; the total illocutionary act.[76] Like Borges's priest, Sade is confined within the enigma of the Writing of God, and there he remains, compulsively tracing and retracing that which lies just beyond the reach of writing.

Section III
BODIES OF RESISTANCE

"Does he know his sentence?" "No," said the officer, eager to go on with his exposition, but the explorer interrupted him: "He doesn't know the sentence that has been passed on him?" "No," said the officer again, pausing a moment as if to let the explorer elaborate his question, and then said: "There would be no point in telling him. He'll learn it on his body."
—Franz Kafka, *In the Penal Colony*

Chapter 4

BETWEEN LAW AND THE SLAUGHTERHOUSE
Kant, Fichte, and the "Absolute" Right of Punishment

[E]very murderer—anyone who commits murder, orders it, or is an accomplice in it—must suffer death; this is what justice, as the idea of judicial authority, wills in accordance with universal laws that are grounded *a priori*.
—Immanuel Kant, *The Metaphysics of Morals*

THE AIM OF THIS CHAPTER is to attend to Kant's philosophical justifications for the death penalty as they appear in the *Metaphysics of Morals*. The practice of "attending" to the text carries with it multiple connotations. The term is generally used to express active relationships between a subject and the object. In this regard it can mean to-expect, to-listen, to-wait, and also to-follow. While it may be used to refer to the simple act of being present (i.e., being "in attendance"), this use does not adequately reflect the term's origins. Etymologically the term means to stretch or bend [*tendere*] towards [*ad-*]. This being so, even its most passive sense carries with it the suggestion of mindfulness or care. After all, to attend to an event is also to bear witness to it. In the case at hand I am using the term to refer both to the practice of attending-to the text and to those whose death it calls for. My concern is that while Kant's text theoretically grounds the death penalty in the law of retribution (*ius talionis*), it does not truly attend to its practical realities. As soon as one asks who has the right to punish, how that right is acquired, or how the punishment is to be carried out (i.e., how the distinction between punishment and vengeance is to be maintained), one is confronted with the silent shadow of sovereign authority. In the case of the death penalty this shadow effectively obscures the distinction between force and law.

In the *Critique of Violence* Benjamin highlights this distinction by pointing out that while the commandment "Thou shalt not kill" can be said to be *a priori* or "absolute," it is necessarily abstract and, as a result, there is no way of deriving a specific judgment from it. According to Benjamin, "It exists not as a criterion of judgment, but as a guideline for the actions of persons or communities who have to wrestle with it in solitude and, in exceptional cases, to take on themselves the responsibility of ignoring it."[1]

The point here is that any and all violations of this commandment—whether framed as self-defence, punishment, or an act of war—are the results of subjective decisions and not of an absolute imperative that would absolve a person or persons of the responsibility for their actions. Considering this, my question is quite simply: How can Kant account for a necessary or *a priori* connection between the idea of the law and its application in the case of capital punishment? To phrase this more generally: Is there an "absolute" right to punish?

The question seems both simple and direct. Its form suggests that one might simply answer yes or no; yet, in either case, whatever response one may choose it must be both preceded and informed by a series of responses to other questions. Obviously such a series must include the basic elements of the main question itself. For this main question to be intelligible, one must have a sense of what both "right" and "punishment" mean, and how they can be related. However, even with such a basic understanding in place, the qualifier "absolute" shifts the very grounds of interpretation.

What can it mean to have a right that is "absolute"? The most common example of such a right is the right to self-defence. I have an absolute right to defend my life against another, but the margins of the "absolute" in this instance are very narrow. Abstractly speaking, my right to defend my life against a threat is unquestionable, but I am accountable for the way I actualize this right. That is, I am responsible for both my determination of what constitutes a threat and for the means I use to defend myself. This brings us to two related problem areas:

1 If the boundaries of self-defence are restricted in such a manner, what would an "absolute" right of punishment look like? Such a right would clearly be positive, it is after all *a right to* punish, but, like the right to self-defence, it may be that it is "absolute" only in the abstract sense. If this is the case, its application would be open to contestation, but what would the bounds of this contestation be? Would it be strictly moral and thus removed from the realm of judicial accountability? Even if we hold off on answering this question, we are confronted with another, related problem, namely: Who can lay claim to this right? That is, even if it is conceded that there is an absolute or *a priori* basis for the right to punish, how does a particular individual gain the ability to enact or enforce this right? Structurally speaking, these questions are very similar: both

pertain to the connection between the universal and the particular. The former questions this connection in terms of actions and the latter in terms of claims. The problem is how either an action or a claim could be "absolute."

2. An "absolute" right must be unquestionable, and thus in some way manifestly evident to "everyone." And yet this simply brings us to the problem of who is included in the indefinite pronoun "everyone." How is this set determined? By what criteria does one become "not-one" and thereby lose the right to contest the determinations of others? Could it be that "absolute" rights begin, that is, gain their "absolute" status, with an "absolute" distinction between "everyone" and "no-one"? What of other forms of life? Would an "absolute" right begin, gain its "absolute" status, with an "absolute" distinction between "human" and the "animal"? And further, how is this distinction—this intimate interval between the terms "rational" and "animal"—practised? How does the "animal"—this impossible singular noun—both constitute and unwork the limits of rights?

As we turn towards and begin to follow these problems we will be drawn into a dense and convoluted series of relationships within the text. This series binds capital punishment to sovereign authority, and finally to the very possibility of "human" rights. Our trajectory will begin with Kant's theory of the death penalty and take us to Fichte's *Foundations of Natural Right*, Benjamin's *Critique of Violence*, and finally Derrida's work on autoimmunity and the "*animot*." By following this course, by waiting at the foot of the "theoretical" scaffold, we will attend to what is silenced in the dark corners of Kant's text. That is, we will attend to the suffering of another that resides just beyond the limits of "everyone" and who must die in silence in order for force to appear as law.

AN "ABSOLUTE" RIGHT?

In part two of the *Metaphysics of Morals* Kant provides us with an example of an "absolute" right: "every murderer—anyone who commits murder, orders it, or is an accomplice in it—must suffer death; this is what justice, as the idea of judicial authority, wills in accordance with universal laws that are grounded *a priori*."[2]

Here we find that there is a specific and necessary equality between murder and the death penalty. As Kant states, "there is no substitute that will satisfy justice."[3] All murderers *must* die. He goes to great lengths to emphasize the necessity of this specific equality to the reader:

> Even if a civil society were to be dissolved by the consent of all its members (e.g., if a people inhabiting an island decided to separate and disperse throughout the world), the last murderer remaining in prison would first have to be executed, so that each has done to him what his deeds deserve and blood guilt does not cling to the people for not having insisted upon this punishment; for otherwise the people can be regarded as collaborators in this public violation of justice.[4]

This so-called "blood guilt" binds the members of civil society together in a manner that extends beyond the wilful formation and dissolution of contracts. What this example serves to demonstrate is that the crime of murder extends beyond the scope of *positive* law (i.e., laws "that do not bind without actual external lawgiving"). It is a *natural* law and, as such, it can be recognized as obligatory *a priori* by reason even without external laws.[5]

Kant's confidence in the rational necessity of retribution in the case of murder is clearly evidenced in the text: "one has never heard of anyone who was sentenced to death for murder complaining that he was dealt with too severely and therefore wronged; everyone would laugh in his face if he said this."[6]

On the surface there is a kind of formal appeal to this argument. How can the murderer complain that death is an excessive punishment? It is after all the very limit that the crime transgressed. But why move from this to laughing in the face of the condemned? There is a troubling hint of glee in this laughter, of *Schadenfreude*, and this in turn suggests a mode of subjective pleasure that threatens to blur the lines between punishment and vengeance. And aside from the issue of laughter, the claim that murderers have no grounds to complain about the severity of their sentence is not entirely convincing.[7] Fichte takes issue with this claim. He responds to Kant's line of reasoning by conceding that

> It is completely true such that we are forced to conclude: in a moral world-order, governed by an omniscient judge in accordance with moral laws, if a person is treated according to *the same* law that he himself established in treating others, then there is no injustice done to him. This conclusion, which forces itself upon all human beings, is based on a categorical imperative. Thus there is absolutely no dispute about whether *a murderer* has been treated unjustly, if he, too, should lose his life in a violent manner.[8]

By drawing attention to the need for a "moral world-order," "moral laws" and an "omniscient judge" this *apparent* concession serves to emphasize the necessary conditions of Kant's own argument and thus sets up his rebuttal: "But an entirely different question to be answered would be: from where does a mortal get the right of this moral world-order, the right to render the criminal his just deserts?"[9]

He continues: "Whoever ascribes this right to a worldly sovereign will surely be required (as Kant's system was) to say that the sovereign's rightful title to it is unexaminable; to derive the sovereign's authority from God; and to regard the sovereign as God's visible representative and every government as a theocracy."[10]

If we, in accordance with Fichte, shift the focus of the question from the just punishment for the crime of murder to the basis of the right to punish, the condemned's complaint is no longer laughable. Nor is it a matter of the "overly compassionate feelings of an affected humanity" that Kant attributes to Beccaria.[11] Rather this question seems to provide the condemned murderer from Kant's example with a "justified complaint." As Kant himself admits, such a complaint opens up a gap between the law and the legislative authority of the state. If the state were to ignore this gap and carry out the execution "it would be in contradiction with itself."[12] Kant attempts to save the state from this contradiction by grounding the death penalty within the moral law. Fichte is keenly aware of the political significance of this move within Kant's theory of punishment. He argues that the *a priori* argument for the death penalty is simply a way of expressing or exhibiting the *a priori* power of the sovereign. It is used as a way of cloaking the arbitrary rule of the sovereign with the appearance of fate. In effect, his concern is that Kant's reasoning is relying on a kind of sleight of hand that makes the "is" of sovereign power suddenly appear to be the "ought" of the moral law.

We get a glimpse of this movement in the introduction to *The Metaphysics of Morals*: "One can therefore conceive of external lawgiving which would contain only positive laws; but then a natural law would still have to precede it, which would establish the authority of the lawgiver (i.e., his authorization to bind others by his mere *choice*)."[13] In effect, the *natural law* enables the force of the sovereign to pass through the body of the condemned and emerge as law. But how is the transition from "mere *choice*" to law accomplished? Even if "Thou shalt not kill" is a *natural* law, how can a specific individual acquire the right to enforce it?

WHO AMONG YOU IS WITHOUT RESPONSIBILITY?

This question brings us to the point at which the "absolute" right to punish intersects with sovereignty. Kant clearly states that "[t]he *right to punish* is the right a ruler has against a subject to inflict pain upon him because of his having committed a crime."[14] This tells us "who" has the right to punish, but not "how" this particular individual acquired this right. There are a series of suggestive statements regarding the transition from a "state of nature" to the "civil condition"—for instance, the claim that enforcing the natural law establishes the authority of the lawgiver or that the "ought" of the civil condition supersedes the consent of those who are in the "state of nature."[15]

But the closest we get to a direct answer can be found at the end of part two of *The Metaphysics of Morals*. Here Kant responds to a question from a reviewer regarding the distinction between the idea of sovereignty and a particular sovereign.[16] The reviewer simply asks how the idea of sovereignty could grant any particular individual the right to be a sovereign. This gap between the universal and the particular presents a unique challenge to Kant because of his epistemological commitments (i.e., the concept of the *thing-in-itself* disrupts the essentialist claims of divine right). He thus concedes that the connection between the *a priori* idea of sovereignty and a particular sovereign is one of *appearance* and not of *essence*. Sovereign power is simply a *fact*: "Unconditional submission of the people's will (which is in itself not united and is therefore without law) to a *sovereign* will (united by means of *one* law) is a *fact* that can only begin by seizing power and so first establishing public right."[17]

So there is no essential relationship; sovereignty is a *fact* that begins by an act of will, and yet despite this, Kant constrains the boundaries of contestation to such a degree that the distinction between *essence* and *appearance* is practically meaningless. This constraint is presented in the very syntax of the text: "*Obey the authority who has power over you* (in whatever does not conflict with inner morality)."[18] The priority here is clear: any and all conflicts between sovereign authority and the individual's "inner morality" are suspended or bracketed. Kant will even employ the *thing-in-itself* to cast doubt upon the ability of the individual to challenge the authority of a particular sovereign: "what can be represented only by pure reason and must be counted among *ideas*, to which no object given in experience can be adequate—and a perfectly *rightful constitution* among human beings is of this sort—is the thing in itself."[19]

This being the case, the idea of a "perfectly rightful" civil constitution effectively shields the actual civil constitution from resistance. But does this make all actual civil constitutions somehow equally imperfect? It is one thing to use the disjunction between the ideal and the actual to check the possibility of what Hegel aptly terms "absolute freedom," but altogether another to bind judgment so tightly that the distinction between tyranny and the rule of law is lost.[20] Kant continues:

> The *idea* of a civil constitution as such, which is also an absolute command that practical reason, judging according to concepts of right, gives to every people is *sacred* and irresistible. And even if the organization of a state should be faulty by itself, no subordinate authority in it may actively resist its legislative supreme authority; the defects attached to it must instead be gradually removed by reforms the state itself carries out.[21]

Kant is obviously aware that there are meaningful differences between actual civil constitutions, but even in the case of tyranny the citizens have no right to resist. The *idea* of a civil constitution is "*sacred* and irresistible," and those that suffer under tyrannical governments are simply told to "have faith and wait." Kant utilizes the progressive historical thesis to reinforce the brackets that bind the individual within the present conditions of the state. In effect, civil freedom is ultimately not the domain of the individual, but of the species.[22] The role of the individual is to simply obey, to publicly submit. The sovereign is exceptional: he cannot be held legally accountable or even publicly questioned.[23] One may morally object in private, follow the prescribed judicial channels, or at most emigrate, but there is no right of resistance of any kind and thus no real responsibility to go beyond a kind of moral quietism.

This wilful suspension of public critique in an effort to maintain the appearance of the universal is intriguing. In effect, Kant admits that sovereign power is a kind of performance maintained by the citizens acting "as if" it were "absolutely" necessary. Much like the concept of duty, this performance requires regulative ideas in order to function: the idea of a prefect civil constitution is combined with the future existence of the state. This combination enables the bare *fact* or sovereign power to retain the appearance of law by shifting the focus from the "now" of the present to the always already "not yet" of the future.

But are there limits to this apparent authority? Is there a point at which sovereign force disrupts this performance and enters the "now"? To answer this question we will have to consider Kant's account of the death penalty more closely.

AT THE LIMITS OF "ABSOLUTE" RIGHT(S)

These problems (i.e., the basis and limits of the law and sovereign authority) converge in the question of the death penalty, as it is at this point that the "absolute" right to punish meets the "absolute" limits of punishment. It is precisely here that the distinction between punishment and vengeance—and with it, law and power—hangs in the balance. Kant is keenly aware of this distinction and tries to establish limits that maintain it. To this end he states, "There is no *similarity* between life, however wretched it may be, and death, hence no likeness between the crime and the retribution unless death is judicially carried out upon the wrongdoer."[24]

Kant begins by openly acknowledging that there is no similarity between life and death. We can quickly see the implications of this lack of similarity. Due to the fact that life and death are unequal, the simple exchange of one for the other is unbalanced and, as such, unjust. And so, he follows this with two stipulations meant to balance the exchange. First, the sentence must be "judicially carried out." The first stipulation is narrowly procedural, as the actual sentence is necessarily death. Therefore the role of the judiciary here is limited to determining "the quality and the quantity" of a specific punishment "in accordance with the strict law of retribution."[25] On its own this stipulation does not provide a limit to the death penalty. It sets the general guidelines that lead up to sentencing, but it does not limit the actual practice of killing the condemned. Kant adds a second stipulation in an attempt to set this limit: "although it must still be freed from any mistreatment that could make the humanity in the person suffering it into something abominable." [26]

In the broadest sense this stipulation can be interpreted as one against what is commonly referred to as cruel and/or unusual punishment. In this sense it can be read as an attempt to limit or at least mitigate the suffering of the condemned, but it is also meant to limit the *signs* of pain and suffering. In order for punishment to be understood as *punishment*—and not vengeance—the apparent "humanity" of the condemned must be maintained. In Kant's words, the punishment must not "dull the people's feeling by the spectacle of a slaughterhouse."[27]

The stakes of this apparent "humanity" could not be higher. If this limit is breached, if "something abominable" is seen, then the "absolute" house of cards begins to fall in upon itself. With the death penalty a kind of constitutive impossibility is exposed. While the law of retribution might well require a life for a life, it does not determine who may kill or how the killing itself is to be done. Kant attempts to bridge this gap by referring us to the fact of sovereign power and "natural" law. This kind of hand-in-glove argument can only maintain itself in the perpetual *différance* of the moral law (i.e., the "moral law" is different from any specific determination and thus its completeness is deferred to the always already "not yet" of the future).[28] The suffering of the condemned interrupts this logic. By bearing witness to this suffering the spectator is confronted by an interval between life and death that radically disrupts the distinction between the will and sensation. Within this moment, this experience of the impossible, the spectator can no longer maintain its distance from the spectacle and the impossibility of the exchange of a life for a life is radically exposed. The "dulling" of feeling that accompanies the abominable spectacle of the slaughterhouse contaminates the very distinction between "human" and "animal." In this moment, the regulative ideas that hold the state together—those necessary "as if" propositions or postulates of "pure practical reason" known simply as *immortality, freedom*, and *God*—are unworked from within.[29]

While Kant does not provide us with a detailed account of the consequences of this suffering—either for the condemned or for those who bear witness—it is clear that his focus is on retaining the "humanity" of both. It is not simply that the spectacle of the condemned's suffering problematizes the distinction between punishment and vengeance by somehow exposing the impossibility of a strictly equal exchange. It problematizes the very boundaries between "humanity" and "animality." This is particularly problematic for Kant because the very concept of freedom hinges on this distinction. Freedom is, in Kant's terms,

> a pure rational concept, which for this very reason is transcendent for theoretical philosophy, that is, it is a concept such that no instance corresponding to it can be given in any possible experience, and of an object of which we cannot obtain any theoretical cognition: the concept of freedom cannot hold as a constitutive but solely as a regulative and, indeed, merely negative principle of speculative reason.[30]

As such, it can only be proven in and through "practical principles." These "practical principles" have their root in the distinction between "human" and "animal." Kant defines "animal choice" (*arbitium brutum*) as being determined by *inclination*—that is, by sensible impulse or *stimulus*—whereas "human choice" can "be *affected* but not *determined* by impulses, and is therefore of itself (apart from an acquired proficiency of reason) not pure but can still be determined to actions by pure will."[31] It is the opposition between the principle of self-love and the "moral law" that provides Kant with the practical determining grounds for freedom. An act is "free" if and only if it is not empirically conditioned, that is, if the object of the act is the "moral law" itself.[32] According to Kant the distinguishing feature of the human species is the capacity for reason (*animal rationale*) and that rationality is demonstrated in and through free choice.[33]

The physical suffering of the condemned—that is, the measureless suffering of dying—fundamentally problematizes these distinctions. It does so by pushing sensation beyond the possibility of endurance, comprehension and measure. Suffering is the experience of impossibility. Blanchot states that

> Suffering is suffering when one can no longer suffer it, and when, because of this non-power, one cannot cease suffering it. A singular situation. Time is as though arrested, merged with its interval. There, the present is without end, separated from every other present by an inexhaustible and empty infinite, the very infinite of suffering, and thus dispossessed of any future: a present without end and yet impossible as a present.[34]

From this he goes on to articulate three characteristics of the experience of impossibility,

1 [T]ime changes direction, no longer offering itself out of the future as what gathers by going beyond; time, here, is rather the

dispersion of a present that, even while being only passage does not pass, never fixes itself in a present, refers to no past and goes towards no future: *the incessant.*
2. [T]he immediate is a presence to which one cannot be present, but from which one cannot separate; or, again, it is what escapes by the very fact that there is no escaping it: the *ungraspable that one cannot let go of.*
3. [W]hat reigns in the experience of impossibility is not the unique's immobile collecting unto itself, but the infinite shifting of dispersal, a non-dialectical movement where contrariety has nothing to do with opposition or with reconciliation, and where the *other* never comes back to the same.[35]

This unending or incessant "now" disorients both the sufferer and those who witness the suffering. It arrests the experience of time in such a way that the orienteering apparatus of morality—consisting of those cardinal points known as *immortality, freedom,* and *God* that together situate the Kantian subject within the developmental movement of historical time—fails. Suffering unto death—the interval of dying—presents us with the experience of a "now" in which the promise of the law can no longer cover over the "fact" of sovereign power. Here, in this moment, the interval between the particular and the universal is experienced as the very impossibility of the moral law. Without the eternal possibility of the future, without the promise of eternal forms, of the timeless completeness of the species or God, the full weight of the moral law bears down on the "now" as an infinite accusation or, to borrow the language of theology, *unforgivable sin (crimen inexpiabile).*[36]

According to Kant, there is one crime that brings us to an experience of the impossible, namely, the execution of the monarch. Kant dedicates an extensive footnote to just this topic in the *Metaphysics of Morals*:

> It is the formal *execution* of a monarch that strikes horror in a soul filled with the idea of human beings' rights, a horror that one feels repeatedly as soon as and as often as one thinks of such scenes as the fate of Charles I or Louis XVI. But how are we to explain this feeling, which is not aesthetic feeling (sympathy, an effect of imagination by which we put ourselves in the place of the sufferer) but moral feeling resulting from the complete overturning of all concepts of rights? It is regarded as a crime that remains forever and can never be expiated (*crimen immortale, inexpiabile*), and it seems to be like what theologians call the sin that cannot be forgiven either in this world or the next.[37]

First the "feeling"—Kant is very specific—is "horror" and not "sympathy." As such, its source is not aesthetic, not an effect of the imagination; rather, it is moral. It is a horror that does not dissipate: it is felt each time one thinks of the event. The distinction between Kant's account of the execution of the condemned and the formal execution of the monarch is immediately apparent. In the former the appearance of formal necessity is maintained by a combination of judicial procedure and "humane" killing. The problem of suffering comes at the level of the phenomenal: it is an aesthetic experience that evokes sympathy.

Referring to Kant's account of sympathy in §34 of the *Doctrine of Virtue* we find that

> humanity can be located in the *capacity* and the *will* to *share in others" feelings* (*humanitas practica*) or merely in the *receptivity*, given by nature itself, to the feeling of joy and sadness in common with others (*humanitas aesthetica*). The first is *free*, and therefore called *sympathetic* (*communio sentiendi liberalis*); it is based on practical reason. The second is *unfree* (*communio sentiendi, servilis*); it can be called *communicable* (since it is like receptivity to warmth or contagious diseases), and also compassion, since it spreads naturally among human beings living near one another. There is obligation only to the first.[38]

It is by no means surprising that Kant divides this "feeling" into voluntary and involuntary components. This division provides him with an order: compassion is linked to the body, it is "mere" receptivity to the communicable "feelings" of others, while sympathy is an active and thus rational capacity to share in those feelings. Kant accuses Beccaria of being moved "by overly compassionate feelings of an affected humanity."[39] He continues: "In fact, when another suffers and, although I cannot help him, I let myself be infected by his pain (through my imagination), then two of us suffer, though the trouble really (in nature) affects only *one*. But there cannot possibly be a duty to increase the ills in the world and so to do good *from compassion.*"[40]

The logic here is puzzling: if another is suffering and I cannot help I should simply refrain from feeling their pain. I should do so because it is a feeling without use or orientation: it is simply needless. Kant even attempts to connect this experience of compassion to pity and thus, to a self-serving attempt to display moral worth. In effect, he attempts to force the reader into an either/or: one either actively chooses to not feel the suffering of others or one displays this feeling as a way of appearing to do good. Yet his caution regarding the spectacle of the condemned's suffering calls this into question. There is obviously a limit to what the subject can consciously choose to not feel. With the spectacle of the condemned's suffering it seems that we arrive at a point where it is no longer possible to divide compassion from sympathy. Here feeling the suffering of the other is not a good, it does not reduce the suffering; rather it is an experience of the impossible that calls the very possibility of orientation into question. There is a convergence here between the uselessness of compassion and the pointlessness of the monarch's execution.

With the formal execution of the monarch we are confronted with a noumenal catastrophe. Here the impossible itself takes the stage: the lawgiver is put on trial. This extends far beyond simply dethroning and killing the monarch—an act that might easily be understood by Kant as an exception to the moral law motivated by a desire for revenge or self-preservation—it folds the law back upon itself exposing a kind of "constitutive anarchy."[41] As Kant states,

> his execution must be regarded as a complete overturning of the principles of the relation between the sovereign and his people (in which the people, which owes its existence only to the sovereign's legislation, makes itself his master), so that violence is elevated above the most sacred rights brazenly in accordance with principle. Like a chasm that irretrievably swallows everything, the execution of a monarch seems to be a crime from which the people cannot be absolved, for it is as if the state commits suicide.[42]

This revolutionary inversion of the law is self-cancelling: it is suicidal. By *formally* executing the monarch the people destroy the legal order that constitutes them as "the people" and not simply an anarchic mass. Kant describes this act as both "wholly pointless" and impossible: "As far as we can see, it is impossible for a human being to commit a crime of this kind, a formally evil (wholly pointless) crime; and yet it is not to be ignored in a system of morals (although it is only the idea of the most extreme evil)."[43]

This act extends beyond the ever-present contamination of "radical evil" to the formal purity "diabolical evil." For Kant, such an act must be formally accounted for, but it remains strictly impossible. It simply "contains too much": "a reason exonerated from the moral law, an *evil reason* as it were (an absolutely evil will), would on the contrary contain too much, because resistance to the law would thereby be elevated to incentive (for without any incentive the power of choice cannot be determined), and so the subject would be made a *diabolical* being."[44]

Paradoxically, the act of "diabolical" evil is formally indistinguishable from the ethical act.[45] Both are *purely* formal and, as such, they are acts of *freedom*. They are not possible "mortal" acts. They are the purview of angels and demons. Were such an act to be committed, it would, in effect, be a collision of two separate orders: the temporal and the eternal. According to Kant, in this moment "violence is elevated above the most sacred rights brazenly in accordance with principle."[46] With this revolutionary inversion the very ground below our feet opens up "like a chasm that irretrievably swallows everything" removing the very possibility of orientation.[47]

By putting the monarch on trial, the pure form of the law is placed in opposition to its actuality. In one moment the full force of the moral law bears down on the now and reveals the impossibility of legality. It exposes the impossible distance between the universal and the particular, between force and law. As Comay argues, "What repels and fascinates Kant about the king's trial is that it reveals an illegality that seems to be both internal to the law and the key to its foundational authority."[48]

The execution of the monarch is both too much and not enough. It is too much in that it attempts to kill a god—to kill the very idea of the monarch—and not enough in that it is simply the death of another. Once done, the act simply exposes what was there all along: law without content. Returning to Comay's text:

> It is only by maintaining the formal indiscernibility between good and evil that the performative force of law can be maintained in the absence of a specific ordinance or injunction: a commitment to law as such, to the form of the law, law in general, the barest possibility of law, but also the monstrous prodigality of a law that must be rearticulated every time it is applied, rejustified and reinvented whenever it is executed, a lawfulness in excess of law—or even, phrased differently, lawfulness without law, *Gesetzmäßigkeit ohne Gesetz*.[49]

The experience of moral horror, this feeling that affects the "soul filled with the idea of human beings' rights," is brought on by the experience of the impossible[50]—that is, of the very impossibility of orientation. Once the monarch is formally executed, the emptiness of the moral law is utterly exposed: the ethical and the diabolical are one in the same. With this the basic coordinates of the moral law—the very coordinates it requires in order to give meaning to the "human"—are lost. Immortality without orientation, without progress, is simply pointless. Here the noumenal catastrophe of moral horror meets the phenomenal experience of compassion. The suffering of the condemned brings with it a useless but irresistible contamination. A breaking point—one impossible to determine or to limit—is shared, communicated, between the condemned and those who bear witness. With suffering the lines between free and unfree, active and passive, "human" and "animal" are forever blurred. The spectacle of abomination, of the slaughterhouse, "dulls" the feeling of those who bear witness. The suffering contaminates them, overriding the distinction between the "free" act of "sympathy" (*communio sentiendi liberalis*) and the communicable affect known as "compassion" (*communio sentiendi illiberalis, servilis*).[51] The pointlessness of shared suffering also brings us to the experience of the impossible. That is, to the point at which there is no meaningful distinction between "human" freedom and "animal choice" (*arbitium brutum*).[52] The suffering of the condemned disrupts the stage play of appearances that allows the hand of sovereign power to enforce the law without being accountable to it. It exposes the very same pointlessness as moral horror: the "now" without coordinates, without the possibility of orientation to the eternal. Without recourse to the ever-receding horizon of infinite progress, the "fact" of sovereign power can no longer take shelter in the moral law. Rather, it is absolutely exposed to it.

This is the force of Benjamin's argument in the *Critique of Violence*:

> For the question "May I kill?" meets its irreducible answer in the commandment "Thou shalt not kill." This commandment precedes the deed, just as God was "preventing" the deed. But just as it may not be fear of punishment that enforces obedience, the injunction becomes inapplicable, incommensurable once the deed is accomplished. No judgment of the deed can be derived from the commandment. And so neither the divine judgment, nor the grounds for this judgment, can be known in advance. Those who base a condemnation of all violent killing of one person by another on the commandment are therefore mistaken. It exists not as a criterion of judgment, but as a guideline for the actions of persons or communities who have to wrestle with it in solitude and, in exceptional cases, to take on themselves the responsibility of ignoring it.[53]

The law simply repeats itself and leaves the means by which it is to be forced open and thus infinitely culpable. The commandment provides us with neither an absolute right to punish nor an absolute right to life. This may seem to render it useless to politics, but in fact *its silence is the political*. It *un*works the claim to necessary violence, to a violence that can serve as a foundation for sovereign power (i.e., Benjamin's "mythic" violence), and leaves us with the responsibility for violence.[54] It leaves us with the pointless openness of life, the constitutive anarchy under the form of law, and the agonism of the political without the comfort of fate.

POINTLESS LIFE: OF TAHITIANS AND SHEEP

In his essay "Idea for a Universal History with a Cosmopolitan Purpose" (1784) Kant articulates a series of nine related historical propositions. Within the body of the fourth proposition we come across an outline of a world without antagonism: "man would live an Arcadian, pastoral existence of perfect concord, self-sufficiency and mutual love. But all human talents would remain hidden forever in a dormant state, and men, as good-natured as the sheep they tended, would scarcely render their existence more valuable than that of their animals."[55]

This line of argumentation is effectively repeated in *Reviews of Herder's Ideas on the Philosophy of the History of Mankind* (1785):

Does the author really mean that, if the happy inhabitance of Tahiti, never visited by more civilized nations, were destined to live in their peaceful indolence for thousands of centuries, it would be possible to give a satisfactory answer to the question of why they should exist at all, and of whether it would not have been just as good if this island had been occupied by happy sheep and cattle as by happy human beings who merely enjoy themselves?[56]

It is easy to read over these selections, ignore the peculiar equations that they offer, accept the broader logic of the text, and continue on. They are presented as obvious examples: a brief aside set into the text to appeal to the reader's common sense. Yet the presentation of this "pointless" form of life should, at the very least, give us some pause, perhaps even a twinge of unease. As soon as we begin to consider the grounds of these equations more carefully, their historical appearance begins to shift, exposing the dimensions of the eternal. The scale of value expressed in these equations is set by the *a priori* logic that binds the terms "nature," "species," "destiny," and "progress." Knowledge of the "truth" of this is constrained to a combination of a postulate of practical reason (i.e., immortality) and the teleological theory of nature.[57] The scale is suspended under the "as if," and yet the frightening implications can be seen in the very form of the question Kant poses to Herder: "Why should they exist at all?"

The question opens up a troubling silence within the text. Kant frames this silence as Herder's inability to answer, and goes on to present the life of Tahitians and sheep as equally lacking in value. But is it possible actually to give a "satisfactory answer" to this question?

1 If we read the question as a comparison of a specific group of individuals with the "destiny" of the human species and hold that a "satisfactory answer" can only be yes or no in absolute terms (i.e., the criterion is identity), the answer is simply no. In this case the terms being compared are of different orders (i.e., historical and eternal) and coincidence is impossible. Kant openly acknowledges this: "no single member of all the generations of the human race, but only the species, attains its destiny completely."[58]

2 If we read the question as a gradational comparison between two historical examples (Tahitians and "civilized nations") that are related to two separate eternal forms (the "human species" and the "animal"), we are provided with the *appearance* of an answer. It is possible to suspend the two historical examples between the eternal forms and thus provide a relative distance between them, but this procedure can be repeated *ad infinitum*. The impossibility of identity between the historical terms and their eternal coordinates means that there will always already be gradational distinctions.

It is thus only the appearance of an answer, because no historical group can be exempt from the question. Additionally, there is a serious epistemological problem: How are the eternal coordinates of these judgments known? The teleological propositions that Kant sets out (in the "Idea for a Universal History" and elsewhere) are provisional and not absolute. Thus, the judgments of the relative value of "life" rest on the tenuous ground of the "as if."

In short, Kant's question to Herder gains its force from the other side of universal history. It sets out to measure the historical from the perspective of the eternal. As soon as the question is asked an unbridgeable distance is set. This can be seen in both the syntax of the question and the selection of examples. The term "they" simultaneously indicates a distinct set of others and separates them from the speaker and the audience. Kant attempts to maximize the distance between the examples to increase the rhetorical effect of the question. He specifically chooses an exotic example to fill the position of "they" (i.e., Tahitians), because the "civilized" audience views their existence as nearly "animal." And, unlike the "animal," they cannot be exempt from the law. Theirs is but the appearance of the "purely animal" being Kant mentions in *Religion Within the Boundaries of Mere Reason*: "*Sensuous nature* therefore contains too little to provide a ground of moral evil in the human being, for, to the extent that it eliminates the incentives originating in freedom, it makes of the human a purely *animal* being."[59]

Sensuous nature contains too little to be the ground of "moral evil": it lacks the "moral" incentives to act. It is clear that animal life—like both angels and demons—exists outside of the bounds of the moral law, but the pointless and bare humanity of Tahitians does not. Their happiness is *almost* innocent, and because of this they are all the more guilty. Their peaceful indolence is a betrayal of their freedom. Their life is pointless, because it does not take on the yoke of destiny and immortality: it is simply not historical, it does not progress, it is dormant. It needs to be awakened, but how?

The answer can be seen in the implications that follow from Kant's question: "Why should they exist at all?" The question does not address those that are collectively referred to as "they." Rather, it establishes a distance, a separation between the "they" and the speaker. From this basis it contests the value of their existence and demands a judgment from the audience. The stakes of this question are high: if "they" have no actual value in this dormant state, if there is no "point" to their continued existence, their awakening can come at any price. In this case, "man is *an animal who needs a master*."[60] Kant opens a space of exception within his moral philosophy to accommodate this need: this space or spacing (as it is a continual and iterative practice) is the *a priori* grounds of the necessary "fact" of sovereign power. It is the distancing and distinguishing of the boundaries between "man" and "animal." It is practised in and through the performance of the "as if": the postulates of pure practical reason (*immortality, God, and freedom*) provide orientation for moral actions and thus bridge the gap between the particular and the universal. It is maintained by continually dividing the self from itself: Kant maintains that the happiness of Tahitians is "pointless" because there is an accord between the body and the will. This accord is the source of their guilt: their happiness is that of animals, not of humans. The rigidity of distinction between the *insignificance* of the "human animal" and the *dignity* of the "rational human being" will lead Kant to claim that masturbation is formally worse than suicide:

> someone casts off life as a burden is at least not making a feeble surrender to animal impulse in throwing himself away; murdering oneself requires courage, and in this disposition there is still always room for respect for the humanity in one's own person. But unnatural lust, which is complete abandonment of oneself to animal inclination, makes man not only an object of enjoyment but, still further, a thing that is contrary to nature, that is, a loathsome object, and so deprives him of all respect for himself.[61]

The "pointless" pleasure of masturbation joins with the "pointless" life of savages. The pointless life of pleasure violates the moral law—it is unfree and, as such, formally impure—it contravenes and contaminates the desire for the impossible: a "pure" moral act. The "civilized" desire of the moral law can be read as a desire for indemnification, or as Derrida refers to it in "Faith and Knowledge," auto-indemnification. It takes on the project of perpetual progress towards the impossibility of the "pure" moral act by setting eternal coordinates (*God, immortality, freedom*). These coordinates make it seem "as if" the moral law has positive content and that content is "man" as a "rational human being." And yet, since "man" is never complete, the eternal coordinates serve to maintain the orientation of the individual. It is only these coordinates that can, at one and the same time, make the execution of the murderer blameless (i.e., naturalize the connection between the formal imperative "Thou shalt not kill" and the death sentence) and forbid the lawful execution of the monarch. In each moment the hand of sovereign power is rendered invisible: it is a necessary condition of that which is always already coming to be. Its invisibility is maintained because of what it promises to bring: movement away from "pointless" life and towards the endless horizon of "man."

What is the role of this "animal" in this incessant progress? Derrida touches on this question in *The Animal That Therefore I Am*:

> The animal (and even the animal in man) cannot be taken to be an end in itself, but only a means. It belongs to the purely sensible order of existence

that must always be *sacrificed* (this is always Kant's word when speaking of the subordination of interests and vital or sensible passions). In a word, and in order to cut straight to the chase, what the nonrational animal is deprived of, along with subjecthood, is what Kant calls "dignity [*Würd*]," that is to say, an internal and priceless value, the value of an end in itself, or if you prefer, a price above any comparable or negotiable price, above any market price.[62]

In short, Kant's account of *freedom* and *progress* are grounded in an allergic reaction to the *"human-animal."* The *"rational human being"* always already different, set apart and against, than the animal-body: it defers, restrains, restricts and opposes itself to its body. It orients itself towards the impossibility of the moral law. And yet it refuses the emptiness of that law. It reads the imperative form in conjunction with "man," and by doing so it blinds itself to the possibility of "diabolical evil." Neither the criminal nor the revolutionary can act freely. Their actions derive from a failure of the will: they are pathological. The motivations behind the formal execution of the monarch cannot be "free":

> There is, accordingly, reason for assuming that the agreement to execute the monarch actually originates not from what is supposed to be a rightful principle but from fear of the state's vengeance upon the people if it revives at some future time, and that these formalities are undertaken only to give that deed the appearance of punishment, and so of a rightful procedure (such as murder would not be).[63]

Yet, even if there are "reasonable" grounds for contesting the motivations of the revolutionary court, the *appearance* of lawful punishment is unforgivable. It is worse than murder. "But this disguising of the deed miscarries; such a presumption on the people's part is still worse than murder, since it involves a principle that would have to make it impossible to generate again a state that has been overthrown."[64]

The formal execution of the monarch effectively exposes the emptiness of the moral law. It is opens and uncouples the *"human-animal"* and with it history. The state falls out of its alignment with the eternal: it is uprooted and it enters the now without an appeal to necessity. All life becomes pointless. Kant struggles to avoid this by refusing the possibility of "diabolical evil." He avoids the formal emptiness of the moral law by shifting his gaze to the arc of the eternal: the species over the individual, the totality over the particular. But the pathological "animal-body" remains constantly in play as that which both inhibits and enables the peculiar contra-natural causality of "freedom." The "animal-body" acts as the "a" of *différance*. This "a" can be thought of as a space, or a spacing, that is held open within meaning and, as such, it is connected to a series of other quasi-concepts in Derrida's work.

From *aporia* to *autrui* and àvenir, the "a" of *différance* is a certain openness, a silent hospitality, or *chora*, within the process of signification that resists the philosophical desire for an absolutely determinate meaning or absolutely delimitable context. But this is only one of the possible reactions to the "a"; it is the reactive, or, to echo Levinas, the "allergic" reaction to the "a." With the "a" there is always an either/or:

> The same unique source divides itself mechanically, automatically, and sets itself reactively in opposition to itself: whence two sources in one. This reactivity is a process of *sacrificial indemnification*, it strives to restore the unscathed (*heilig*) that it itself threatens. And it is also the possibility of the two, of $n + 1$, the same possibility as that of the *testimonial deus ex machina*. As for the response, it is either or. *Either* it addresses the absolute other as such, with an address that is understood, heard, respected faithfully and responsibly; or it retorts, retaliates, compensates and *indemnifies itself* in the war of resentment and of reactivity. One of the two responses ought always to be able to contaminate the other. It will never be proven whether it is the one or the other, never in an act of determining, theoretical or cognitive judgment. This might be the place and the responsibility of what is called belief, trustworthiness or fidelity, the fiduciary, "trust" <*la "fiancé"*> in general, the tribunal <*instance*> of faith.[65]

On the individual level Kant's moral philosophy expresses itself as a "war of resentment and reactivity" against the pointless life of the "human animal." It gathers its resources from the other side of universal history and asks the "human-animal": "Why should you exist at all?" And yet, when it comes to correcting or reorienting this "pointless" life to rational dignity—to the actual event of sovereign power in the form of violence—the Kantian subject must abstain. This perspective—which, Arendt refers to as the "world spectator"—can only be maintained if it can retain a distance from certain spectacles.[66] It requires a distance in order to retain its *innate shared feelings*. It must not become dull and thereby totally numb to the suffering of others. Were it to become immune to the suffering of others, nothing would restrain it from the absolute freedom hiding just behind that insidious question: "Why should they exist at all?" Hegel brings the terror of this stance into stark relief: "In this absolute freedom, therefore, all social groups or classes which are the spiritual spheres into which the whole is articulated are abolished; the individual consciousness that belonged to any such sphere, and willed and fulfilled itself in it, has put aside its limitation; its purpose is the general purpose, its language universal law, its work the universal work."[67] And from that point putting others to death has "no more significance than cutting off a head of cabbage or swallowing a mouthful of water."[68] In order to save itself from that fate, the "rational human being" must retain its "feeling" for life by abstaining from the spectacle of cruelty. Maintaining the orientation towards the eternal requires selective blindness.

Kant's "world spectator" sets his sights on the totality of the "human species" in order to decipher the arc of universal history in the seemingly meaningless repetition of violence. As Kant states, "Nature should thus be thanked for fostering social incompatibility, enviously competitive vanity, and insatiable desires for possession or even power. Without these desires, all man's excellent natural capacities would never be roused to develop. Man wishes concord, but nature knowing better what is good for his species, wishes discord."[69] Hegel echoes this use of historical reason, "The History of the World is not the theater of happiness. Periods of happiness are blank pages in it, for they are periods of harmony—periods when the antithesis is in abeyance."[70]

How can Kant know the ends of "nature"? How is he able to distinguish perpetual progress from perpetual violence? The answer to this is found at the very basis of the so-called *"absolute"* right of punishment. In Arendt's words: "at the center of his philosophy of history (or, rather, his philosophy of nature) stands the perpetual progress of the human race, or mankind."[71]

At the base it is the distinction of a life that lacks value that enables Kant to read the world as the text of a universal history. If "man" is the meaning of history then it is written with the blood of the "animal," that is, at one and the same time, internal and external to the "rational human being." With the "absolute" distinction between "man" and the "animal," force is able to appear as law. Animal life is sacrificed so that "man" is possible as an orientation. What is "not" man—that which does not and cannot count—is only preserved by his duty to himself. The needless destruction of "what is *beautiful* in inanimate nature" is wrong because "it weakens or uproots that feeling in him which, though not of itself moral, is still a disposition of sensibility that greatly promotes morality or at least prepares the way for it: the disposition, namely, to love something (e.g., beautiful crystal formations, the indescribable beauty of plants) even apart from any intention to use it."[72]

This auto-violation is even greater when it comes to the "animate but nonrational part of nature": "violent and cruel treatment of animals is far more intimately opposed to a human being's duty to himself, and he has a duty to refrain from this; for it dulls his shared feeling of their suffering and so weakens and gradually uproots a natural predisposition that is very serviceable to morality in one's relations with other men."[73]

In order to continue to see reason in acts of violence a certain set of (impossible) distinctions must be maintained. The execution of the condemned must not be a theatre of cruelty. It must preserve the boundary between "man" and the "animal." It must invoke the *voluntary* sympathy of those who witness the execution, but not arouse their compassion. Compassion (*communio sentiendi, servilis*) overwhelms reason, it is involuntary, it contaminates, spreading like a disease from one body to another. It is disorienting, because it interrupts the active and/or willful displacement of the historical gaze. Here in a moment without orientation the spectacle of execution meets with the moral horror of the formal execution of the monarch. According to Kant each is catastrophic and to be avoided at all costs, and yet it is these impossible moments that open up the possibility of political action.

This possibility is exposed in the very moments that Kant wishes to avoid. For him, there are moments in which we must avert our gaze or risk being too close to the spectacle and losing track of our "humanity." Once they have passed we can gain some distance, return to our seats, and read the course of fate into these gaps. But there is another course. If we pause within such a moment, if we do not merely "tarry" (waiting on the magic of the *aufgehoben* to resume the course of being) but rather attend to its silence, we leave both the eternal light of Kant's moral law and the magic circle of dialectics.[74] Within this departure or hiatus we arrive within a "now" without the possibility of orientation. Kant's description of conscience in §13 of the *Doctrine of Virtue* captures this experience:

> Every human being has a conscience and finds himself observed, threatened, and in general, kept in awe (respect coupled with fear) by an internal judge; and this authority watching over the law in him is not something that he himself (voluntarily) *makes*, but something incorporated in his being. It follows him like his shadow when he plans to escape. He can indeed stun himself or put himself to sleep by pleasures and distractions, but he cannot help coming to himself or waking up from time to time; and when he does, he hears at once its fearful voice. He can at most, in extreme depravity, bring himself to *heed* it no longer, but he still cannot help *hearing* it.[75]

If we shift Kant's account of the voice of conscience and no longer hear it as the voice of "man" (the *"rational human being"*), but as that which is, in the words of Levinas, *otherwise than being*, that is, as absolute, non-dialectical difference, then we begin to touch on the "now" without the possibility of orientation. In this moment, outside the bounds of "man," politics enters the open of unlimited responsibility.

Chapter 5

BETWEEN THE JUDGE AND THE EXECUTIONER
Revisiting the Silent Foundations of Hegel's Moral Point of View*

[A]lthough retribution cannot aim to achieve specific equality, this is not the case with murder, which necessarily incurs the death penalty. For since life is the entire compass of existence [*Dasein*], the punishment [for murder] cannot consist [*bestehen*] in a *value*—since none is equivalent to life—but only in the taking of another life.
—G. W. F. Hegel, *Elements of the Philosophy of Right*

THE INITIAL SITE OF OUR PROBLEMATIC is §104 of Hegel's *Grundlinien*.

> Thus, it now has its *personality*—and in abstract right the will is no more than personality—as its *object* [*Gegenstand*]; the infinite subjectivity of freedom, which now has being *for itself*, constitutes the principle of the *moral point of view*.[1]

Here we find a condensed summary of the transition from Right to Morality. We are told that in this moment *personality* (i.e., the formal universality of the "I" as detailed in §§34–40) becomes an *object* of knowledge.[2] Further we find that by becoming an *object* of knowledge personality is sublated [*Aufheben*], but this immediately leads us to two related questions. First, on a conceptual level, how exactly does personality become an object of knowledge? Simply put, what immediately precedes and thus conditions the possibility of this moment? Secondly, and following from this, how does this overcoming occur at a practical level, that is, how is it accomplished? If we pause at this point in the text and take up the first question, we can quickly see that personality becomes an object of knowledge through punishment. That is, punitive justice sublates the contradiction between Right,

---
* This chapter first appeared in *Idealistic Studies* 41:3 (Fall 2011): 149–60.

which is up until this moment abstract and thus *in-itself*, and "the *individual* [*einzelnen*] will which has being *for itself* in opposition to the universal."[3] Punishment *actualizes* right; this much is given quite clearly in §104 and its corresponding *Zusätze*. However, as soon as we ask which punishment exposes the "truth" of personality, who sets this punishment, who carries it out, or even how it is carried out, we are confronted by a puzzling mixture of shadows and silence.

It is not that Hegel simply leaves these details out of the text—in fact there are a series of partial answers to these questions—but as soon as we look for the specifics of this transition, the text falls silent. One might attempt to excuse the lack of specifics by arguing that the *Grundlinien* is a text that concerns itself with the *principles* of right and not the practices thereof; but as Hegel states in §282, some practices uniquely relate to the principle of right. He goes so far as to refer to §§95–102 as an example of such an application, and, this being so, we are clearly dealing with a practice that, like the Monarch's right to pardon criminals, is related directly to the principle of right. This makes the lack of a clearly articulated account of the practices that fulfill the conceptual requirements of this transition even more puzzling.

Adriaan Peperzak, one of the most thorough and systematic scholars of the *Grundlinien*, has attempted to shed some light on this moment by claiming that it is the figure of the judge that resides in these shadows (i.e., as the unnamed character detailed in §103).[4] While this thesis provides us with a possible answer to the question of "who" determines the "how" of punishment, it still leaves us with the problem of where the judge's authority is derived from. That is, if we claim that the character in §103 is the judge that emerges as a central figure of civil society in §§209–229, we are left asking where the judge obtains its authority from within this moment. In civil society the court of law will derive its authority from the ability of moral subjects to recognize and affirm the actuality of right, but at this stage right is still *in-itself* (cf. §§218–19).[5] The judge's purview is the administration of law; he or she can neither proclaim law nor affirm its moral status as either just (punitive) or unjust (avenging). As a result, with this thesis we seemingly have a judge enforcing formal penal laws that lack moral recognition; but without this recognition there is seemingly no way to distinguish between vengeance and punishment. Furthermore, without this distinction personality cannot become an object of knowledge and the dialectic of right is unable to progress beyond the level of contract. Despite these apparent problems, we are told in §104 that this transition occurs; personality is overcome in the dialectical exchange of crime and punishment and as a result the persons who enter this moment leave it as subjects of a moral community.

Given this state of affairs we are left with the option of either simply shrugging our shoulders at this apparent *aporia*, and moving on to the next moment in hopes of finding our answer in the next fold of the dialectic, or pausing here to carefully reexamine the precise contours of this moment. The latter option will require a close reading of the section on coercion and crime in the *Grundlinien* (§§90–104).

On the basis of this account we can propose an alternative reading of the transition from Right to Morality. In our reading, the character in §103 is not the judge, but rather the executioner.[6] This interpretation is grounded in both Hegel's conceptual requirements for this particular transition and his views on the relationship between murder and capital punishment as presented in the *Zusätze* for §101.[7] At the same time it provides us with a clear account of the source of the authority of the character in §103 and it puts this authority into question.[8]

To both substantiate and clarify this thesis, we will begin by providing the reader with a more detailed account of the transition as presented in the text. In the concluding section we will briefly touch on the critical problems this interpretation of Hegel's political philosophy raises with respect to the more general relationship between capital punishment, sovereign authority, and moral community.

REVISITING THE TRANSITION FROM RIGHT TO MORALITY

In order to thoroughly examine Hegel's account of the transition from Right to Morality, we must take our time and consider the specific details of §104. Hegel opens this section by summarizing the confrontation between crime and avenging justice: "Thus, crime and avenging justice represent the *shape* of the will's development when it has proceeded to the distinction between the universal will which has being *in itself*, and the *individual* [*einzelnen*] will which has being *for itself* in opposition to the universal."[9]

This confrontation is, at least at this point, an antinomy, as the relationship between crime and avenging justice is, in Hegel's terms, one of the subjective will.[10] In short, both crime and revenge are subjectively motivated, and the resulting social condition is dominated by cyclical violence. In order to appreciate the more specific details of this problem, it is necessary to consult Hegel's discussion of crime and punishment as given in the section on coercion and crime in the *Grundlinien*.

As Hegel details in §95 crime constitutes a *"negatively infinitive judgment in its complete sense,"* in that it is not only the victim's personal property that is negated, but more importantly his or her capacity for rights.[11] By committing a criminal act, an agent is effectively caught in what we can refer to as a performative contradiction. This is due to the fact that such an act violates the conditions of his or her own possibility (i.e., the criminal act violates the "commandment of right"—"*be a person and respect others as persons*"—in §36 and thus violates its own capacity for rights). According to

Hegel's dialectical theory of punishment only coercion can cancel [*Aufgehoben*] coercion and positively manifest right (cf. §93). Seeing as the function of punishment is to negate the initial coercion, the question of proportionality becomes central. If the punishment is excessive (e.g., the laws of Draco), it constitutes a new infringement of right. Hegel is careful to stipulate in §96 that the qualitative and quantitative degree of the objective infringement *does vary*, and therefore crimes such as robbery and theft are different in degree from "murder, slavery and religious coercion, etc."[12] In most cases (the exception being absolute infringements) establishing the specific proportionality of crimes and punishments can only be accomplished in a positively determined legal code, as they do not possess a specific or necessary equality (cf. §101).[13] In short, the antinomic deadlock that marks the limit of Abstract Right is brought on by the problem of finding a proportional punitive response to crime.

Continuing on with §104, we can begin to consider Hegel's account of the dialectical transition that sublates [*Aufgehoben*] this problem: "They [crime and avenging justice] also show how the will *which has being in itself*, by superseding this opposition, has returned into itself and thereby itself become *actual* and *for itself*. Having proved itself in opposition to the individual will *which has being only for itself*, right accordingly *is* and *is recognized* as *actual* by virtue of its necessity."[14]

Pausing at this point, we find that Hegel is addressing the *results* of the *solution*. That is, he is addressing the conceptual changes that occur as a result of superseding this opposition [*Aufheben dieses Gegensatzes*] and not the specific details of the supersession itself.[15] As Hegel clearly reiterates later on in same paragraph, the opposition is between the universal will, which has being *in itself* [*an sich*], and the individual will, which has being *for itself* [*für sich*]. If right remains abstract (i.e., *in-itself*), the social condition remains effectively anomic, but we are told that right does not remain abstract; rather, it becomes actual [*wirklich*] and *for itself* [*für sich*].[16] Hegel closes this section by providing us with a more detailed account of exactly what this actualization entails on a conceptual level:

> by superseding this opposition—the negation of the negation—it determines itself as will *in its existence* [*Dasein*], so that it is not only a free will in itself, but also *for itself*, as self related [*sinch auf sich bezie-hende*] negativity. Thus, it now has its *personality*—and in abstract right the will is no more than personality—as is *object* [*Gegenstand*]; the infinite subjectivity of freedom, which now has being *for itself*, constitutes the principle of the *moral point of view*.[17]

Here it is clear that in the process of this supersession [*Aufheben*] the universal will "determines itself as *will in its existence* [*Dasein*]" and thus becomes *for-itself*. The reiteration of the transition of right (the universal will which is up until this point abstract or, in Hegel's terms, *in-itself*) from being abstract to being "*actual*" (in Hegel's technical sense of the term) adds emphasis to the fact that this transition entails a *determination* of right in existence. It is in this determination that personality becomes an object [*Gegenstand*] of knowledge. That is, the *inner truth* of personality (that it is only *for itself* and thus a deficient mode of being) becomes explicitly available to cognition. This presentation or exposure of the limits of personality sets up the transition of right to morality, in that right moves from being *abstract* (formal) to being *actual* (internalized) in the moral point of view. Simply put, in this moment *formal persons* become *moral subjects*. Now the question is *how* exactly does personality become an object of knowledge?

What is clear at this point is that avenging justice cannot fulfill the conceptual requirements of this moment, because it is subjectively motivated and, as Hegel specifies in §102, it constitutes a *new infringement* of right.[18] In §103 Hegel clearly states that what is needed to resolve [*Aufhebens*] this contradiction is "a justice freed from subjective interest and subjective shape and from the contingency of power—that is, a *punitive* rather than an *avenging justice*."[19] Furthermore this type of justice requires a specific type of actor: it requires "a will which, as a particular and *subjective* will, also wills the universal as such."[20] Given this orientation of the will this character (the judge/executioner) has obviously superseded the limits of *formal* personhood and has attained the moral point of view, but at this point this reorientation of the will is *unique* to this character.[21] That is, in order to fulfill the (onto)logical requirements of this moment there must be a negation of the negation; the criminal must be negated and in this negation right must become *actual* (*Wirklichkeit*). Without the act of punitive justice there is no *negation of the negation*. Hegel is careful to specify that, punitive justice is not to be understood as simply a "requirement" (something formally needed but practically unavailable); rather, it emerges from the dialectical movement itself—it is (onto)logically *necessary*. This being so, we now have a partial answer to our question; that is, personality becomes an object of knowledge in the act of punitive justice. Furthermore, a moral subject is required to carry out the act of punitive justice (i.e., the judge/executioner from §103). This fits with the account given in §104, as it clarifies how right moves from being abstract to being actual, and yet this answer is only *partial* because we have yet to establish which crime is being punished.

This question is deceptively simple. While it may at first seem that any crime can fulfill the requirements of §104 as long as it is responded to punitively, a problem arises as soon as we get to the question of determining what that punishment is (i.e., sentencing). As we noted earlier, (most) crimes *do not* have a specific equality with punishments and, as a result, a legal code needs to be positively determined (cf. §101 and §214). In a legal code, crimes are converted into a value and exchanged for punishments, but how can we ensure that a specific legal code is punitive? In civil society there is a court of law *precisely because* at this stage "property and personality have legal recognition and validity," but at the stage of Abstract Right there is only the *formal* requirement of such recognition (right has not yet become *for-itself*).[22] In short, if the individuals at this stage do not possess the *moral point of view*, there is no way to get them to recognize a particular legal code as valid. Without this recognition there is no way to preserve the distinction between punitive and avenging justice—that is, unless there is an exceptional type of crime (i.e., one with a specific equality with its punishment). As we have already seen, this type of crime is first mentioned in §96 and then elaborated on in the *Zusätze* for §101.

MURDER AND CAPITAL PUNISHMENT

In this *Zusätze* we find that, " although retribution cannot aim to achieve specific equality, this is not the case with murder, which necessarily incurs the death penalty. For since life is the entire compass of existence [*Dasein*], the punishment [for murder] cannot consist [*bestehen*] in a *value*—since none is equivalent to life—but only in the taking of another life."[23]

Here murder is presented as an exceptional type of crime. This exceptional status is corroborated in §96 as it is listed—along with slavery and religious coercion—as a total or infinite infringement of the will. For Hegel, the difference between these types of crimes and crime in general is one of degree. That is, while *all* crimes infringe on my *formal* capacity for rights, the degree of the *objective* [*Dasein*] infringement varies. For example, in a crime like theft the objective infringement is different in degree from robbery, because the latter includes a threat to my life. With crimes like murder, slavery, and religious coercion, the infringement simultaneously violates both the *formal* and the *objective* aspects of the will completely. Even among these murder is unique. Whereas in slavery I become the property of another and in religious coercion I am denied both my freedom of belief and expression, only in the case of murder do I cease to exist.[24] This distinction has a direct effect on the type of retributive response required in order to restore right. In the case of both slavery and religious coercion, individuals are *required* to resist the coercive force being exerted on them.[25] The specific form of this resistance cannot be conceptually predetermined and thus, like (most) crimes, it must be positively determined in practice. This is not the case with murder. By ending the life of the victim, murder destroys the very possibility of their resistance and, as such, it is the *only* crime that has a specific equality with its punishment.

At this point we can return to the questions we had concerning the transition from Abstract Right to Morality. The central problem we highlighted with this transition is that of punitive justice. That is, how can an act of punitive justice be carried out when right is still abstract? Part of this answer is given in §103. The unnamed character (judge/executioner) provides us with a moral actor to carry out the act of punitive justice, but this still leaves us with the question of the actual punishment. This is a problem, because (most) punishments are positively determined and, in order to be considered just, these determinations require the moral recognition of those to whom they apply. Due to the fact that at this point this recognition is still only a *formal* requirement and not a lived actuality (i.e., right is not yet *for-itself*), we are seemingly left with no explanation of how persons become moral subjects. And yet, as we have just seen, the unique qualities of the crime of murder offer a solution. Since murder has a *specific equality* with its punishment, we no longer have to deal with the issue of determining a "just" sentence. In fact, all that is needed to enact the punishment is a moral actor, and §103 provides us with just that. The solution to our problem is now clearly in place; in the *Grundlinien*, the execution of the murderer is the advent of moral subjectivity.

AFFIRMATION, DEATH, AND MORALITY

What are the consequences of this? To an extent, the answer depends on the context. There are specific consequences for the interpretation of the *Grundlinien*. The most pressing consequences—at least for our purposes—will pertain to the parallels that exist between Abstract Right and Hegel's account of External Sovereignty. The fact that the transition from right to morality occurs with the punitive execution of the murderer helps to explain why international law remains abstract.[26]

In addition to the consequences for the interpretation of Hegel's texts, there are also consequences for the relationship between these texts and lived practices. Here we undoubtedly confront the most difficult of tasks. After all, in order to begin to inquire as to the relevance of a particular political philosophy, we first have to acquire a high degree of proficiency within that theory itself. With regard to Hegel, this is in and of itself an immense undertaking. Reading his texts, that is, reading them well, requires a level of patience and dedication that will undoubtedly bring the reader "to the point where one would like just to emit an inarticulate sound."[27] When we are considering the moments within the *Grundlinien* that deal with instances of "legitimate" or "necessary" lethal violence, this frustration can quickly become an outright refusal to read. Hegel's view on "savages" and his celebration of the positive value of execution and war are admittedly unsettling, but this is precisely why they demand our attention. In fact, we would argue there is a twofold ethical duty in reading these moments. On the one hand they deal with legitimated instances of lethal violence, and therefore as readers we face the ethical duty of seeking out the principles and arguments that ground this claim to legitimacy. On the other hand we have an ethical duty to Hegel's text: to present his arguments to the very best of our ability. These duties are inseparable. If we simply dismiss or omit these moments, we not only neglect to read Hegel's text, but we fail those he condemns. Simply put, if our aim is to raise the question of ethics in Hegel's text we must practise an ethics of reading.

Once we raise the question of the practical implications of this moment in the text, we should make no mistake that the question that we are dealing with is the question of the boundaries of moral community. We are being told that the moral subjectivity begins with and is accomplished through the *punitive* execution of the murderer. It is through the negation of the exposed and, as Hegel will refer to it in the *Zusätze* for §97, *vulnerable* body of the condemned that right "proves itself as a necessary and mediated existence [*Dasein*]."[28] The claim is seductive; in just this once instance we are told we can go beyond the absurd and repugnant visage of the one-eyed and toothless miscreant that the more literal version of the *lex talionis* forces us to confront and have *real* justice.[29]

The frightening symmetry of this idea brings to mind the officer and his remarkable apparatus in Kafka's "*In der Strafkolonie*" ("In the Penal Colony"). The promise of the apparatus was also the spectacle of justice. By literally *writing out* the sentence on the flesh of the condemned it also laid claim to a *specific equality* with the crime it responded to; but the truth of its work remained locked between the illegibility of the guiding plans and the silent "enlightenment" [*Verstand*] of the condemned.[30] The apparatus draws in the crowds with the *promise* of justice, but what is initially a spectacular show soon loses its novelty and becomes little but the monotonous repetition of death. The truth of the apparatus is exposed when the officer enters it. Whereas the apparatus was set up to inscribe a specific imperative ("HONOUR THY SUPERIORS") on the condemned, the officer sets it up to inscribe a universal imperative ("BE JUST!") on himself.[31] With this shift from a specific to a universal imperative, the apparatus fails to write out its sentence. In place of the "exquisite torture" the officer desired, there is "plain murder." In effect the attempt to actualize a universal imperative exposed the performative contradiction that was there all along.

We must ask ourselves how Hegel's scene differs from this one. That is, how can he balance the scales of this impossible exchange of life for life? How can the crowd of "persons" witness this exchange and become "moral subjects"? What of those that cannot affirm the equality of this exchange? Are they simply cast out of the community? Is there not some ineffable excess here? A kind of irreducible remainder that defies the very concepts of equality and identity? Perhaps it is in this moment that we can catch a brief glimpse of the non-identity that Hegel's remarkable dialectical apparatus was constructed to negate and see that it also bleeds. Like the blood of Abel, this blood saturates the ground, calling out for justice, and thus—much like the remain(s) in Derrida's *Glas*—it provokes the very action of Hegel's apparatus.[32] The heterogeneity of the remain(s) demands a response, and the dialectical apparatus is constructed to respond by *writing-out* difference in the name of identity. Yet, like Kafka's apparatus, it can never be finished with its work. In Kafka's story it is only the *belief* of the officer that enables him to see the positive "truth" of the apparatus. Without this *belief* we see the apparatus from the eyes of the explorer and witness nothing but the negativity of "plain murder." It is the blood of the non-identical that should bring us to question the nature of our participation in Hegel's text. In the end, Hegel's response to our troubled conscience is written on the tomb of the Old Commandant: "Have faith and wait!"[33]

Chapter 6

TO READ THE WRITING OF RIGHT
An Excursus on Death and the Foundations of Law in the Penal Colony

[A]an attack on capital punishment assails, not legal measure, not laws, but law itself in its origin. For if violence, violence crowned by fate, is the origin of law, then it may be readily supposed that where the highest violence, that over life and death, occurs in the legal system, the origins of law jut manifestly and fearsomely into existence.
—Walter Benjamin, "Critique of Violence"

READING KAFKA'S "IN THE PENAL COLONY" ("In der Strafkolonie") is, much like the "apparatus" that it details, both remarkable and disturbing. One cannot help admire the frighteningly logical precision of the text's composition. The arrangement of its constituent parts (i.e., the officer, the explorer, the old and the new Commandant, etc.) displays a kind of mechanical synchronicity in which each action both entails and amplifies the next. This accelerative quality serves to accentuate the growing unease of the reader. With each sentence what is initially presented as distant and foreign becomes all too intimate. Like the explorer in the story we are progressively deprived of the space that allows us to simply observe. The strange and the familiar blend together in such a way that neither is retrievable and what we are left with is an unbearable proximity.

It is this proximity that the explorer flees but cannot escape. Proximity—or rather, the very problematization of distance, the *Unheimliche*—both structures the work of the apparatus and ultimately undoes it. But what is the nature of this proximity? What is the relationship between the proximity that the officer desires—both in leaning close to watch the condemned at the "sixth hour" and, ultimately, entering the apparatus himself—and that from which the explorer flees? Provisionally, we can say that the "what" that each holds in common and that binds them together is silence. This is an openly paradoxical answer. Silence is not a "what" in the sense of a localizable object or thing, and yet it permeates the colony. There is the silence of the mystifying "guiding plans," the silence of the condemned's "enlightenment" [*Verstand*], the officer's death, and the old Commandant's promise to return. In each case silence is, figuratively speaking, close at hand. This being so, it is silence provides us with a point of entry that will lead us into the inner most workings of the colony. But, before we begin, we must give a clear account of the stakes. That is, we must explain why the fate of this fictional colony matters.

Even taken at a distance, the conceptual topography of the colony is not as strange as it may first seem. The characters are fantastically drawn. Their movements strangely amplified, concentrated, and somehow pushed to the very limits of the possible. And yet despite this they are not incomprehensibly "foreign." The colony is here—that is, it is a possible place, a *topos*—but it is also no place in particular. In terms of its conceptual arrangement, the colony is clearly guided by the transcendental promise of law. There are two orders, that of the new Commandant and that of the old. The former is mentioned, but few details are given. It is clearly an order of liberal penal reform, but its movements towards this reform are slow and take the form of a kind of purposeful neglect, in which the unwanted components of the colony's architecture are simply cordoned off and ignored. In the old order, spoken of by the officer, the entire colony is centred on the apparatus. The community is drawn to the apparatus not simply to behold the spectacle of an almost unimaginable cruelty, but by the promise of justice. With every sentence the apparatus writes, the law gains expression; it is determined or manifested, and thus is no longer an empty or silent ideal. The paradoxical twist is that with every sentence the distance between the formal promise of the law and its lived actuality becomes more evident. With every sentence written out, the meaning of the law becomes less stable, because every sentence requires further sentences to secure its meaning. In effect, the colony and the apparatus form a positive feedback loop. The system is grounded on the demand for and promise of justice, but with every sentence the demand for justice is redoubled. It is the inability of the apparatus to write an absolute sentence—that is, a sentence without silence, in which law and justice completely coincide—that secures its ultimate fate. At this point the seemingly strange topography of the colony becomes all too familiar. Like the modern state the colony exists at the crossroads of the necessity of law and the singular demand of justice. And like the modern state, it carries its past within it, despite all its attempts to forget or pass beyond it and make the colony "new"; the connection between the law and the death penalty remains bound to the very foundations of its law.

The importance of this fictional colony is this connection between the foundation of law, death and the claim to justice. The issue here is the role of capital punishment in the foundations of law. As Benjamin notes, " an attack on capital punishment assails, not legal measure, not laws, but law itself in its origin. For if violence, violence crowned by fate, is the origin of law, then it may be readily supposed that where the highest violence, that over life and death, occurs in the legal system, the origins of law jut manifestly and fearsomely into existence."[1]

With capital punishment, law juts—that is, it extends, projects, or protrudes into existence—as *necessity* itself. Violence here appears crowned as "fate," but at the same time "in this very violence something rotten in the law is revealed."[2] Kafka's story seizes upon this exposure and draws it into the open. The colony concentrates, condenses, and thereby accelerates the relationship between the death penalty and the "mystical foundation of authority"; it accelerates it to the point of silence, that is, to the point at which its silence begins to speak. The officer presents the apparatus as *the* means through which justice can be done. Its work of literally *writing-out* the sentence on the body of the condemned takes punishment beyond a simple deterrence or reformation. The promise of "enlightenment" or "understanding" [*Verstand*] honours the condemned as a *rational being*. Referring to §100 of Hegel's *Gundlinien* we find: "[t]he injury [*Verletzung*] which is inflicted on the criminal is not only just *in itself* (and since it is just, it is at the same time his will as it is in itself, an existence [*Dasein*] of his freedom, *his* right); it is also a *right for the criminal himself*, that is, a right *posited* in his *existent* will, in his action."[3]

The promise of retribution, of justice as equality—or borrowing an image from Kant, the promise of balancing the scales of justice—is uniquely connected to the death penalty. Kant clearly articulates this in *The Metaphysics of Morals*:

> Even if a civil society were to be dissolved by the consent of all its members (e.g., if a people inhabiting an island decided to separate and disperse throughout the world), the last murderer remaining in prison would first have to be executed, so that each has done to him what his deeds deserve and blood guilt does not cling to the people for not having insisted upon this punishment; for otherwise the people can be regarded as collaborators in this public violation of justice.[4]

In the case of murder the punishment of death is *necessary* in the fullest sense. The law cannot begin, cannot be founded, without this punishment. The same argument is essentially repeated in the *Zusätze* for §101 of Hegel's *Grundlinien*:

The Eumenides sleep, but crime awakens them; thus the deed brings its own retribution with it. But although retribution cannot aim to achieve specific equality, this is not the case with murder, which necessarily incurs the death penalty. For since life is the entire compass of existence [*Dasein*], the punishment [for murder] cannot consist [*bestehen*] in a *value*—since none is equivalent to life—but only in the taking of another life.[5]

The formal equality between murder and the death penalty is determined *a priori*; it is "fate." And yet it is this very claim of "necessity" or "fate" that is *unworked* in the colony. As Deleuze and Guattari observe, "it is not the law that is stated because of the demands of a hidden transcendence; it is almost the exact opposite: it is the statement, the enunciation, that constructs the law in the name of an immanent power of the one who enounces it—the law is confused with that which the guardian utters, and the writings that precede the law, rather than being the necessary and derived expression of it."[6]

Our focus in reading "In the Penal Colony" will be on how this "unworking" or "dismantling" [*démontage*] brings us back—by way of repetition—to a position that we have actually never left; that is, to the silence of the scaffold and the foundations of law.

A MACHINE FOR WRITING-*OUT*

"Read it," this imperative, given twice by the officer in Kafka's "In the Penal Colony," marks out the impossible position of the apparatus. It "marks out" in the sense of setting the coordinates or mapping the position the apparatus occupies within a field of relations. We can begin to gain a sense of orientation within this field simply by asking what the imperative is referring to. In both cases the officer's imperative refers to the "guiding plans" hand written by the former Commandant. The plans contain the sentence(s) that apparatus is designed to inscribe. Like a program or template they provide the officer with the precise instructions necessary for operating the apparatus. The content of the plans is highly specialized. The explorer attempts to read the plans but can only see "a labyrinth of lines crossing and recrossing each other."[7] The officer can read the plans but even he admits, "it's no calligraphy for school children. It needs to be studied closely."[8] As such, the apparatus is the mediator, it gives expression to the sentence by literally writing it out; but it cannot accomplish this "work" without a medium. The medium is the body itself. The body bears the sentence, and in doing so the "truth" of the sentence becomes intelligible. As the officer exclaims, "you have seen how difficult it is to decipher the script with one's eyes; but our man deciphers it with his wounds."[9] The apparatus is thus placed between the law and justice. Its "work" is to *write-out* the law by *writing-out* the body, but as the story unfolds it becomes clear that this "work" is always already an *unworking*, which is to say a *démontage* or *désoeuvrement*.[10] Within the penal colony this *unworking* is accelerated to the point of rupture—the apparatus collapses on the officer and the explorer flees the colony—but why does this rupture occur? Why, or more precisely, *how* does the apparatus collapse? How is the work of the apparatus an *unworking*?

To answer this, we must first take a closer look at both the composition and the operation of the apparatus. With regard to the former, the officer provides a detailed description. The apparatus itself is composed of three parts: the Designer, the Harrow, and the Bed. The Bed is covered with a layer of "cotton wool," it has straps to secure the hands, feet, and neck as well a gag—also made of "cotton wool"—to prevent the condemned from "screaming and biting his tongue."[11] It is motorized and powered by an "electric battery." Once the condemned is strapped in, the Bed is set into motion. As the officer explains, "'It quivers in minute, very rapid vibrations, both side to side and up and down. You will have seen similar apparatus in hospitals; but in our Bed the movements are all precisely calculated; you see, they have to correspond very exactly to the movements of the Harrow.'"[12]

The Designer is identical in size to the Bed and sits approximately two metres above it. Together they are described as looking like "two dark wooden chests" bound together at the corners with four brass rods.[13] It is also powered by an "electric battery," which, in this case, powers the movements of the Harrow, which is suspended between the Bed and the Designer by a ribbon of steel. Within the Designer's rather unassuming contours are "all of the cogwheels that control the movements of the Harrow."[14] In order to set the Harrow to work on a particular inscription, the complicated inner machinery of the Designer must be properly calibrated. For this the officer uses the mysterious "guiding plans" that were drawn by the former Commandant.

The final component is the Harrow. Its purpose is to inscribe the sentence onto the body of the condemned and, as such, it is the "instrument for the actual execution of the sentence."[15] It is constructed from both steel and glass and its shape corresponds to the human form. There are two types of needles, long and short, fixed into the glass and arranged in "multiple patterns." For each long needle there is a short one beside it. The long needles do the actual writing whereas the short ones spray "a jet of water to wash away the blood and keep the inscription clear."[16] This function is important as the purpose of setting the needles into the glass is to make it so the "actual progress of the sentence can be watched."[17] In addition the long "writing" needles can be used to disperse acid. The purpose of this is to increase the pain of the condemned to such a degree that his sighs can be heard even with the gag firmly in place. But, under the new Commandant, this practice is no longer permitted.[18] The final detail of Harrow's construction is the small single spike that is set in the position of the condemned's head. Its function is not to write, but to mark the end of the sentence by delivering the *coup de grâce*.

Moving on from the composition of the apparatus we can now begin to address its operation. In the most general terms its operation is linear, in that there is a beginning and an end to each sentence. It has three basic variables: frequency, intensity, and sentence. That is, while the operator can select from a range of sentences the actual process of inscription can only vary in the number of repetitions and the intensity of those repetitions (i.e., the use of acid versus water in the Harrow). Simply put, the apparatus is a machine for repeating sentences. It has a very well defined, if not narrow, operational capacity. And yet any attempt to provide an account of the "operation" of the apparatus—its manner of working or activity—must also account for its context. The operation of the apparatus can only have meaning within a larger socio-historical process. Quite simply, one cannot clearly separate the operation of the apparatus from the operation of the colony itself. The repetitive operation of the apparatus must be put in relation to the context that calls for or demands this repetition. At this level the question of the operation of the apparatus involves a set of social actors: the condemned, the operator(s), the audience, and the commandant(s). The operation or work of the apparatus binds these actors into a shared social context (the colony). The difference at this level of operation is that the repetitive and linear work of the apparatus is not received as a repetition pure and simple, that is, without difference. There is a difference between repetitions that exceeds their semantic content, and this difference determines the fate of the colony. For the sake of clarity we will begin with the mechanical operation of the apparatus itself and then put this operation in relation to the socio-historical process of the colony.

In order to set the apparatus to work, an appropriate sentence must be selected. The selection of a sentence is dictated by the nature of the offence. In the words of the officer: "Our sentence does not sound severe. Whatever commandment the prisoner has disobeyed is written on his body by the Harrow."[19]

Once the sentence is determined the officer selects the corresponding inscription from the "guiding plans drawn by the former Commandant" and sets the Designer.[20] It is important to keep in mind that these plans are mysterious, in that they are illegible to the uninitiated. As the officer explains the highly complicated nature of the plans does have an operational effect:

> Of course the script can't be a simple one; it's not supposed to kill a man straight off, but only after an interval of, on an average, twelve hours; the turning point is reckoned to come at the sixth hour. So there have to be lots and lots of flourishes around the actual script; the script itself runs around the body only in a narrow girdle; the rest of the body is reserved for the embellishments.[21]

Now, barring any mechanical difficulties, each sentence requires a cycle of twelve hours to complete, but the "turning point" occurs at the sixth. In the six hours leading up to this moment, the condemned "stays alive almost as before, he suffers only pain."[22]

> But how quiet he grows at just about the sixth hour! Enlightenment comes to the most dull-witted. It begins around the eyes. From there it radiates. A moment that might tempt one to get under the Harrow oneself. Nothing more happens than that the man begins to understand the inscription, he purses his mouth as if he were listening. You have seen how difficult it is to decipher the script with one's eyes; but our man deciphers it with his wounds. To be sure, that is a hard task; he needs six hours to accomplish it.[23]

The German is more specific on this point: it is not "enlightenment" [*Aufklärung*] but "understanding" [*Verstand*] that comes to the condemned and he does not "begin to understand the inscription" rather he "deciphers" [*entziffern*] it.[24] So, at the "turning point," the condemned begins to understand the meaning of the inscription by deciphering it with his wounds. This is a crucial moment, because if in fact he does *understand* the meaning of his punishment, the work of justice is indeed done. The condemned does not know the sentence when he enters the apparatus and the script that it is inscribing on his body is difficult (if not impossible) to read. And yet, if we are to take the officer at this word the condemned "deciphers it with his wounds." The emphasis thus falls directly on what, if anything, the condemned "understands" at this moment. One possibility is that he *understands* the content of the sentence as the law and accepts it as the law. In this version his *understanding* would reaffirm the legitimacy of both his punishment and the law. The apparatus would thus effectively transcend the gap between the sensible and the intelligible, bringing understanding to even "the most dull-witted" of offenders. Those that bear witness to this scene would see the work of justice itself. The understanding of the condemned becomes his confession; at the "turning point" he accepts and thus participates in his own punishment, absolving others of their guilt by reaffirming the law. In this way the punishment becomes a manifestation of the condemned's own will. This model of punishment as retribution is clearly articulated by Hegel in §100 of the *Grundlinien*:

> The injury [*Verletzung*] which is inflicted on the criminal is not only just *in itself* (and since it is just, it is at the same time his will as it is *in itself*, an existence [*Dasein*] of his freedom, *his* right); it is also a *right for the criminal himself*, that is, a right *posited* in his *existent* will, in his action. For it is implicit in his action, as that of a *rational* being, that it is universal in character, and that, by performing it, he has set up a law which he has recognized

for himself in his action, and under which he may therefore be subsumed as under *his* right.[25]

While Hegel would find the law of the penal colony barbaric (in much the same manner as the laws of Draco, which punished every crime with death), there is a striking similarity. For both Hegel and the officer the function of punishment is not simply deterrence, but rather retribution: it restores the balance of right and honours the "will" of the condemned as a *rational will* in and through the act of punishment.

There are, of course, other possibilities. The condemned could simply *understand* that he is going to die and the *meaning* of his pain is simply meaningless. He could *understand* that in his pain he has become a scene for others and, as a consequence, his cries are simply a part of the performance they have come to watch. In this case his silence can be read as a refusal to participate in their theatre of punishment. There is, quite simply, no way of limiting the interpretive possibilities, because the meaning of the condemned's "understanding" is being determined by another. He does not speak or whisper his confession to the officer kneeling down beside him. It is the look "around the eyes," the way he "purses his mouth as if he were listening," that enables the officer to read, or rather decipher, the content of his "understanding."[26] In reality what we are left with is twelve hours of cruelty strung between two silent ciphers. This is the reality that the colony cannot face; that there is nothing to decipher, no ultimate *understanding* to reach, that the work of the apparatus is not that of justice, but "plain murder."[27] And yet, if this is the reality of the apparatus, why does the colony continue to use it?

To answer this question we will have to turn our attention to the sociohistorical context of the apparatus. This will require an examination of the changes in this context over the course of three temporal periods: the foundation of the colony by the old Commandant, its present existence under the new Commandant, and the future.

FROM THE LABYRINTH TO A SINGLE SPIKE: "FATE" AND THE *UNWORKING* OF THE COLONY

The officer keeps the history of the colony. This is not to say that he is simply an archivist preserving traces of what has past. Rather, the past of the colony is alive within him. He maintains the apparatus because, like it, he is a component of the former colony. As he clearly states, he was present at the beginning, "'This apparatus,' he said, taking hold of a crank handle and leaning against it, 'was invented by our former Commandant. I assisted at the very earliest experiments and had a share in all the work until its completion. But the credit of inventing it belongs to him alone.'"[28]

This provides us with an indication of his relation to the apparatus. While he admittedly played no role in its invention, he did assist with its construction from the very earliest stages. He continues:

> Have you ever heard of our former Commandant? No? Well, it isn't saying too much if I tell you that the organization of the whole penal colony is his work. We who were his friends knew even before he died that the organization of the colony was so perfect that his successor, even with a thousand new schemes in his head, would find it impossible to alter anything, at least for many years to come. And our prophecy has come true; the new Commandant has had to acknowledge its truth. A pity you never met the old Commandant![29]

This details the scale of the old Commandant's role in founding the colony. He was not only the designer of the apparatus, but of the entire colony. As the explorer later exclaims, "Did he combine everything himself, then? Was he soldier, judge, mechanic, chemist, and draughtsman?"[30]

The apparatus is thus not an *ad hoc* addition to an existing penal framework; rather, it is only one component, one cog, within a much larger machine. In fact, the divisions that exist between the current colony and its past are far from clear. The officer suggests that there is a "we" ("we who were his friends") remaining within the colony that opposes any changes to its original design. This being so, it seems that there are internal ideological divisions we should be aware of (a point we will return to later when we address the future of the colony). What is clear is that the officer and the apparatus he operates have been a constant presence within the colony.

There have, of course, been changes in the administration of the colony. The apparatus is now neglected, it still functions, still does its work, but it remains, for the most part, unseen. For the current administration its continued existence is a shameful concession to the integral nature of its role within the original architecture of colony. As the officer states,

> "How different an execution was in the old days! A whole day before the ceremony the valley was packed with people; they all came only to look on; early in the morning the Commandant appeared with his ladies; fanfares roused the whole camp; I reported that everything was in readiness; the assembled company—no high official dared to absent himself—arranged itself around the machine; this pile of cane chairs is a miserable survival from that era.[31]

During the reign of the old Commandant the apparatus was the centre of the colony. Its activity was not shamefully concealed; rather, it was celebrated. In short, the execution was a festival. The officer continues:

> The machine was freshly cleaned and glittering, I got new spare parts for almost every execution. Before hundreds of spectators—all of them standing on tiptoe as far as the heights there—the condemned man was laid under the Harrow by the Commandant himself. What is left today for a common solider to do was then my task, the task of the presiding judge, and was an honor for me. And then the execution began! No discordant noise spoiled the working of the machine. Many did not care to watch it but lay with eyes in the sand; they all knew: Now Justice is being done.[32]

The details of this description serve to indicate the significance of the apparatus within this era of the colony's history: it is clean to the point of "glittering," its constituent parts are constantly maintained and replaced, operational tasks are symbolic of social rank and the spectators are silent. The last sentence is of particular importance; according to the officer many of the individuals within the crowd avert their eyes to the spectacle of the execution. The gesture of attending the execution but turning away can be read in a number of ways: from a state analogous to the divided will of Leontius in Plato's *Republic* to the combination of mandatory attendance and disgust or moral dissent. Despite the inherent instability of this gesture, the officer claims that they all know that justice is being done.[33] Continuing:

> In the silence one heard nothing but the condemned man's sighs, half-muffled by the felt gag. Nowadays the machine can no longer wring from anyone a sigh louder than the felt gag can stifle; but in those days the writing needles let drop an acid fluid, which we're no longer permitted to use. Well, and then came the sixth hour! It was impossible to grant all the requests to be allowed to watch nearby. The Commandant in his wisdom ordained that the children should have the preference; I, of course, because of my office had the privilege of always being at hand; often enough I would be squatting there with a small child in either arm. How we all absorbed the look of transfiguration on the face of the sufferer, how we bathed our cheeks in the radiance of that justice, achieved at last and fading so quickly![34]

Here, at the sixth hour, we have the *dénouement* of the execution. This moment, signalled by a "look" on the face of the condemned, is said to be the moment in which, the condemned begins to "decipher" [*entziffern*] the inscription being written on him. The spectators struggle to get closer to see this moment, because in it the condemned is said to achieve both "understanding" [*Verstand*] and "transfiguration" [*Verklärung*]. And yet, as we have already stated, there is no evidence to support the officer's interpretation of this moment. With such little evidence to support the interpretation (i.e., a "look" on the face of the condemned), it speaks more to the desired than to the actual significance. The officer believes that the condemned "deciphers," "understands," and is thereby "transfigured" by the transcription because this transfiguration would expiate the colony. If his belief were in fact true, the work of the apparatus would be that of fate itself. There would be no question of guilt left unaccounted for. In effect, the colony would be just. This reading is disrupted not only by the silence of the condemned, but also by the desire of the officer himself. After all, it is this moment that, he exclaims, "might tempt one to get under the Harrow."[35] Why would this be a temptation, if all that there was to understand was the inscription? He can decipher any and all of the inscriptions that the apparatus can write out by simply reading the former Commandant's "guiding plans." Thus, this desire suggests that even for the officer there is a silence in this moment that exceeds his interpretive grasp, and it is this silence that he must end.

Turning our attention from the history of the colony, we can now begin to consider its present. The changes to the colony have, to a certain degree, been addressed. The apparatus is no longer the centre of the colony; rather, it is concealed and strategically neglected. The officer still operates and maintains it, but the new Commandant is gradually cutting off the supply of necessary resources in an apparent effort to suspend its use and thereby reform the colony in some unspecified manner. The explorer thus arrives in the colony during a time of internal conflict. The new Commandant invites him to witness the execution of "a solider condemned to death for disobedience and insulting behavior to a superior," and he accepts this invitation out of what, at least initially, seems like mere politeness.[36] For the officer his attendance is an opportunity to demonstrate the "truth" of the apparatus. He believes that if he can convince the explorer of this "truth," then he will be able to halt the new Commandant's attempts to reform the colony and preserve its original design.

Thus, in effect the story takes the form of a trial. What is on trial is the method of administering justice. We are given only partial access to the proceedings of this trial, in that we have access to the perspective of the officer and the explorer, but not to that of the new Commandant. The officer sees the stakes of this trial and acts as the sole advocate—he states that there are other adherents within the colony, but they remain silent—for the apparatus and the general methodology of the old Commandant. For his part, the explorer is conflicted about interfering with the internal politics of the colony:

> The explorer thought to himself: It's always a ticklish matter to intervene decisively in other people's affairs. He was neither a member of the penal colony nor a citizen of the state to which it belonged. Were he to denounce the execution or actually try to stop it, they could say to him: You are a foreigner, mind your own business. He could make no answer to that, unless he were

to add that he was amazed at himself in this connection, for he traveled only as an observer, with no intention at all of altering other people's methods of administering justice. Yet here he found himself strongly tempted. The injustice of the procedure and the inhumanity of the execution were undeniable.[37]

The officer senses the explorer's aversion to his legal procedures and punitive methods, and consequently he must play his role to the hilt. He knows that the judgment of the explorer will be the deciding factor in the future of the colony, and so he openly solicits the explorer's aid in arguing his case to the new Commandant. The officer's foremost desire is to use the conviction of the explorer to get the new Commandant to fully concede and thus effectively state, "Old Commandant, I humble myself before you."[38] The explorer openly refuses the officer's request to act as an advocate for the apparatus. In response to this refusal the officer frees the condemned man and enters the apparatus himself. This act is not simply suicidal, the officer is not accepting defeat and simply opting to disappear; he is attempting to finally make the "truth" of the apparatus speak for itself.

At this point we must pause and carefully consider the trajectory that brings the officer to this point. This is after all the final *un*working of the apparatus. It is the result of a dynamic that has been, figuratively speaking, *working-itself-out* form the very beginning. The work of the apparatus has always been an interval between two ciphers (the "guiding plans" and the sixth hour in which the condemned "deciphers," "understands" and is thus "transfigured"). It did its work under the auspices of justice, and yet it is constantly confined to the limits of reading and interpretation.[39] The officer, an acolyte of the old Commandant, can read the "guiding plans," but something remains within the "look" of the condemned that tempts him. Something remains out of his reach. He interprets the "look" as "understanding," as the work of "justice," but he cannot fully grasp its significance. It is as if his own need to read the "look" as "understanding" compels him to read beyond the limits of reading itself—to know in the fullest possible sense, to know absolutely, the meaning of the "look." Only this knowledge, knowledge beyond interpretation, could fully expiate the colony. The silence of the "look" both drives the work of the colony-machine (the apparatus and the social arrangement that makes it work) and *un*works it. The silence of the "look" both differs from the meaning imposed on it and defers it. It leaves a space, a gap; it is incomplete and thus tempting.[40] It "tempts" the officer to enter the apparatus himself, because he believes that he can finally go beyond it, just as initially it temps the crowds to draw near and see the work of justice being done. Yet in the end it is this same "silence," the silence of the "look," that makes the crowd abandon the apparatus. The procedures of the former Commandant promise them the spectacle of justice achieved, but all it can offer is twelve hours of cruelty and a repetition of the "look." In each instance the reading of the "look" becomes less convincing, because it can go no further. The apparatus can vary frequency and intensity, but beyond that it is powerless. This being so, it is in the "look" that it confronts the limit that it will never leave; the colony-machine, despite all appearances to the contrary, is static. Its work is to reveal the "truth" of the order that it imposes, to show that it is "just," in and through the execution of the condemned; and yet, in the end, all it can show is what was there all along: death and cruelty. In short, the colony-machine claims to exhibit the power of the law but its "truth" is the law of power.[41]

The officer attempts to breach this limit (that imposed by "silence") by entering the apparatus and changing the semantic content of the inscription from a particular imperative ("HONOR THY SUPERIORS") to a universal imperative ("BE JUST!").[42] At this point the explorer witnesses the apparatus completely fail: "The Harrow was not writing, it was only jabbing, and the Bed was not turning the body over but only bringing it up quivering against the needles. The explorer wanted to do something if possible, to bring the whole machine to a standstill, for this was no exquisite torture such as the officer desired, this was plain murder."[43]

The officer attempts to make the apparatus finally speak, that is, to speak without silence. He attempts to expose the "truth" of the "look" and he actually does. There was no meaning hidden in the "look," at least, not the meaning that he sought. There was no completion, no absolute or total meaning that would finally expiate the colony. Like Benjamin's account of "mythic" violence, the officer and the tradition he represents demands sacrifice. They always demand more. There can never be an end to the *writing-out* of the condemned, because there is always a "silence" in the "look." The ground of their authority rests on the "truth" of their procedures. This "truth" must be absolutely just. It must be the work of fate. Unlike "divine" violence it cannot simply accept sacrifice and all of the doubt that it entails. It cannot accept the "silence" of the condemned. It needs to *sound-out* this silence: to both *write-beyond-the-limits-of-writing* and *read-beyond-the-limits-of-reading*. "Divine" violence builds nothing on the "silence" of the condemned. It accepts it as "silence" and must always struggle with its unfathomable responsibility. It can only destroy law, because it *un*works the connection between law and violence. It exposes the impossible "silence" that separates the law and violence.[44] This "silence" is driven home by the explorer's reading of the officer's corpse:

> And here, almost against his will, he had to look at the face of the corpse. It was as it had been in life; no sign was visible of the promised redemption; what the others had found in the machine the officer had not found; the lips

were firmly pressed together, the eyes were open, with the same expression as in life, the look was calm and convinced, through the forehead went the point of the great iron spike.[45]

This "great iron spike" is supposed to be the last stroke the apparatus delivers. It is the period; the grammatical mark that indicates the end of the sentence. The apparatus gives the officer nothing but inarticulate, repetitive jabbing, and finally the mark of the end. With this the officer's *a priori* claim to justice, that is, to necessity or fate, is shown for what it always was and yet could never accept: the "silence" of "plain murder."

Now we can begin to address the future of the colony. We can do this by asking a somewhat deceptively simple question, namely, what can follow this silence? Kafka himself struggled with this question. This struggle is evidenced by the alternative endings he composed in his diary, but before we get to those we will consider the ending of the published version. The explorer leaves the apparatus and enters the teahouse. The teahouse does not just suddenly appear within the topography of the colony; in fact, the officer mentions the teahouse earlier on when referring to the adherents of the tradition of the former Commandant who choose to remain silent.[46] As the explorer observes, "Although this teahouse was very little different from the other houses of the colony, which were all very dilapidated, even up to the Commandant's palatial headquarters, it made on the explorer the impression of a historic tradition of some kind, and he felt the power of past days."[47]

The built environment of the colony carries with it the memory of its purpose. The buildings are dilapidated and the adherents are currently silent, but there remains the possibility of a return to the old traditions. As the soldier informs the explorer, the old Commandant is buried in the teahouse:

> "The old man's buried here," said the soldier, "the priest wouldn't let him lie in the churchyard. Nobody knew where to bury him for a while, but in the end they buried him here. The officer never told you about that, for sure, because of course that's what he was most ashamed of. He even tried several times to dig the old man up by night, but he was always chased away."[48]

The old Commandant is deprived of a sanctified resting place. His power remains confined within the architecture and arrangement of the colony. As the explorer reads the inscription—written in "very small letters"—on his tomb he discovers the nature of this power: "Here rests the old Commandant. His adherents, who now must remain nameless, have dug this grave and set up this stone. There is a prophecy that after a certain number of years the Commandant will rise again and lead his adherents from this house to recover the colony. Have faith and wait!"[49]

The messianic call ("Have faith and wait!") promises the return of the apparatus. It attempts to salvage the meaning of "silence" by calling for a return to the foundations of the colony. The current Commandant can cover over these foundations, but they remain in place. The apparatus may be cast off in order to maintain the veneer of the "rule of law," but this is little more than a reflex. It is a temporary change of the apparent structure, which leaves the fundamental connections in place. That is, it remains a system in which *power is law*. The mode of this power simply shifts from the scaffold to the "ghostly presence" of the police.[50] This shift is only apparent because, if the conditions of the system change in such a way that power is threatened, the scaffold returns.

In response to this discovery the explorer flees the colony. At least this is the conclusion of the published version. In an unpublished fragment the explorer is transformed by his guilt. In this version the Commandant sends out men to retrieve him from the site of execution and they find him lying down beside the pit.

> He jumped up when they spoke to him as if revived. With his hand on his heart he said, "I am a cur if I allowed that to happen." But then he took his own words literally and began to run around them on all fours. From time to time, however, he leaped erect, shook the fit off, so to speak, threw his arms around the neck of one of the men, and tearfully exclaimed, "Why does all this happen to me!" and then hurried to his post.[51]

This transformation refers back to the initial description of the condemned man at the beginning of the story: "the condemned man looked so like a submissive dog that one might have thought he could be left to run free on the surrounding hills and would only need to be whistled for when the execution was due to begin."[52]

In both cases there is no "end," no real escape, from the colony. Here the explorer's position of foreign observer is shown to be just as superficial as the "reformed" façade that the new Commandant brings to the colony. The non-violence of both is only apparent. Each remains bound to the latent "truth" of the old Commandant. To borrow Benjamin's formulation, beneath both "violence crowned by fate, is the origin of law."[53] And yet can there be another avenue available in this indictment of punishment? Is there another way, a non-violent praxis that is not merely a temporary forgetting or concealing of the mystical foundations of law? Kafka's story uses the "truth" of the old Commandant to *un*work the lie of both the new Commandant and the explorer. This leaves us with a difficult question: Is law possible without the colony?

OF SILENCE, SCAFFOLDS, AND THE LAW

"Is law possible without the colony?" Why is this hard to answer? One might think the draconian nature of the colony (the lack of a trial, the severity of the punishment, etc.) would make it easy to answer "Yes": the manner in which justice is administered in the colony is so violent that it bears no resemblance to our own "modern" penal system.

But this ignores the problem posed by the colony. The text itself demonstrates the superficial nature of this argument. This is after all the position that the explorer holds to for most of the story, but by the end (and in all versions thereof) his position changes. Despite the conflict that exists between the penal procedures of the old and the new Commandant, they have a common foundation. For each, violence is the means by which the "truth" of the law is revealed. It is necessary, "crowned by fate," and thus, it *must* be done.[54]

At its base this line of reasoning relies on the impossible scales of the *lex talionis* to set the measure of "justified" violence. Variations on this logic exist in both Hegel and Kant. While Hegel will explicitly acknowledge the absurdity of a *specific equity* between crimes and punishments (in part by asking us to imagine a one-eyed or toothless criminal), he will nonetheless appeal to a modified version of this logic.[55] His solution relies on the positivity of dialectics: the fundamental claim is that *"coercion is cancelled [aufgehoben] by coercion"* and thus the only matter to be settled is the exchange value of crimes in relation to their punishments.[56] And yet there is one exception to this penal economy, one crime that does in fact have a *specific equity* with its punishment, and that is murder. Murder has *a priori* connection with capital punishment. Here Hegel is essentially in line with Kant: "Accordingly, every murderer—anyone who commits murder, orders it, or is an accomplice in it—must suffer death; this is what justice, as the idea of juridical authority, wills in accordance with universal laws that are grounded *a priori*."[57]

Kant is decidedly more liberal (or perhaps simply more explicit) with the types of crimes that must be punished with death, as he includes both accomplices to murder and crimes against the state. And yet, despite their (frequently vast) differences, they are unified on the *a priori* connection between murder and the death penalty. As Benjamin notes, with this *"a priori"* argument for capital punishment "the origins of law jut manifestly and fearsomely into existence."[58] The colony is founded on the "truth" of this *a priori*. It requires it because it is this "truth" that can convert power into the law (not merely positivistic laws, but "the" law). This conversion can be thought of in three stages: first, there is the law of power, law is simply proclaimed and the condemned is sentenced to execution without trial; second, the apparatus is used to miraculously turn the situation and make *arbitrary* judgments seem *necessary*; and finally, the appearance of necessity makes the law-of-power seem to be the power-of-the-law. This appearance grants those that have designed and/or operate the apparatus a type of political legitimacy that extends far beyond the brute reality of power. With this appearance in place the former Commandant was not only a soldier, judge, mechanic, chemist, and draughtsman, but a sovereign and messiah as well.[59]

The problem is that this legitimacy is conditional. It is grounded in a claim to the *a priori* truth of the law, but the only proof that the apparatus can offer is the repetition of silence. There is no way to close off the interpretive possibilities of the "look," and thus the repetition simply widens the gap between "law" and "justice." To defer this problem, the former Commandant relies on stagecraft. The apparatus is a magical device. Its fearsome elegance draws in the audience, it misdirects their gaze, as the officer swiftly moves from the mysterious "guiding plans" to the ineffable "look" of the condemned and claims that "justice" has been done. Yet, like any magical act, this conversion relies on sleight of hand. Its twelve-hour act of blood-drenched logomancy leaves the crowds in awe, and for a time it unites the colony in the celebration of "just" death. That is, until they have seen all that the trick has to offer. In order for the trick to be more than just that—that is, in order to balance the scales and be *necessary*—the condemned must read the inscription with his body, he must "decipher" it, and by deciphering it "understand" and be "transfigured" by it. But even this would not be enough. It is not that he must simply "understand" and be "transfigured," but that the colony must *know*, in the fullest possible sense, that he has "understood" it. His "silence" both compels them and limits them; it draws them closer, brings them to demand execution after execution, and yet they never get beyond this "silence."

The colony makes us confront the impossible idiocy of this *a priori* argument. Even reduced to the single exchange of murder for death, it faces two impossibilities: (1) the exchange of one death for another occurs under the assumption that because neither can be assigned a determinate value they are equal, (2) it presents the actual execution of the sentence as in some way distinct from vengeance and thus just. It is interminably bound to the question of measure: it must use measure to both distinguish punishment from vengeance and claim that the exchange of death for death balances the scales of justice. And yet, how can the measure be established without the use of an *a posteriori* judgment? Once this judgment enters the stage and sets the measure how can it not be responsible? What is needed is an execution in which blood is spilled and yet miraculously no hands are stained by it. In order for the *lex talionis* to be "just" it must be both judged and enforced by fate. As soon as one asks how this miracle is achieved—that is, how the judge, the executioner, and the crowd can see nothing but "fate" or the "work of justice"—they are accused of being "moved by overtly compassionate feelings of an affected humanity (*compassibilitas*)."[60] But even Kant will state that even in the case of just executions the "spectacle of a slaughterhouse" dulls the people's "feeling" and should thus be minimized in some way.[61] So, paradoxically, those horrified by the spectacle of the singular execution are too compassionate and those that are subjected to multiple executions risk losing their compassion. Once again we are left with a question of measure that only the majesty of the sovereign can settle. The struggle of measure is, in fact, the struggle to maintain the boundary between arbitrary power and the rational necessity of the law. For Kant, the colony and the law remain bound *a priori* (i.e., capital punishment *must* be carried out). This effectively transfers the question of proof to a "mysterious" combination of executive power and procedure.

So can there be law without the colony? Is the colony part and parcel of the categorical imperative? This question can be rephrased into a slightly more recognizable form, namely: Is there an absolute right of punishment? Fichte takes up just this question in the *Foundations of Natural Right*, and his answer will help us bring some focus to the issue. He immediately takes issue with Kant's characterization of Beccaria as being mere sentimentality and affected humanitarianism, by pointing out that the basis of Kant's own position is simply a statement and not an argument. By grounding the death penalty on the categorical imperative it takes on the appearance of an unexaminable end. Fichte quotes Kant's argument from the *Metaphysics of Morals*: "one has never heard of anyone who was sentenced to death for murder complaining that he was dealt with too severely and wronged; everyone would laugh in his face if he said this."[62]

Fichte responds to this by conceding that

> It is completely true such that we are forced to conclude: in a moral world-order, governed by an omniscient judge in accordance with moral laws, if a person is treated according to *the same* law that he himself established in treating others, then there is no injustice done to him. This conclusion, which forces itself upon all human beings, is based on a categorical imperative. Thus there is absolutely no dispute about whether *a murderer* has been treated unjustly, if he, too, should lose his life in a violent manner.[63]

By drawing attention to the need for a "moral world-order," "moral laws" and an "omniscient judge," this *apparent* concession serves to emphasize the necessary conditions of Kant's own argument and thus sets up Fichte's rebuttal: "But an entirely different question to be answered would be: from where does a mortal get the right of this moral world-order, the right to render the criminal his just deserts?"[64]

He continues: "Whoever ascribes this right to a worldly sovereign will surely be required (as Kant's system was) to say that the sovereign's rightful title to it is unexaminable; to derive the sovereign's authority from God; and to regard the sovereign as God's visible representative and every government as a theocracy."[65]

Fichte thus effectively lays out the necessary conditions of the colony's relationship to the law. The *a priori* argument for the death penalty is simply a way of expressing or exhibiting the *a priori* power of the sovereign. It can be used as a way of cloaking the arbitrary rule of the sovereign with the appearance of fate. This argument provides the condemned murderer from Kant's example with a "justified complaint"; and thus, as Kant himself admits, it opens up a gap between the law and the legislative authority of the state. If the state were to ignore this gap and carry out the execution "it would be in contradiction with itself."[66] And so, it would seem that the colony and law are not *necessarily* connected; in fact, they may even be in contradiction.

Fichte's solution to this is worth reviewing, as it clearly separates the death penalty from the law. According to Fichte the most serious sentence the state can legally impose is exclusion from the state; that is, it can (and in the case of murder *must*) revoke the civil status of the criminal. This effectively alters the status of the individual from criminal to outlaw. It may permanently brand the outlaw if it finds this measure necessary, but it must be done "as painlessly as possible, for the state must not appear to engage in torture." Such individuals are quite literally placed outside of the law, but what follows from this? Fichte answers: the

> completely arbitrary treatment of the person thus condemned. It is not that one *has a right to treat him in this way*, but there is also no *right against it*; therefore, the condemned person is to be declared a thing, a piece of livestock.... Within the context of (external) right, there is no reason at all why the next person who comes along and gets the idea in his head should not arbitrarily apprehend, torture, and kill him; but nor is there any reason why he should do so.[67]

This leads us to two questions concerning the outlaw. First, what if a private individual does choose to kill an outlaw? Secondly, what role does the state play in relation to the outlaw? In answer to the first question, Fichte argues that such an individual could not be held legally liable by the state, because the outlaw has no rights. That said, the actions of this individual would be morally judged by others, and as a result they would be held in moral contempt. As Fichte states, "Whoever tortures an animal for the pleasure of it, or kills an animal without any purpose or benefit, is held in contempt as an inhuman barbarian, is shunned and abhorred, and rightfully so. How much more so if someone should do the same to a being that, in spite of everything, still has a human countenance!"[68]

In a sense this type of moral limitation also applies to the behaviour of the state. Seeing as the outlaw is no longer a citizen of the state, the two parties do not confront one another on legal grounds. They "are no longer anything to each other, and if the state kills the criminal, it does so not *as a state, but as the stronger physical* power, as a mere force of nature. The state's reasons for killing him are the same as those of the private person; it is not because of the outlaw's rights, for he has none, but rather because of its respect for itself, as well as for its citizens and other states."[69]

While the state might find it necessary to kill the outlaw to protect itself or its citizens, "it does so not by virtue of its judicial authority, but through the police."[70] Accordingly Fichte will clearly state that the death penalty "is *not a form of punishment*, but only a means of ensuring security."[71] In fact, because it cannot be seen as the consequence of a positive right, it should, "like everything that is dishonorable," be carried out "with shame and in secret."[72]

Fichte's model provides a clear separation between judicial and police powers. It does this by arguing for a contract model of the state and eliminating the capacity of the state to use lethal violence against its citizens. By doing so he can effectively save the law from the contradiction of *a priori* punishments and the *lex talionis*, but this can only be done by placing the condemned outside of the law. This repositioning enables us to see violence as violence and not the work of fate. Yet it only does so by simultaneously placing the criminal outside of humanity and limiting the scope of rights to citizens. This leaves this model with the considerable burden of clearly defining the boundary between the animal and human. This points up a problem in Fichte's system of absolute idealism, as the "I" and its "other" are the *same* (consider the opening sentence of the introduction to the *Foundations of Natural Right* or the utopian proclamations of the posthumously published *Doctrine of the State*). The limitation of rights also creates serious problems for stateless people. Despite the serious nature of its shortcomings, Fichte's text does provide us with two important insights in regards to our current inquiry: first, law cannot be founded by an act of lethal violence, as this can only be an act of power and not of law; second, if a state attempts to use lethal violence as a legal punishment it contradicts itself by conflating judicial and police powers. This being so, states can act against the law and citizens can hold it accountable by revolutionary force if necessary (an implication Fichte was well aware of).

Using Fichte's arguments against Kant's *a priori* argument for the death penalty and applying them to the colony, we can see that the work of the apparatus is not that of the law, but of power. Its purpose is to amplify the immanent power of the former Commandant by making it seem to originate in the "demands of a hidden transcendence."[73] It conceals the nature of power and makes it appear to be necessity. In short, the colony-machine produces sovereign power. It does so by supplementing speech acts. By making the death of the condemned seem determined *a priori*, it makes the performative acts that surround it—declarations, commands, promises, et cetera—look absolute (despite the impossibility of a "pure" speech act within a "total" context).[74] It makes it seem as if the "truth" of the situation comes from outside of language, that language simply *gives voice* to the "truth," while iteration demonstrates the inverse to be the case. The demand for iteration (for further executions) demonstrates that the claim to being absolute is in fact false. The colony-machine can continue by placing the blame on language (i.e., language is incapable of transmitting the fullness of the "truth"), but this can only stand if there is the promise of an eventual completeness. In order to fully ground the law—to justly unite law and force the *a priori*—"truth" must transcend the limits of language. It must become the "word" of God, a "word" that would be in and of itself absolute (i.e., without either syntagmatic or associative meaning). Fichte is thus incorrect when he asserts that the absolute right to punish requires a sovereign regarded as "God's visible representative."[75] This right would still be bound to the limitations of language and thus could only extend its claim to this right via messianism. Even with the promise of messianism in place, the system of justification—the interpretive system of writing-out the condemned in order to read the "look"—is autoimmune.[76] It requires that language exceed the conditions of its own possibility. It demands the end of *différance*, the end of silence, and with this demand it runs itself into the ground. The silence of the "look" (the "a" of *différance*) tempts the officer to enter the apparatus. It promises a "truth" that the mysterious calligraphy of the "guiding plans" cannot communicate. The colony is built upon the need for this "truth." Each execution is authorized in the name of this "truth," and yet with each execution there is only silence. The silence of the "look" threatens to draw the entire colony into the apparatus, and so the new Commandant cordons it off. He retains the foundations of the colony and simply maintains its power by other, less explicit means. At base there is still the claim to the absolute right to punish, still the claim to absolute sovereign power, to a power that precedes and transcends linguistic meaning. But it is this very claim that the story interrupts.

The liberalization of the colony is not the solution to the injustice and cruelty of the apparatus. In fact, it simply conceals it in order to preserve the foundations of its authority. The explorer's reaction(s) merge with the officer's reading of the new Commandant's administration of the colony. He may well cordon off the apparatus and opt for the use of more "civilized" method of punishment, but the basis of his right to punish remains unchanged. That basis is power. The shift in means is superficial, as violence is still employed under the auspices of justice. At any time the new Commandant can return to the methods of the former Commandant. His prophesized return does not require him to be literally resurrected from the grave: he *is* his methodology.

And so we return one last time to our question: Is law possible without the colony? And the answer depends on how the "law" is to be understood. If it is simply a set of arbitrary rules enforced by the strongest, law and the colony are one and the same. On the other hand, if the law must be just in order to retain its claim to being law, they are of different orders. The story of the colony provides an account of what happens when those orders are superimposed (i.e., when power dons the mask of justice). Power becomes bound to the logic of the very masquerade that establishes it as law. By laying claim to the absolute right to punish, it gains a means by which it can communicate the absolute nature of its sovereign power. But the power it gains is contingent upon its basis remaining *unexaminable*. In effect, it must obscure the basis of its own authority; it must maintain the "mysterious" nature of the foundations of law, because if the "mysterious" basis of the *a priori* argument (claims to God's will or the sovereign will of the "people") is set aside, all that remains is simply a claim or assertion.

As the colony clearly shows, these foundations are a mystery not only to the crowd but also to the officer (hence his belief in its "truth" and desire to experience the apparatus himself). As a result, the distinction between the reality and the performance is soon lost. The awful work of the colony continues, but it is not free to set either the rhythm or the tempo of its work as both are set by the demands of justice. Its claim to being just is predicated on the impossible measure of the *lex talionis*. It struggles to find a mode of violence that will fulfill this standard and thus exhibit the "truth" of the colony (i.e., that the work of the apparatus is the fulfillment of the law, that it balances the scales). But the repetitive exchange of crime and punishment is never balanced. Each execution is compelled by the demand for justice and each simply increases that demand: the colony forms a positive feedback loop. In effect, the work of the apparatus is always that of vengeance (violence for violence) and not that of the law. The law distinguishes itself from vengeance by not setting the measure of punishment. This is the force of Benjamin's argument:

> For the question "May I kill?" meets its irreducible answer in the commandment "Thou shalt not kill." This commandment precedes the deed, just as God was "preventing" the deed. But just as it may not be fear of punishment that enforces obedience, the injunction becomes inapplicable, incommensurable once the deed is accomplished. No judgment of the deed can be derived from the commandment. And so neither the divine judgment, nor the grounds for this judgment, can be known in advance. Those who base a condemnation of all violent killing of one person by another on the commandment are therefore mistaken. It exists not as a criterion of judgment, but as a guideline for the actions of persons or communities who have to wrestle with it in solitude and, in exceptional cases, to take on themselves the responsibility of ignoring it.[77]

The law simply repeats itself and leaves the means by which it is to be enforced open and thus infinitely culpable. The commandment provides us with neither an absolute right to punish nor an absolute right to life.

This might seem to render it useless to politics, but in fact its *silence is the political*. It *un*works the claim to necessary violence, to a violence that can serve as a foundation for sovereign power (Benjamin's "mythic" violence), and leaves us with the responsibility for violence.[78] It leaves us with the agonism of the political without the comfort of fate. Kafka leaves us in the open of political agonism.

NOTES

Notes to Introduction
1. Sophocles, "Antigone," 80; Plato, *Republic*, 1071; Kafka, "In the Penal Colony," 166.
2. Foucault, *Abnormal*, 14.
3. Ibid.
4. Foucault, *Society*, 46.
5. Marx, *Later Political Writings*, 126–7.
6. Derrida, *Margins of Philosophy*, 7.
7. Beckett, *Letters*, 518.
8. Derrida, *Acts of Religion*, 242.
9. Ibid., 241.
10. Ibid., 242.
11. Kafka, "In the Penal Colony," 167.
12. Nancy, *Inoperative Community*, 35.

Notes to Chapter 1
1. Derrida, *Politics of Friendship*, 47.
2. Ibid., 48.
3. Ibid., 304–5.
4. On this point it is interesting to note that the word "community" makes a rather prominent appearance in his early essay "Violence and Metaphysics." While it is not altogether clear that this appearance contradicts Derrida's claim, this "community of the question"—the question being the relationship between philosophy and its end(s)—does raise questions about the relationship between community and the democracy-to-come (cf. Derrida, *Writing and Difference*, 79–80).
5. Derrida, *Politics of Friendship*, 298.
6. Derrida, *Rogues*, 35.
7. Derrida, *Politics of Friendship*, 298–9.
8. Ibid., 33.
9. Ibid., 111.
10. In *Rogues* Derrida addresses Jean-Luc Nancy's *The Experience of Freedom* and not *The Inoperative Community*. Nonetheless, his tack is very close to the one he takes with Nietzsche's Sons in *Politics of Friendship* (i.e., the general focus is the threat of fraternity). *On Touching—Jean-Luc Nancy* takes up the question of auto-affection and the other within the philosophical register of touch. While it does not explicitly address the question of community, it does deal with *compearance* (the ecstatic reflexivity expressed in Nancy's syntagma from *Corpus* "to *self-touch* you"). Derrida's text could well have been entitled *The Meaning of Community in Nancy*, as this

text reaches towards the very heart of the ontological-transcendental (non)logic of *being-with*.
11 Derrida, *Politics of Friendship*, 105.
12 Nancy, *Inoperative Community*, 35.
13 Ibid., 61.
14 Derrida, *Politics of Friendship*, 47.
15 Bataille, *On Nietzsche*, 3.
16 Derrida, *Politics of Friendship*, 81.
17 Ibid., 32.
18 Ibid., 37.
19 Nietzsche, 147.
20 Ibid., 73.
21 Derrida, *Politics of Friendship*, 38.
22 Ibid., 42.
23 Ibid., 42–3.
24 Ibid., 37.
25 Ibid., 32.
26 Ibid., 81.
27 Ibid.
28 Nancy, "The Confronted Community," 21.
29 Ibid.
30 Ibid., 24.
31 Nancy, *Inoperative Community*, xxxviii.
32 Ibid.
33 Ibid., 10–12.
34 Ibid., 10–11.
35 Ibid., 29.
36 Ibid., 35.
37 Ibid., 12.
38 Ibid., 9.
39 Ibid., 3.
40 Ibid.
41 Beckett, *Waiting for Godot*, 1.
42 Ibid., 61.
43 In this sense it echoes Hegel's account of finitude in the *Logic*:

> Finite things are; but their relation to themselves is this, that being negative they are self-related, and in this self-relation send themselves on beyond themselves and their being. They are, but the truth of this being is their end. The finite does not only change, like Something [*Etwas*] in general, but it perishes; and its perishing is not merely contingent, so that it could be without perishing. It is rather the very being of finite things, that they contain the seeds of perishing as their own being-in-self [*Insichsein*]: the hour of their birth is the hour of their death. (Hegel, *Science of Logic*, 142)

44 Nancy, *Inoperative Community*, 12.
45 Nancy, "*La Comparution*," 392.
46 One could of course claim, in line with Hegel, that the speculative resources of the German language offer us a solution with *Aufheben*. This most untranslatable of words—which is, one should note, the term Luther uses to translate Paul's *katargein*—simultaneously contains, negates, and lifts up. As Derrida states in his essay "The Ends of Man," "*Aufheben* is *relever*, in the sense in which *relever* can combine to

relieve, to displace, to elevate, to replace and to promote in one and the same movement" (Derrida, *Margins of Philosophy*, 121). And yet, in this movement, *Aufheben* is overextended; or, to use a common metaphor, it "bites off more than it can chew." As Derrida points out in *Glas*, there is always a question of the remain(s):

> Forces resistant to the *Aufhebung*, to the process of truth, to speculative negativity must be made to appear, and as well that these forces of resistance do not constitute in their turn relievable or relieving negativities. In sum a remain(s) that may not be without being nothingness: a remains that may (not) be. (Derrida, *Glas*, 43)

The resistance of the remain(s)—that inexplicable remainder that lays on the stage after each act of Hegel's dialectical theodicy and which can only be explained by the subsequent act *ad infinitum, ad nauseam*—opens up a non-dialectical, or rather, non-dialectizable entry point into Hegel's text. Derrida's *Différance* takes up the question of the remain(s) in Hegel's text:

> Writing "*différant*" or "*différance*" (with an *a*) would have the advantage of making it possible to translate Hegel at that particular point—which is also absolutely decisive point in his discourse—without further notes or specifications. And the translation would be, as it always must be, a transformation of one language by another. I contend, of course, that the word *différance* can also serve other purposes: first, because it marks not only the activity of "originary" difference, but also the temporizing detour of deferral; and above all because *différance* thus written, although maintaining relations of profound affinity with Hegelian discourse (such as it must be read), is also, up to a certain point, unable to break with that discourse (which has no kind of meaning or chance); but it can operate a kind of infinitesimal and radical displacement of it. (Derrida, *Margins of Philosophy*, 14)

This translation of Hegel (the one that *différance* makes possible) displaces the text by tracing the impossible course of the remain(s) within the system. This "a" of *différance* might be thought of as a space, or spacing, held open within meaning and, as such, it would be connected to a series of other quasi-concepts in Derrida's work. From *aporia*, to *autrui*, and *àvenir* the "a" of *différance* is a certain openness, a silent hospitality, or *chora*, within the process of signification that resists the philosophical desire for an absolutely determinate meaning or absolutely delimitable context. There is a distinct resonance—and this resonance must not be mistaken for equivalence—between the resistance of the remain(s) and Nancy's claim that "community is, in a sense, resistance itself: namely, resistance to immanence" (Nancy, *Inoperative Community*, 35). We will take up this particular resonance in more detail later on.

47 Marx, *Communist Manifesto*, 16.
48 Nancy, *Inoperative Community*, 4.
49 Ibid.
50 Ibid.
51 *Ply* here being used in its multiple senses: to *pursue*, to *assail*, to *address persistently*, to *travel a fixed course*, and so on.
52 Levinas, 233.
53 Nancy, *Corpus*, 49.
54 It is useful to remember that in Genesis God punishes Cain by marking him with the very law that he transgressed (i.e., not to commit murder). In receiving this mark, both his mortality—the condition he shared with Abel—and his responsibility are exposed. This multiplication of the law, in the sense of both its repetition and the promise of a sevenfold vengeance, seals Cain's fate as fugitive and vagabond on the

earth. The ground—from which Abel's blood cries out—is forever cursed to him. Cf. Genesis 4:1–16.
55 Derrida, *Archive Fever*, 78.
56 Nancy, *Being Singular Plural*, 20.
57 Ibid., 20–1.
58 Nancy, *Inoperative Community*, 12.
59 Ibid., 4.
60 Ibid., xxxix.
61 Ibid., 11.
62 Nancy, *Finite Thinking*, 19.
63 Nancy both rejects Marx's formulation of "alienation"—by decoupling it from "species-being" and replacing it with his own transcendent-ontological model of finitude—and retains its uncompromising critique of the "living-conditions" of capital (cf. Nancy, *Finite Thinking*, 20–21).
64 Nancy, *Finite Thinking*, 21.
65 Nancy, *Inoperative Community*, xxxix.
66 Ibid., 15.
67 Ibid., 14.
68 Heidegger, *Being and Time*, 303, 298.
69 Ibid., 298.
70 Nancy, *Inoperative Community*, 15.
71 Ibid.
72 Ibid.
73 Ibid.
74 Ibid., 16.
75 Bataille, *Inner Experience*, 21.
76 Ibid., 23.
77 Nancy, *Inoperative Community*, 18; Bataille, *The Accursed Share*, 430.
78 Nancy, *Inoperative Community*, 18.
79 Bataille, *Inner Experience*, 46.
80 Ibid., 61.
81 Ibid.
82 Nancy, *Inoperative Community*, 28.
83 Ibid., 23.
84 Bataille, *Inner Experience*, 194.
85 Ibid., 196.
86 For more on Nancy's problematization of the concept of sacrifice refer to *Corpus* and his essay "The Unsacrificable."
87 Nancy, *Inoperative Community*, 27.
88 Nancy, *Finite Thinking*, 14.
89 Ibid., 189.
90 While Heidegger will hold that *Mitsein* is co-originary with *Dasein*, the analysis proceeds from the position latter instead of from what Nancy refers to as the "plural singularity" of *being-with* (Nancy, *Finite Thinking*, 194). Consider the following parenthetical remark from *The Inoperative Community*:

> when it came to the question of community as such, the same Heidegger also went astray with his vision of a people and a destiny conceived at least in part as a subject, which proves no doubt that Dasein's "being-toward-death" was never radically implicated in its being-with—in *Mitsein*—and that it is this implication that remains to be thought. (Nancy, *Inoperative Community*, 14)

91 Nancy, *Finite Thinking*, 100.
92 Ibid., 93, 230.
93 Nancy, *Inoperative Community*, 27–8.
94 Ibid., 29.
95 Ibid., 4.
96 Ibid.
97 Ibid., 35.
98 Nancy, "*La Comparution*," 391.
99 Nancy, *Inoperative Community*, 41.
100 Ibid., 39.
101 Nancy, "*La Comparution*," 392.
102 Nancy, *Inoperative Community*, 39.
103 Bataille, *Inner Experience*, 46.
104 Bataille, *The Accursed Share*, 430.
105 Nancy, "*La Comparution*," 393.
106 Nancy, *Inoperative Community*, 41.
107 Nancy, *Multiple Arts*, 33.
108 Ibid.
109 Ibid., 33–4.
110 Nancy, *The Sense of the World*, 110.
111 An analysis made all the more puzzling by Hegel's own renouncing of politics and history as being an impossible slaughter-bench (i.e., "objective spirit"), the "truth" of which leads consciousness to the elevated realm of art, religion, and philosophy (i.e., "absolute spirit"). In this there is more than a trace of Kant's own quietistic reverence for sovereign power, but these connections will have to be explored elsewhere.
112 There is a similar staging of the intractable problem of politics in the legend of the Gordian Knot. As in the Arthurian legend the solution also involves a sword—the symbol of sovereign power or the force of law—but the relation of the sword and the problem are shifted. In the first staging, it is fate or divine providence that places the sword in the hand of the sovereign. In the second, the sovereign cannot untie the knot and thus employs the so-called "Alexandrian solution" (i.e., to simply cut the knot with the sword). Read in this manner, in the first staging the divine chooses a man and in the second a man chooses to become divine. In each case the problem of political-theology (i.e., the categorical separation of "community" and "number") is resolved by the use of a sword.
113 Nancy, *The Sense of the World*, 111.
114 Ibid., 114.
115 Ibid. The *fasces* (the plural form of *fascis* meaning "bundle" or "pack") was a bundle of wooden rods bound around an axe that served as a symbol of power and authority in ancient Rome. According to Livy, Romulus appointed twelve lictors (from *ligāre* meaning "to bind") to guard the magistrates. Each lictor was assigned a *fascis*, which symbolized their power to execute (cf. Livy's *The History of Rome, Books 1–5*). Since that point it has been generally employed as a symbol for jurisdiction and the administration of justice (i.e., the current emblem of France, the official seal of the U.S. Senate, etc.), but its most notable modern use is undoubtedly that of Benito Mussolini's National Fascist Party (*Partito Nazionale Fascista* or PNF). Nancy's use of the term centres on the binding of the several into one—a "binding" that authorizes the use of lethal force—or logic of fusion that characterizes both this symbol and fascism.
116 Nancy, *The Sense of the World*, 114.

117 The history of the inclusion of *"fraternité"* in the motto is a complicated one. Unlike *"liberté"* and *"égalité,"* its roots are decidedly Christian. And, much like the concept of brotherhood itself, these roots both bind and divide. While the association between *"liberté"* and *"égalité"* is seen as essential—one insuring the other, as in isolation there can be "liberty for some" and/or "equality in servitude"—the inclusion of *"fraternité"* is much less direct. In fact, within the host of mottos the revolutionary period produced, *"fraternité"* was by no means a constant. And yet, while there was the suggestion of both less specifically Christian terms (i.e., *amitié*) and Christian terms that were not gender-exclusive (i.e., *charité*), it was ultimately *"fraternité"* that remained. For a more detailed examination, refer to Mona Ozouf's article on "fraternity" in *A Critical Dictionary of the French Revolution* and the chapter entitled "In Human Language, Fraternity ..." in Derrida's *Politics of Friendship*.
118 Nancy, *The Sense of the World*, 114.
119 Nancy, *The Truth of Democracy*, 51.
120 Derrida, *Aporias*, 22.
121 Nancy, *The Sense of the World*, 115.
122 Nancy, *Being Singular Plural*, 25.
123 Nancy, *The Truth of Democracy*, 54.
124 Derrida, *On Touching*, 309.
125 Derrida, *Politics of Friendship*, 48.
126 This shift in register also serves to mark a specific text, namely, *The Experience of Freedom*. In §7—which is entitled: "Sharing Freedom: Equality, Fraternity, Justice"— Nancy relates freedom to the *-in* or *co-* of community and to fraternity,

> It is also fraternity, if fraternity, it must be said, aside from every sentimental connotation (but not aside from the possibilities of passion it conceals, from hatred to glory by way of honour, love, competition for excellence, etc.), is not the relation of those who unify a common family, but the relation of those whose *Parent*, or common substance, *has disappeared*, delivering them to their freedom and equality. Such are, in Freud, the sons of the inhuman Father of the horde: becoming brothers in the *sharing* of his *dismembered* body. Fraternity is equality in the sharing of the incommensurable. (Nancy, *The Experience of Freedom*, 72)

Nancy is far from settled on his own use of the French motto (i.e., *Liberté, Égalité, Fraternité*). In fact in §14 he states that the motto "seems to us somewhat ridiculous and difficult to introduce into philosophical discourse, because in France it remains official (a lie of the State) and because it is said to summarize an obsolete 'Rousseauism'" (ibid., 168).

Despite this he defends its use in relation to Heidegger in that he reads the analysis of *Mitdasein* (§26 of *Being and Time*) as a linking of both freedom and equality. He continues:

> As for fraternity, which gives one even more to smile about: should it be suspected of coming from a relation to murdering the Father, and therefore of remaining a prisoner as much of the sharing of hatred as of a communion with an identical substance/essence (in the totemic meal)? The interpretation of the community as "fraternal" must be carefully dismantled. But it is possible, even with Freud, to interpret it otherwise: as a sharing of a maternal thing which precisely would not be a substance, but sharing—to infinity. In this respect, Chapter 7 above has only gone halfway. Perhaps the "mother" must also be abandoned, if we cannot avoid her being "phallic" (but is this certain?). We must also think of the fraternity in abandonment, of abandonment. (Ibid., 168)

Derrida's concerns with this mode of brotherly inheritance are given in the quote from *Politics of Friendship* (which we just considered above) and in §5—whose very title is addressed directly to Nancy: "Liberty, Equality, Fraternity, or, How Not to Speak in Mottos"—of *Rogues*. And yet, even here—prior to the publication of those texts—there is a kind of a response to Derrida's concerns. In fact, it is quite possible that this selection is a direct response to Derrida, as §14 (entitled "Fragments") is a collection of responses to questions and concerns that were given by friends and other early readers. The fragments themselves were originally meant, according to Nancy, "to be read for a thesis defense," and, as such, they are meant not as concluding remarks but as a series of openings or prolegomena (ibid., 206). The selection itself goes to show that Nancy is far from settled on either the meaning of "fraternity" or his specific use of it. As we will see, Nancy extends his response to Derrida in *The Sense of the World* by further qualifying his use of Freud's totemic meal.

127 Nancy, *The Sense of the World*, 115.
128 In fact, in a footnote to *Being Singular Plural* Nancy openly states that he agrees with Derrida's critique of fraternity in *Politics of Friendship*: "But I must point out that I have also, on occasion, raised the question of Christian fraternity. Moreover, I have reversed my position again and again on the possibility of looking into whether fraternity is necessarily generic or congenital" (198).
129 Nancy, *The Sense of the World*, 193. In this footnote Nancy presents a more extended response to Derrida's invocation of Freud's *Totem and Taboo* and Kafka's parable "*Before the Law*" in *Politics of Friendship* (cf. Derrida, *Politics of Friendship*, 46–8) by referring to texts by Jacques Lacan and Nicolas Abraham. This shift into the psychoanalytic register can be outlined here only provisionally. A more comprehensive account of this "fraternal" exchange would require a paper of its own.
130 Nancy, *Finite Thinking*, 284.
131 This trajectory is mapped out very clearly in Victor Hugo's *La Conscience*. The poem charts Cain's course away from his brother's murder. He flees seeking shelter and safety—one might even say immunity—and yet, at every point at which he stops to rest he is confronted. He initially seeks shelter at the foot of a mountain, and not being able to sleep he looks up,

> Lifting his head, he looked up and saw an eye
> Entirely open, in the depths of the sky,
> Which stared at him fixedly from out of the night.
> "I am too close," he said, shuddering at the sight. (*Selected Poetry*, 215)

He flees from the mountain "as if fleeing for his life." The eye follows him from the mountains to the coast, it drives him to seek shelter of tents, to set his children out to hunt down and rip out the eyes of every person that they meet, to commission the construction of a wall of bronze and a city "that looked as if it were a city from hell":

> Its towers caused a night to fall on outlying fields.
> Its walls were like mountains. For the built them not to yield
> To anything. They scrawled above its gate: "No Gods allowed." (217)

But the eye followed him even here, and so he says,

> "I want to live underground
> Like a hermit in his tomb—in some place without sound
> Where no one will see me, and I won't see them as well." (Ibid.)

And so they dig a hole for him and he goes "down into the black crypt alone":

> And when he was sitting in the darkness on his throne,
> And they had sealed the vault in which he would remain,
> The eye was in the tomb there and looked straight at Cain. (Ibid.)

The "high seat" in the poem is Cain's final refuge from the "eye." It is set within his own crypt and yet, even there, he is exposed.

132   Nancy, *Inoperative Community*, 4.
133   Ibid., 4.
134   On this point—among others—there are distinct parallels between Nancy's rethinking of "fraternity" and Derrida's work on *auto-immunity*. If we understand "fraternity" as follows—

- First, "anterior rather than posterior to all law and common substance," or, "were it possible ... *as* Law and *as* substance" (Nancy, *The Sense of the World*, 115).
- Second, that it is *not* the positing of a particular "substance" or "essence," but of the very impossibility of such a positing. That is, the *sense* of "fraternity" is not fixed nor is it fixable. Nor, for that matter, can it be declared null and void (i.e., set apart as the space of the messiah). Rather, it is the shared impossibility of the *in-* or *-with* of *being-in-common*.
- Third, and finally, that it is *resistance to* or *unworking of* (*désoeuvrement*) any attempt to close off, complete, or set the figure of the common. For example, "the relation (the community) is, if it *is*, nothing other than what it undoes, in its very principle—and at its closure or on its limit—the autarchy of absolute immanence" (Nancy, *Inoperative Community*, 4).

—then it seems that it is far from being, as Derrida suspects, a *sealing off* or *in* (i.e., a determining of the "who" or an "I can") of a singularity that might lay claim to autonomy (Derrida, *Rogues*, 44–45). Rather, it seems to parallel Derrida's *auto-immunity* or autoimmune process. For example, consider the following selection from *Rogues*:

> For what I call the autoimmune consists not only in harming or ruining oneself; indeed in destroying one's own protections, and in doing so oneself, committing suicide or threatening to do so, but more seriously still, and through this, in threatening the I [*moi*] or the self [*soi*], the *ego* or the *autos*, ipseity itself, compromising the immunity of the *autos* itself: it consists not only in compromising oneself [*s'auto-entamer*] but in compromising the self, the *autos*—and thus ipseity. It consists not only in committing suicide but in compromising *sui-* or *self*-referentiality, the *self* or *sui-* of suicide itself. Autoimmunity is more or less suicidal, but, more seriously still, it threatens always to rob suicide itself of its meaning and supposed integrity. (Ibid., 45)

Here auto-immunity is presented as a kind of impossibility of auto-affection (i.e., of the self feeling or sensing—and thus, finally, *knowing and grounding*—itself and only itself). Like a series of other terms in Derrida's work—*aporia*, *double bind*, or *différance*—there is something like an essential heteronomy, an "internal contradiction, an indecidability, that is, an internal-external, nondialectizable antinomy that risks paralyzing and thus calls for the event of the interruptive decision" (ibid., 35). Now compare this articulation with this selection from *The Inoperative Community*:

> The logic of the absolute violates the absolute. It implicates it in a relation that it refuses and precludes by its essence. This relation tears and forces open, from within and from without at the same time, and from an outside that is nothing other than the rejection of an impossible interiority, the "without relation" from with the absolute would constitute itself.... Excluded by the logic of the absolute-subject of metaphysics (Self, Will, Life, Spirit, etc.), community comes perforce *to cut into* this subject by virtue of the same logic. The logic of the absolute *sets it in relation*: but, this, obviously, cannot make for a relation between two or several absolutes, no more than it can make an absolute of the relation. It undoes the absoluteness of the absolute. (Nancy, *Inoperative Community*, 4)

Needless to say, these parallels do not constitute an equivalence—in fact, they deserve a much more thorough account than can be offered here—but they do suggest a sustained and close relationship. Each renders autonomy—in the sense of absolute, sovereign, self-grounding, and self-authorizing—impossible by virtue of a prior (and non-dialectical) heteronomy. For Derrida, community is *auto-co-immunity* precisely because, by his account, the "common" of community has "the same duty or charge [*munus*] as the immune" (Derrida, *Rogues*, 35). That is, by determining what is "common," an *omphalos* is put in place (i.e., the stone that marks the centre or navel of all fraternity). It is a closing off of the *autos* by virtue of its extension to the plural. But this closing off cannot occur without naming that which is not included (i.e., identity requires difference). Paradoxically every move that the self makes to separate itself from the other only serves to multiply the implication of this relationship and mark off the impossibility of absolute identity. For Nancy, this movement will be called "communion" and will mark off a certain strand of both "community" and "fraternity." But, unlike Derrida, he will take the *risk* of retaining the names. We will detail both this *risk* and the difference between Derrida and Nancy later on.

135 Nancy, *The Confronted Community*, 24–5.
136 Ibid., 25.
137 Nancy, *Inoperative Community*, 4.
138 Nancy, *The Experience of Freedom*, 16.
139 Nancy sets "evil" in opposition to "fraternity" in §12 of *The Experience of Freedom*: "Wickedness does not hate this or that singularity: it hates singularity as such and the singular relation of singularities. It hates freedom, equality, and fraternity; it hates sharing. This hatred is freedom's own (it is therefore also the hatred that belongs to equality and fraternity; sharing hates itself and is devoted to ruin)" (Nancy, *The Experience of Freedom*, 128).

This opposition does not contradict the equation offered above (i.e., evil = fraternity). Rather, it indicates the amphibology of "fraternity" in Nancy's work. As we have seen, he will use it to refer both to the "additional element" (i.e., the fraternity suspended by "perhaps" and without father or mother) and to the logic of communion (i.e., the brotherhood that sets its bonds in blood and soil and is symbolized by the *fasces*). The latter—as the paradoxical logic of the absolute—is, like evil, "*the hatred of existence as such*" (ibid., 128). This hatred is not constitutive (i.e., evil in Nancy's terms is not an involuntary defect or perversion); rather, it is—despite Kant's claim that such a position or act is not possible—a *positive act* of freedom (ibid., 123). It is—like Kant's diabolical evil—evil in principle and, as such, it is self-cancelling. As Nancy puts it, "*it is freedom that unleashes itself against itself*" (ibid., 126).

140 Nancy, *The Sense of the World*, 115.
141 Hegel, *Philosophy of Right*, 38–9.
142 Ibid., 21.
143 Nancy, *Finite Thinking*, 296.
144 Ibid.
145 By taking jurisdiction over the here and now via the logic of the absolute "fraternity," the sovereign implicates itself in a relationship with what it refuses to recognize. The symbolism of the fasces is a testament to the primacy of this exclusion: at its centre is an axe. This instrument of execution is the symbol of the sovereign's exceptional power (i.e., to kill without responsibility). At the centre of the fraternal bond is the power to kill, but this "power" is self-issued. Those who resist, question, or

contest the right of the brotherhood are confronted with this power. Yet death does not put an end to the question; it multiplies it. It marks those who wield its power with the very question that they have claimed to answer: Who are you? It cannot answer: "I am your God." Its violence is not divine (as Benjamin notes, to be "divine" violence must meet the impossible qualification of being "lethal without spilling blood") (Benjamin, "Critique of Violence," 297). There is no possibility of justification, because there can be no dialogue with the corpse: there is only the ellipsis without return. It remains there as the only one left standing in the blood that demands (without measure) an account.

146 Hegel, *Phenomenology*, 360.
147 Ibid.
148 Derrida, *Politics of Friendship*, 298–9.
149 Ibid., 48.
150 Nancy puts forward his own set of concerns about Derrida's work in his essay *"Borborygmi."* Consider the following:

> Derrida is always susceptible to surprising himself from behind. He watches himself, watches out for himself, gets himself caught. He is on the trail of the trace, which he effaces insofar as he leaves its imprint behind him. He is on the scent of effacement itself: he effaces an enormous overload of traces, marks, and gilded letters. His mania for marking is the madness of effacing the mark in marking effacement, in one fell swoop always knocking himself out from behind. (Nancy, *Finite Thinking*, 122)

The characterization—which at times seems (almost) to venture into the realm of caricature—that Nancy offers presents Derrida as both an ingenious detective and paranoid skeptic. He follows the trace, and not by virtue simply of a disciplinary or technical proficiency, but also of a "gut feeling" (*Boborygmi* is, as Nancy reminds us, a Greek onomatopoeia that can be used to refer to both "a rumbling in the bowels" and "incomprehensible and inarticulate remarks") (ibid., 112). While this "gut feeling" or "hunch" enables the detective to follow the trace with preternatural ability, it also—as any good detective story will clearly show—brings with it an almost paralyzing skepticism. Can this hunch be trusted? Is it a figment of the imagination, a mirage of desire, or a barely caught glimpse of the "truth"? We are given the distinct image of a detective afflicted with a debilitating skepticism that manifests itself in both his gastronomic discomfort and his penchant for mumbling while thinking. The danger associated with such a manner, or way, of going about things is that one might lose track of the trace and end up chasing phantoms or, for that matter, one's own tail (Nancy does invoke the image of the *Ouroboros*). It can lapse into "mumbled incantations"—as Nancy puts it, "poetry in the worst sense"—or a nihilistic dissolution of any and all concepts (ibid., 113). On this account Derrida is both Holmes, ingeniously tracking down Moriarty, and Clouseau stumbling over his own feet. And yet, despite all of its pitfalls, there is also a palpable sense of admiration here. While Nancy notes the pitfalls of Derrida's *modus operandi*, he clearly also sees it (at least in part) as a virtue. Like a good detective he refuses to accept what is simply presented as being true, or to simply look for the easiest explanation or nearest conceptual handhold and deem it true because it holds his world together. Derrida's pursuit of the trace runs the risk of crossing over into madness—which is to say that he puts himself at risk—in an effort to discover the "truth." It is this "truth" that threatens to unravel him. Despite these risks he follows it.

151 Nancy, *Finite Thinking*, 299.
152 Nancy, *The Experience of Freedom*, 23.

153 Ibid. For more on this *risk*, refer to the chapters entitled "Politics I" and "Politics II" in Nancy's *The Sense of the World*. Aside from the *risk* of reserving the space there is also the *risk* of abandoning the task of judgment (i.e., allowing indeterminacy to lapse into the empty discourse of "tolerance" that excuses misogyny and racism on the basis of "cultural difference").

154 While it may seem that Derrida's *democracy-to-come* does precisely this (i.e., it opens up a void that cannot be filled). For instance, if we refer to the closing page of *Politics of Friendship*, we find that

> For democracy remains to come; this is its essence in so far as it remains: not only will it remain indefinitely perfectible, hence always insufficient and future, but, belonging to the time of the promise, it will always remain, in each of its futures, to come: even when there is a democracy, it never exists, it is never present, it remains the theme of a non-presentable concept. (Derrida, *Politics of Friendship*, 306)

Were one to confine analysis to this example, or others like it, it would seem to lend support to the contention that Derrida's *democracy-to-come* leads to the very type of *sanctum sanctorum* that Nancy is concerned with (i.e., a thinking of "number" that lacks a thinking of "community" or "fraternity" as *co-*, *-with*, or *-in* of the "common"). But such a reading would have to ignore the very question that concludes the text: "Is it possible to open up to the 'come' of a certain democracy which is no longer an insult to the friendship we have striven to think beyond the homo-fraternal and phallogocenric schema?" (ibid.).

Derrida—like Nancy—does not stop at a thinking of "freedom" and "equality." That is, he does not stop with the empty space left by the question of "number" (i.e., Who counts?). He approaches a thinking of "community," but, as he himself notes, he is reticent to write this word. In fact, community forms "fundamentally the essential part of the disquiet which inspires" *Politics of Friendship* (ibid., 305). This does not mean there is an unbridgeable divide between Derrida's work on friendship and Nancy's on fraternity; rather, I contend that this is an essential line of communication between them. It is not simply the case that they pass one another without noticing, and thus require the judgment of a third party to put the continuity of their paths into perspective. Nor is it that they meet at a particular point only to take divergent paths and never meet again. While each takes a different path and adopts different tactics, they remain in touch at a shared limit. They both struggle with the question of the *demos*—that is, the freedom and responsibility of existence as *being-with*—and neither is willing to accept it either as solid all through (i.e., a specific quality or substance) or as a pure void (i.e., the space held open for the advent of the messiah).

155 In this respect, it might be thought of not as *sanctum sanctorum*, but a "house of commons." This would of course call for a radical rethinking of both this term and its boundaries. (In other words asking: Does the "house" somehow delimit this questioning?—aside from all the problematic questions of "representation" in figuring the "common.")

156 Nancy, *The Sense of the World*, 115.

Notes to Chapter 2

1 Derrida, *Writing and Difference*, 272.
2 Löwith, 1.
3 Augustine, 189.
4 Lyotard, 76.

5 Augustine, 283.
6 Ibid., 244.
7 Bataille, *Inner Experience*, 46.
8 Ibid., 179.
9 Bataille, *On Nietzsche*, 150.
10 Ibid., 19.
11 Bataille, *Inner Experience*, 24, 60–1. This re-thinking of the limits of community draws us towards a rich series of texts that correspond with Bataille's work; this series extends from Jean-Luc Nancy's *The Inoperative Community*, to Maurice Blanchot's *The Unavowable Community*, Giorgio Agamben's *The Coming Community*, and Jacques Derrida's *The Politics of Friendship*. For a partial exploration of this series, refer to Chapter 1.
12 Derrida, *Writing and Difference*, 271.
13 Cf. Augustine, 94–6, 226, 295–6, 300.
14 Augustine, 152.
15 Ibid., 92.
16 Ibid., 94.
17 The disorientation that takes hold of the subject at this point is captured by Alcibiades: "I swear by the gods, Socrates, I have no idea what I mean—I must be in some absolutely bizarre condition! When you ask me questions, first I think one thing, and then I think something else" (Plato, *Alcibiades*, 573).

Through the course of the dialogue Alcibiades is brought to the point of aporia, but Socrates attempt at utilizing philosophy to reorient him to the "good" fails. Alcibiades remains within-out the "true" orientation and, as such, he suffers:

> My whole life has become one constant effort to escape from him and keep away, but when I see him, I feel deeply ashamed, because I'm doing nothing about my way of life, though I have already agreed with him that I should. Sometimes, believe me, I think I would be happier of if he were dead. And yet I know that if he dies I'll be even more miserable. I can't live with him, and I can't live without him! What *can* I do about him? (Plato, *Symposium*, 498)

Alcibiades exists as a failed convert; he cannot turn away from the surface of things and yet he remains dissatisfied with them. He is caught between the apparent and the essential, but unlike Augustine he has no way to escape this aporia. Like Augustine prior to his conversion he suffers at the precipice, but he does not fall.
18 Augustine, 140.
19 Ibid., 95.
20 Ibid.
21 Ibid., 96.
22 Heidegger, *Religious Life*, 209.
23 A useful point of reference in regard to this absent-presence is Augustine's discussion of memory and forgetting in Book X.
24 Lyotard, 72.
25 By operating in this manner the *Confessions* is bound by the logic of *différance*.
26 Lyotard, 72.
27 Augustine, 152.
28 Ibid., 152–3.
29 Ibid., 153.
30 Ibid., 171.
31 Ibid.
32 Ibid.

Notes to Chapter Two

33 The verb *inhiamus*, translated as "panting after" in the Chadwick edition, comes from the stem *inhiare* meaning "to gape at or for" and is related to *hiare* "to gape" and *hiatus* "gaping, gap, opening." This is interesting, as what occurs at this point in the text can be interpreted as a hiatus in that there is a gap or interruption in the continuity of the text (*Oxford English Dictionary*, 2nd ed., s.v. "Inhiate," "Hiate," "Hiatus").
34 Augustine, 172.
35 Ibid.
36 Ibid., 225.
37 Ibid.
38 Ibid.
39 Ibid., 226.
40 Ibid., 283.
41 Ibid., 300.
42 Ibid., 240.
43 Ibid., 289.
44 Ibid., 296.
45 Ibid., 223–4.
46 Ibid., 226–7.
47 Ibid., 243.
48 Ibid., 189.
49 Ibid.
50 Ibid., 186–7.
51 Ibid., 243.
52 Ibid., 245.
53 We should clearly state that from within the confessant's belief structure the epistemological question cannot be raised. Once one accepts the broader metaphysical framework (i.e., *Deus incommutabilis substantia*), the problem of knowledge (epistemology) is as inappropriate as the problem of meaning. From within this framework the question of how Augustine *knows* the meaning of any given "sign" (i.e., how he is able to go beyond the precipice of polysemy) is effectively deflected towards the one who poses the question. That is, the very act of asking the question is interpreted by the confessant as an indication of that individual's fallen state. Just as when Ambrose "was reading, his eyes ran over the page and his heart perceived the sense," the confessant experiences the "truth" via the "inner" senses (Augustine, 92). The argumentative structure is thus self-sealing. The epistemological question can only be asked if one refuses the "now" of *incommutabilis substantia* (the absolute or total "now" that the confessant orients itself towards and that guarantees the sense of the "signs" it reads). In and through this refusal, the meaning of "now" becomes an open question. And it is precisely as an *open* question that it becomes the finite "now" of the *timens praecipitium*.
54 Augustine, 179.
55 In *La Communauté désœuvrée* (*The Inoperative Community*) Jean-Luc Nancy states that will to communion (understood as absolute immanence and/or fusion with *incommutabilis substantia*) "contains no other logic than that of the suicide of the community that is governed by it" (Nancy, *Inoperative Community*, 12). In the context of the *Confessions* this immanence finds its expression in the "day when, purified and molten by the fire of your love, I flow together to merge into you" (Augustine, 244). If this day were to arrive, the result would be the instantaneous end of both communication and community. To quote Nancy, "Death is not only an example of

this, it is its truth" (Nancy, *Inoperative Community*, 12). Nancy un-works this logic by exploring the (non-dialectical) difference between communion and community. We will return to this later on.

56 This trajectory of language finds a critical parallel in Benjamin's concept of "pure language":

> In all language and linguistic creations there remains in addition to what can be conveyed something that cannot be communicated; depending on the context in which it appears, it is something that symbolizes or something symbolized. It is the former only in the finite products of language, the latter in the evolving of the languages themselves. And that which seeks to represent, to produce itself in the evolving of languages, is that very nucleus of pure language. Though concealed and fragmentary, it is an active force in life as the symbolized thing itself, whereas it inhabits linguistic creations only in symbolized form. While that ultimate essence, pure language, in the various tongues is tied only to linguistic elements and their changes, in linguistic creations it is weighted with a heavy, alien meaning. To relieve it of this, to turn the symbolizing into the symbolized, to regain pure language fully formed in the linguistic flux, is the tremendous and only capacity of translation. In this pure language—which no longer means or expresses anything but is, as expressionless and creative Word, that which is meant in all languages—all information, all sense, and all intension finally encounter a stratum in which they are destined to be extinguished. (Benjamin, *Illuminations*, 79–80)

In the *Confessions* this "nucleus of pure language" is interpreted as "meaningful" or, at the very least, indicative of a non-linguistic meaning that is *yet-to-come*. Augustine refuses openness of "pure language" by reading the silence of each linguistic fragment as a "secret opening" that leads to Absolute meaning. The levity of "pure language," the levity of an opening without orientation within the moment is as unacceptable to him as a word that does not mean anything. Cf. Giorgio Agamben's essay "Language and History: Linguistic and Historical Categories in Benjamin's Thought."

57 Lyotard, 41.
58 Ibid., 42.
59 Bataille, *Inner Experience*, 16.
60 Augustine's exegetical method is "cryptomantic" in the sense that it avoids the problem posed by the inadequation of sign and sense (i.e., the precipice of polysemy) by reading-over it. He reads any and all inadequation as a "hidden" or "secret" opening that leads towards Absolute meaning. His means of accessing this "hidden" opening are mantic (i.e., through divine inspiration), and thus the only justification he can offer for any meaning he derives in this manner is promissory in the messianic sense. That is, unlike a standard promissory note, the guarantee that his reading is "true" (that it is the "*natural law*") is not bound to a specific date, but rather infinitely deferred.
61 Saussure, 67. It is interesting to note that Saussure's second principle is the linear character of the sign: "The linguistic signal, being auditory in nature, has a temporal aspect, and hence certain temporal characteristics: (a) *it occupies a certain temporal space*, and (b) *this space is measured in just one dimension: it is a line*" (Saussure, 69–70).

Augustine understands this principle of language as an indication of the fallen state of human language (i.e., it is the distention of the *incommutabilis substantia*). The *Confessions* can be read as a strategic manipulation of this principle against the first principle (the arbitrary nature of the sign). That is, if the meaning of any given term or sequence of terms is determined negatively by syntagmatic (i.e., the meaning of any given term within a sequence is determined by its negative relation to the other terms in that sequence) and associative relations (mnemonic associations that connect a term of sequence to terms to others) (ibid., 121–2). The only way to override the play of linguistic meaning is to form a chain that does not end. The *Confessions* represent an attempt to secure absolute meaning by obliterating silence; hence the compulsive and repetitive nature of the text. If it were possible the repetitive pattern of the text would form a single unending sound: the present would be the present of the line and not the point. Only then would the confessant be fused into communion with the Absolute: no longer present in any particular time or space, no longer contestable, and thus no longer responsible.

62 Bataille, *Inner Experience*, 14.
63 Derrida, *Writing and Difference*, 265–6.
64 Bataille, *Inner Experience*, 50. One cannot help but notice the parallels with the final propositions of Wittgenstein's *Tractatus Logico-Philosophicus*. For example, the propositions are to be used "as steps" that one must discard—"so to speak, throw away the ladder after he has climbed up it" (Wittgenstein, *Tractatus*, 89). And yet, Wittgenstein's final proposition ("What we cannot speak about we must pass over in silence") is effectively reversed. For Bataille, "the inadequation of all speech ... at least must be said" and thus, as Derrida states, "we must find a speech which maintains silence" (Derrida, *Writing and Difference*, 262). The imperative of retreat (i.e., passing over in silence) is replaced by one of deconstruction.
65 Derrida, *Writing and Difference*, 267.
66 Ibid., 242.
67 Bataille, *Inner Experience*, 46.
68 Ibid.
69 Ibid.
70 Ibid., 37.
71 Ibid., 46.
72 Ibid., 24.
73 Ibid.
74 Ibid., 37.
75 In his later work Derrida refers to this entropic dynamic as "autoimmunity." In *Rogues* Derrida details two modes of "autoimmunity"; the first being a constitutive form he associates with the undecidable openness of democracy, and the second a suicidal form he associates with sovereignty. In its constitutive mode autoimmunity works to maintain the porosity or openness of democracy: "democracy is what it is only in the différance by which it defers itself and differs from itself" (Derrida, *Rogues*, 38). The second is the result of an autocratic or sovereign assertion of strict boundaries that divide the same from the other. In this mode the silent "a" of *différance* is interpreted as a barrier to onto-theo-logical purity, and a system is set in place to annul this silence. Whether this "system" is one of cognition or of security and governance, its activity is the same, namely the repetitive assertion of the *autos* in the negation of the other. This radical assertion of autonomy is suicidal, as in proclaiming and enforcing itself as law it compromises itself (i.e., Augustine's identification with his "soul" entails the progressive regulation of both the world of temporal things and his own body). To quote Derrida:

> what I call the autoimmune consists not only in harming or ruining oneself, indeed in destroying one's own protections, and in doing so oneself, committing suicide or threatening to do so, but more seriously still, and through this,

in the threatening the I [*moi*] or the self [*soi*], the *ego* or the *autos*, ipseity itself, compromising the immunity of the *autos* itself: it consists not only in compromising oneself [*s'auto-entamer*] but in compromising the self, the *autos*—and thus ipseity. It consists not only in committing suicide but in compromising *sui*- or *self*-referentiality, the *self* or *sui*- of suicide itself. Autoimmunity is more or less suicidal, but, more seriously still, it threatens always to rob suicide itself of its meaning and supposed integrity. (Ibid., 45)

The self denies the other and effectively claims (like Augustine), "What I am not yet, I am" (Augustine, 57). As a result it attacks the other as its self and itself as the other (i.e., as the mortal "body" it refuses). It does this in order to gain pure *auto-affection*: a pure "living feeling" of its self as it is yet to be (the completely silent *auto-affection* of Augustine's angels and the momentary experience of this self-proximity in his vision). I deal with this, to some degree, in Chapters 1, 4, and 6. I plan take up a more comprehensive consideration of "autoimmunity" in relation to Derrida's earlier work another time, but for now it is useful to refer to Michael Naas' essay "'One Nation ... Indivisible': Jacques Derrida on the Autoimmunity of Democracy and the Sovereignty of God."

76 Nancy, *Inoperative Community*, 12.
77 Agamben, 53.
78 Bataille, *Inner Experience*, 37.
79 The unknowable culpability of "inner experience" is similar to the guilt Father Zosima speaks of: "For you must know, my dear ones, that each of us is undoubtedly guilty on behalf of all and for all on earth, not only because of the common guilt of the world, but personally, each one of us, for all people and for each person on this earth" (Dostoyevsky, 164).

It is even possible to argue that the condition of the community of those without community is one in which a form of communication that is "infinite, universal, and that known no satiety" is shared (ibid.). There is a twofold tension that suspends this argument: (1) it depends upon both the reading of Zosima's knowledge of "guilt" (i.e., is there a method of measuring and expiating guilt hidden here, that is, of getting beyond it?) and "love" (i.e., is this the insatiable love of communion with and in the absolute or is it insatiable precisely because it maintains a communicative distance?); (2) as Derrida suggests in *Politics of Friendship*, there may be a hidden "brotherhood" within the logic of this community, and this risk forces us to carefully retrace and reconsider the articulations of "community" from Bataille to Nancy and Blanchot—to retrace in an effort to ensure there is no concealed "sign" that would serve to re-found the community-of-order. In addition to or conjunction with the question of "brotherhood," such a retracing would have to account for both the position of Nietzsche and the role of Acéphale in Bataille's thought (cf. Derrida, *Politics of Friendship*, 37, 47–8, 54, 80–2, 295, 298). Refer to Chapter 1 for my own exploration of these questions.

80 Benjamin, *Illuminations*, 257.
81 Bataille, *Inner Experience*, 52.
82 Ibid., 60.
83 Ibid., 61.
84 Cf. Derrida, *Politics of Friendship*, 37, 47–8; Blanchot, *Unavowable Community*, 1.
85 Dostoyevsky, 69. In Bataille's terms, Ivan's resignation ("It's not that I don't accept God, Alyosha, I just most respectfully return him the ticket") is simply the evasion of experience (ibid., 245). By "returning the ticket" he maintains a distance from the world that enables him to expiate himself. His position is paradoxical in that

he "believes neither in God nor in his own immortality," but he cannot accept a world without divine justice (ibid., 69, 245). In short, Ivan refuses responsibility in the name of divine vengeance. Like the Grand Inquisitor of his poem, Ivan can imagine the community-of-order: "There are three powers, only three powers on earth, capable of conquering and holding captive forever the conscience of these feeble rebels, for their own happiness—these powers are miracle, mystery, and authority" (ibid., 255).

In the absence of these powers, he (much like the Marquis de Sade) can see only the law of egoism. In his longing for the immanence of communion Ivan retains the perspective of the absolute. His view of human nature is formed by the very dualist arguments he claims to reject; that is, he has retained the metaphysical view of human finitude. For him all that remains if God is an illusion is man as beast, but the very idea of both "man" and "beast" are constructed in relation to God. The leap from the community-of-order to the lawless state of nature is by no means logically consistent. This becomes clear once we recontextualize the logic of his argument in relation to language. Effectively he is arguing that, if absolute meaning cannot be determined, language is without meaning. He refuses to communicate the inadequacy of communication, and by doing so he, like Pilate, makes the empty gesture of refusing to partake in that which he is already both active in and responsible for.

86 Nancy, *Inoperative Community*, 4.
87 Ibid., 15.
88 Ibid., 28.
89 Antelme, 88.
90 Ibid., 93–4.
91 Blanchot, *Unavowable Community*, 9.
92 Benjamin, *Reflections*, 297.
93 Augustine, 244.

Notes to Chapter 3

1 Sade, *Reflections*, 97; Sade, *Idée*, 3–4. Due to the limited reliability of the current English translations of Sade's major works, I have cited both the English and the French for each quote and amended the translations where necessary.
2 It should be noted that I am using the English term "novel" in place of Sade's term "roman." Sade uses the term to refer to fiction in general, and thus replacing it with the English cognate "romance" would be much too limited because it refers to a specific type of fiction (cf. Sade, *Sodom*, 97).
3 Barthes, 36–7.
4 Bataille, *Erotism*, 188.
5 There has been a series of important studies on the relationship between Sade's work and that of his contemporaries in terms of both philosophy and literature. For a detailed examination of these connections, one should consult the work of authors such as Jean Deprun, Michel Delon, Caroline Warman, Annie Le Brun, Hans-Ulrich Seifert, Maurice Lever, and Jean-Marie Goulemot.
6 In *Sade: From Materialism to Pornography* Caroline Warman argues that Sade should be read as a "sensationist materialist." This philosophical position connects him with a series of other 18th-century empiricists who viewed the body, and more specifically sensation and perception, as the means to access the laws governing the natural world. Her study offers a wealth of contextual detail, but it leaves a number of crucial differences between Sade and other "sensationist materialists" unaccounted for. For instance, she argues that "Sade's 'desire' is 'attraction' in all its

principle points, the difference being that Sade means human bodies where Buffon means material ones" (Warman, 147).

This is problematic; physical attraction relies on the presence of the objects to generate attraction, whereas Sade clearly articulates that the object of desire is not, strictly speaking, present. Consider this quote from *The 120 Days of Sodom*: "[S]ince my arrival here my fuck has not once flowed because of the objects I find about me in this castle. Every time, I have discharged over what is not there, what is absent from its place, and so it is" (Sade, *Sodom*, 362; Sade, *Sodome*, 163).

This problem extends to his anthropomorphic characterization of Nature as desiring her own final end. This reading also does not account for Sade's own outrage towards the laws of nature (a feature of Sade's text that Blanchot reads as paradigmatic to his entire project; cf. "Sade's Reason"). I also find the concluding sentence of this text completely puzzling: "none of us naturally inhabits Sade's cultural 'house' any longer" (Warman, 170). Beyond all of the questions pertaining to the "us," is it simply that the cultural context of Sade is in the past? Does that imply that despite all of Sade's connections to philosophy and literature from the 18th century on, he is somehow simply a neutralized "historical" curiosity? That "we" can simply access his texts like impartial and bemused observers? If so, I am much more inclined to agree with Klossowski and argue that Sade remains very much "our" neighbour.

7   Hénaff, "Excess," 151.
8   Blanchot, "Sade's Reason," 33–4.
9   Ibid., 36–7.
10 In "Coldness and Cruelty" Gilles Deleuze states:

> Underlying the work of Sade is negation in the broadest sense. Here we must distinguish between two levels of negation: negation (the negative) as a partial process and pure negation as a totalizing idea. These two levels correspond to Sade's distinction between *two natures*, the importance of which was shown by Klossowski. Secondary nature is bound by its own rules and its own laws; it is pervaded by the negative, but not everything in it is negation. Destruction is merely the reverse of creation and change, disorder is another form of order, and the decomposition of death is equally the composition of life. (Deleuze, 26–7)

Conversely, "original nature is necessarily the object of an Idea, and pure negation is a delusion; but it is a delusion of reason itself" (ibid., 27). Much like Blanchot, Deleuze does not read Sade's writing as the product of an idiosyncratic madness that could be easily distinguished from reason. Nor is he to be read as some puzzling and benign outgrowth of the tradition of empiricism and materialism. Rather, Sade's writing finds its basis in the speculative idea of totality.

11 Sade, *Reflections*, 113; Sade, *Idée*, 42.
12 Sade, *Reflections*, 107; Sade, *Idée*, 27.
13 For a detailed account of the broader context of Sade's appeal to the authority of sensation, consult Warman's *Sade: From Materialism to Pornography*. Also, for an account of the transgressive elements of this appeal, refer to Blanchot's essay "Sade's Reason" as he focuses on the move from the authority of sensation to that of desire.
14 Rousseau, *Émile, or Treatise on Education*, 193.
15 Derrida, *Of Grammatology*, 17.
16 Sade, *Juliette*, 780; Sade, "Histoire de Juliette," 883–4.
17 Derrida, *Of Grammatology*, 17.
18 Sade, *Juliette*, 340–1; Sade, "Histoire de Juliette," 428.
19 Sade, *Reflections*, 102; Sade, *Idée*, 26.

Notes to Chapter Three

20 Sade, *Reflections*, 110–1; Sade, *Idée*, 36–7.
21 Sade, *Reflections*, 109; Sade, *Idée*, 34.
22 Sade, *Reflections*, 109; Sade, *Idée*, 34–5.
23 Sade, *Reflections*, 110; Sade, *Idée*, 34–5.
24 Derrida, *Of Grammatology*, 26.
25 Blanchot, "Sade's Reason," 9.
26 Ibid.
27 Derrida, *Margins of Philosophy*, 19.
28 Lacan, *Ecrits*, 323.
29 Lacan, *Seminar XI*, 182–5.
30 Sade, *Juliette*, 778; Sade, "*Histoire de Juliette*," 882.
31 Sade, *Sodom*, 254; Sade, *Sodome*, 60–1.
32 Sade, *Juliette*, 525; Sade, "*Histoire de Juliette*," 650. Emphasis added.
33 Sade, "Bedroom," 304; Sade, "*Boudoir*," 118–9.
34 Sade, *Juliette*, 340–1; Sade, "*Histoire de Juliette*," 482.
35 Sade, *Juliette*, 340–1; Sade, "*Histoire de Juliette*," 482.
36 Sade, *Reflections*, 99; Sade, *Idée*, 9.
37 Sade, *Reflections*, 98–9; Sade, *Idée*, 5–8.
38 Sade, *Sodom*, 362; Sade, *Sodome*, 163.
39 Sade, *Sodom*, 361–2; Sade, *Sodome*, 163.
40 Klossowski, *Sade My Neighbor*, 97–8.
41 Sade, *Juliette*, 640–1; Sade, "*Histoire de Juliette*," 752–3.
42 Sade, *Juliette*, 340; Sade, "*Histoire de Juliette*," 482.
43 Deleuze's characterization of Sadean apathy emphasizes this point: "The 'apathy' of the sadist is essentially directed against feeling: all feelings, even and especially that of doing evil, are condemned on the grounds that they bring about a dangerous dissipation which prevents the condensation of energy and its precipitation into the pure element of impersonal and demonstrative sensuality (Deleuze, 51).

Hénaff analyzes the function of Sadean apathy in depth in chapter three of his *Sade: The Invention of the Libertine Body*. According to him the role of the libertine's apathy is

> to split the instinctual nucleus, refine it, and diversify it in this catalytic-cracking device. The passions would emerge purified, cleansed, allocated to precise objectives within the program of pleasures. They would become operational. But their passage through this rational fast-breeder reactor would not leave them intact, nor would their new way of functioning be without consequences: reason proposes no means without also imposing its own ends, and what would emerge from this passage through apathy was apparently a plan for unlimited mastery, mastery to the death. (Hénaff, *Sade*, 85)

44 Sade, *Juliette*, 781–2; Sade, "*Histoire de Juliette*," 885.
45 Sade, *Sodom*, 364; Sade, *Sodome*, 165.
46 Sade, *Juliette*, 771; Sade, "*Histoire de Juliette*," 875–6.
47 Lacan, *Seminar I*, 102.
48 Sade, *Juliette*, 49; Sade, "*Histoire de Juliette*," 223.
49 Derrida, *Of Grammatology*, 26.
50 Sade, "Bedroom," 234–5; Sade, "*Boudoir*," 51.
51 Sade, *Reflections*, 111; Sade, *Idée*, 36–7.
52 Sade, *Reflections*, 110–1; Sade, *Idée*, 36–7.
53 Sade, *Reflections*, 98–9; Sade, *Idée*, 5–8. Bold emphasis added.

54 Sade, *Reflections*, 113; Sade, *Idée*, 42–3. Bold emphasis added.
55 Sade, *Reflections*, 99; Sade, *Idée*, 8.
56 Sade, *Reflections*, 109–10; Sade, *Idée*, 34–5.
57 Sade, *Reflections*, 106; Sade, *Idée*, 25–6.
58 Sade, *Reflections*, 107; Sade, *Idée*, 27.
59 Sade, *Reflections*, 99; Sade, *Idée*, 8.
60 Rousseau, 1.
61 Sade, *Reflections*, 99; Sade, *Idée*, 8.
62 Sade, *Reflections*, 115; Sade, *Idée*, 46–7.
63 Sade, *Reflections*, 114; Sade, *Idée*, 43–4.
64 Nancy, "Exscription," 327.
65 Sade, *Reflections*, 106; Sade, *Idée*, 8.
66 Sade, *Reflections*, 107; Sade, *Idée*, 27.
67 Sade, *Reflections*, 106; Sade, *Idée*, 26.
68 Borges, 250–4.
69 Derrida, *Of Grammatology*, 18.
70 Ibid., 26.
71 Sade, *Juliette*, 778; Sade, "Histoire de Juliette," 882.
72 Sade, *Sodom*, 199; Sade, *Sodome*, 9.
73 Disavowal is key in Sade's writing, as it is by disavowing his right as author of the text that he is able to imbue his text in the force of law. He recognizes that the God of the Book is impotent, yet he simply transfers the function of the absolute to Nature and the neurogrammatic inscription. Through disavowal he gains the knowledge of the absolute; he is shown the indissoluble connection between the signifier and signified. He is chosen, he is the subject that knows; his proof is invincible. He straddles the gap between the signifier and the signified and struggles to complete their fusion. This process consumes him to the point of total deafening silence (cf. Deleuze, 31).
74 Austin, 101.
75 Ibid., 52.
76 Nancy, "Exscription," 331.

Notes to Chapter 4

1 Benjamin, "Critique of Violence," 298.
2 Kant, *Metaphysics of Morals*, 107.
3 Ibid., 106.
4 Ibid.
5 Ibid., 17.
6 Ibid., 107.
7 First, there is the rather surprising omission of Cain's dialogue with God in Genesis. Second, what of complaints pertaining to pain and suffering? Kant is clearly aware of the latter problem. He responds to it by placing the responsibility for determining the actual measure and practice of punishments with the judiciary under the puzzling proviso that punishment does not "make the humanity of the person suffering it into something abominable" (Kant, *Metaphysics of Morals*, 106). We will be addressing the problem of suffering and the distinction between "humanity" and "abomination" in detail later on.
8 Fichte, *Foundations of Natural Right*, 246.
9 Ibid.
10 Ibid.
11 Kant, *Metaphysics of Morals*, 108.

12. Ibid., 107.
13. Ibid., 17.
14. Ibid., 104.
15. Ibid., 17, 85.
16. Ibid., 136–7.
17. Ibid., 137.
18. Ibid., 136.
19. Ibid., 137.
20. Hegel, *Phenomenology*, 361.
21. Kant, *Metaphysics of Morals*, 137.
22. Kant clearly articulates this point in his essay "Idea for a Universal History with a Cosmopolitan Purpose" and his reviews of Herder's *Ideas on the Philosophy and History of Mankind*. His association of reason with the species effectively enables him to see progress in the so-called *"unsocial sociability* of men" (Kant, *Political Writings*, 44). From this perspective the suffering of the individual serves the ends of the rational species: murder, war, and tyranny are thus simply nature's way of awakening "man" and prodding him forward to his true end.
23. Kant explicitly argues that it is a punishable offence to question the historical origins of authority with a view to challenging its legitimacy (cf. Kant, *Metaphysics of Morals*, 111–2, 136). He will even go so far as to parenthetically state that such an inquiry is pointless because "we can already gather from the nature of uncivilized men that they were originally subjected to it by force" (Kant, *Metaphysics of Morals*, 112). This response betrays a rather narrow conception of the possibilities of the historical question. It is not simply a matter of whether the foundational act was contractual consent or force. Rather, it extends to the very processes that generate the civilized/uncivilized distinction, which in turn enables an act of force to appear as necessary.
24. Kant, *Metaphysics of Morals*, 106.
25. Ibid.
26. Ibid.
27. Ibid., 107.
28. The fact of sovereign power gains legitimacy by serving a "natural law," and the "natural law" gains expression from the fact of sovereign power. Hegel echoes this reasoning with his concept of the "cunning of reason" (cf. the introduction to Hegel's *Philosophy of History*).
29. Kant, *Practical Reason*, 110.
30. Kant, *Metaphysics of Morals*, 14.
31. Ibid., 13.
32. Cf. Kant, *Practical Reason*, 28; Kant, *Metaphysics of Morals*, 18.
33. Kant, *Anthropology*, 226.
34. Blanchot, *Infinite Conversation*, 44.
35. Ibid., 46–7.
36. With the experience of impossibility there is no promise of eternity, which Kant preserves in the form of the postulates of pure practical reason. There is no way to displace or transfer the force of the moral law into an eternal horizon, no way to orient oneself to a known or knowable point outside the movement of time. And so there is no way to divide the "animal" from the "rational," no way of dividing the self into higher and lower desires. The weight of the moral law shifts into the "now," and what was once called the activity of "freedom" (that wilful overcoming of stimulus, inclination, desire, and passion) becomes the passivity of responsibility.

37 Kant, *Metaphysics of Morals*, 97.
38 Ibid., 204–5.
39 Ibid., 108.
40 Ibid., 205.
41 Comay, 42.
42 Ibid., 97.
43 Ibid.
44 Kant, *Rational Theology*, 82.
45 For more on this paradox, refer to the following texts: Comay, 42–6; Zupančič, 70–104; Žižek, 206–9.
46 Kant, *Metaphysics of Morals*, 97.
47 Ibid.
48 Comay, 41.
49 Ibid., 44.
50 Kant, *Metaphysics of Morals*, 97.
51 Ibid., 204–5.
52 Ibid., 13.
53 Benjamin, "Critique of Violence," 298.
54 Benjamin's "divine violence" is not violence without responsibility. Rather, it is violence without the claim to necessity or fate. It is violence in the open. It can neither actualize its ideal (i.e., the bloodless violence of the Old Testament) nor set the boundaries of law. It can destroy the boundaries of the law (and with it the state) by exposing the rottenness that exists at the core of "mythic" violence. This "rottenness" is, as Benjamin argued, most clearly seen in the "highest violence," that is, capital punishment. Here with the power over life and death we find the true character of "mythic" violence: it is power passing itself off as fate (Benjamin, "Critique of Violence," 286). The "true" character of this violence is revealed by the state's reaction to the non-violent praxis (i.e., civil disobedience or the general strike) as it is by war. Consider Benjamin's closing sentence from the *Critique of Violence*: "Divine violence, which is the sign and seal but never the means of sacred execution, may be called sovereign violence" (ibid., 300). It may be the "sign and seal, but never the means"; that is, it may model itself on the ideal of the bloodless violence of God, and be done in the name of divine justice, but it cannot be *just*. It must live with the responsibility of its actions because it is *not* fate that guides its hand.
55 Kant, *Political Writings*, 45.
56 Ibid., 219–20.
57 The presumption of "purpose in nature" forms the very first proposition in Kant's "Idea for a Universal History with a Cosmopolitan Purpose": "All the natural capacities of a creature are destined sooner or later to be developed completely and in conformity with their end" (Kant, *Political Writings*, 42).
58 Kant, *Political Writings*, 220.
59 Kant, *Rational Theology*, 82.
60 Kant, *Political Writings*, 46.
61 Kant, *Metaphysics of Morals*, 179.
62 Derrida, *Animal*, 100.
63 Kant, *Metaphysics of Morals*, 98.
64 Ibid.
65 Derrida, *Acts of Religion*, 66.
66 Arendt, 58.
67 Hegel, *Phenomenology*, 357.
68 Ibid., 360.

69 Kant, *Political Writings*, 45.
70 Hegel, *Philosophy of History*, 26–7.
71 Arendt, 58.
72 Kant, *Metaphysics of Morals*, 192.
73 Ibid., 192–3.
74 Hegel, *Phenomenology*, 19.
75 Kant, *Metaphysics of Morals*, 189.

Notes to Chapter 5

1 Hegel, *Philosophy of Right*, 131–2.
2 For Hegel *Objekt* differs from *Gegenstand*, as the former is a real object whereas the latter is an object of knowledge (cf. the "Object and Objectivity" article in Michael Inwood's *A Hegel Dictionary*).
3 Hegel, *Philosophy of Right*, 131.
4 Peperzak, 294. Most commentators omit a detailed discussion of this particular transition, focusing instead on determining what is "living" and what is "dead" in Hegel's text (an approach stemming from the work of Benedetto Croce that has dominated much of the Anglo-American reception of Hegel). While this particular mode of Hegel scholarship has yielded a number of important studies that have brought Hegel into the current Anglo-American philosophical conversation, its particular interpretive commitments (a rejection of Hegel's "metaphysics") have made the interpretation of Hegel's own system even more difficult. As regards the *Grundlinien*, the most notable exception to this trend is Adriaan T. Peperzak's *Modern Freedom*, which provides the most detailed and scholarly commentary on the *Grundlinien* available in the English language. Those interested in the history of the reception of Hegel's political philosophy in the Anglo-American context should refer to the introduction to this invaluable text.
5 This "recognition" [*Anerkennung*] is not to be confused with Hegel's account of the "struggle for recognition" in the *Phenomenology*. The latter is a transitional phase in the development of self-consciousness, and thus in terms of Hegel's own system it *precedes* Objective Spirit. In fact, in §§8, 35, 57, and 71 Hegel explicitly states that the phenomenological "struggle for recognition" belongs to a pre-spiritual stage of the system. For a comprehensive account of the difference between recognition [*Anerkennung*] as used in the *Grundlinien* and the *Phenomenology*, refer to Peperzak, 139–42, 250–4.
6 The distinction, in this instance, being that the unnamed figure in §103 does not set the punishment in accordance with an established legal code; rather, it simply recognizes the specific equality that the crime of murder has with the death penalty and enacts it. The argument here is that by enacting the death penalty as the punishment for murder, this figure effectively sublates contradiction between abstract Right and crime with an act of punitive justice.
7 At this point I should plainly state that, like many commentators, I believe that the *Zusätze* (student notes of Hegel's lecture courses) should be used with a degree of caution. For purposes of scholarly interpretation they should only be treated as an application, confirmation, or reiteration of Hegel's own work (written and/or published) if they do not contradict the explicit theoretical positions of his authorized texts. As Peperzak clearly states in the introduction to *Modern Freedom*, "Only in cases where authentic texts are unavailable may they be accepted as indications of Hegel's answers to questions that are not treated in his handwritten or published work" (Peperzak, 29).

With regard to the particular case we are dealing with in the present work, the *Zusätze* in question *does not* contradict the explicit theoretical position, but rather provides the reader with the specific application of the conceptual principles detailed in the closing sections (§§101–4) of the first part of the *Grundlinien*. In fact, the content of this specific *Zusätze* (i.e., that there is a specific equality between murder and the death penalty) is supported implicitly by the conceptual structure of the surrounding sections and explicitly in §96 (murder is listed as a type of crime that infinitely negates right). The aim of this book is to make the connection between the explicit theoretical position and the comments pertaining to capital punishment in the *Zusätze* for §101 (capital punishment as the conceptually necessary response to murder) as clear as possible.

8 That is, by offering an interpretation of the transition from Abstract Right to Morality the thesis opens up a series of questions relating to this transition. For instance, if execution is the practice that *presents* or *exposes* personality as an object of cognition and thus the practice through which the *moral point of view* is made possible, we are seemingly drawn into an extensive, if not practically infinite, number of problems concerning the actual practices of execution and how this act communicates the principle of right to those that witness it. Due to the confines of the current interpretive analysis, a more thorough treatment of this empirico-critical approach to Hegel's text will have to be taken up in a separate but related piece.

9 Hegel, *Philosophy of Right*, 131.

10 On this point we should keep in mind Hegel's distinction between *Willkür* (will as arbitrarily choosing) and *Wille* (*rational* autonomy) (cf. Peperzak, 203–7, 277; Hegel, *Philosophy of Right*, 47–52).

11 Hegel, *Philosophy of Right*, 121–2.

12 This distinction is important to keep in mind when we consider the role of punishment as a retributive response to crime, as these absolute infringements cannot be positively valued in the same manner as lesser infringements. We will develop this point in more detail later on.

13 While Hegel's theory of punishment is predicated on retribution, it must not be confused with the more simplistic versions of this theory. On this point it is useful to consult §101 as Hegel explicitly criticizes *lex talionis* as a model of retributive justice: "[I]t is very easy to portray the retributive aspect of punishment as an absurdity (theft as retribution for theft, robbery for robbery, an eye for an eye, and a tooth for a tooth, so that one can even imagine the miscreant as one-eyed and toothless); but the concept has nothing to do with this absurdity, for which the introduction of that [idea of] *specific equality* is alone to blame" (Hegel, *Philosophy of Right*, 128).

14 Hegel, *Philosophy of Right*, 131.

15 Hegel, *Grundlinien*, 198.

16 For Hegel, actuality [*Wirklichkeit*] has a precise meaning; that is, it is the unity of essence and appearance, interiority and exteriority, and thus is not to be confused with a reference to a sensed world of external objects (cf. Peperzak, 93; Inwood, 33–35).

17 Hegel, *Philosophy of Right*, 131–2.

18 If we attempt to solve this problem by presenting this transition as an *inner* revolution of the will (an internal rejection of the spectacle of revenge that would echo Hegel's account of the Terror in the *Phenomenology*), we are immediately faced with a series of interpretive problems. First, if Hegel's own (onto)logical system requires an *actualization* of right. This being so, what practical event satisfies this requirement? The *Grundlinien* clearly details the contradiction between abstract right and

the contingency of the arbitrary will, but it does not present revolutionary terror as the practical consequence of this contradiction. In fact, there is no mention of either the Terror or revolution. Attempting to use the *Phenomenology* as support for this interpretation requires that we account for the changes that occur within Hegel's own work from the *Phenomenology* in 1807 to the *Encyclopaedia* in 1816 and the *Grundlinien* in 1821 and the fact that in Hegel's system the *Phenomenology* is an account of the development of Consciousness (the second moment in Hegel's account of Subjective Spirit) and not of Objective Spirit. Even if we disregard the development of Hegel's work and the structure of his system, we simply find no account of absolute freedom and moral terror in this section of the *Grundlinien*. The prerequisites (tyranny followed by revolution) that would be necessary for such a situation are not present. Without a revolution there is no way to account for a stopping mechanism that would force such an inner revolution to occur (i.e., no description of the Terror or any other situation of unlimited negation would expose the inner truth of absolute freedom). In the *Phenomenology* the transition is set up by absolute freedom (a mode of consciousness that refuses any and all determinations of the will and thus results in unlimited negation) and "the death that is without meaning, the sheer terror of the negative that contains nothing positive" (Hegel, *Phenomenology*, 362). At this point in the *Grundlinien* we have the cyclical exchange of crime and revenge, which does share some of the characteristics (i.e., the transition in the *Phenomenology* is also a practical exposure of the ultimate emptiness of the arbitrary will, albeit *from the perspective of self-consciousness*) but without an account that exposes the "truth" of avenging justice (i.e., that it constitutes a new infringement of right) by pushing it to the limits of the Terror there is no way of accounting for this transition *without* an act of punitive justice. In addition there is also a reference in §282 that indicates that Hegel views punitive justice as a *practice that relates to the principle* of right (like the Monarch's right of pardon). This lends support to the interpretation being put forward in this chapter (that the transition is accomplished by an act of punitive justice).

19 Hegel, *Philosophy of Right*, 131.
20 Ibid.
21 The sudden and unexplained development of a character with a moral point of view preceding the act of punitive justice parallels Hegel's account of the hero. There are two references to the "right of heroes" in the *Grundlinien* and they occur in the following locations:
 - §93 in section three ("Coercion and Crime") of part one ("Abstract Right")
 - §350 in the third subsection ("World History") of section three ("The State") in part three ("Ethical Life")

 Hegel provides a detailed account of the hero and its role in history in 1830 in the second draft of his *Lectures on the Philosophy of World History* (cf. Hegel, *World History*, 68–93).
22 Hegel, *Philosophy of Right*, 250.
23 Ibid., 130.
24 In addition, slavery and religious coercion are *social crimes*, that is, they necessarily involve multiple actors, and thus in Hegel's terms they must be historically surpassed [*Aufgehoben*], whereas murder is an individual crime and cannot be historically surpassed (cf. §§57, 66).
25 For Hegel, resistance is a "requirement" or "duty" [*Sollen*] because *not* to resist is to fail to actualize the concept [*Begriff*] (cf. *Modern Freedom*, 98–9, 301). An example of such a failure is given in §93 when Hegel addresses the use of "pedagogical coercion"

against the "uncivilized" [*ungebildeten*] (*Philosophy of Right*, 120). His view of the "uncivilized" or "natural will" is closely linked to his (onto)logical interpretation and use of the Christian doctrine of "original sin" (cf. *Philosophy of Right*, 50–1, 167–70; *Encyclopaedia Logic*, 60–3; *Philosophy of Religion*, III, 104–8, 207–11, and 300–304).

26. This particular implication problematizes Adriaan Peperzak's argument concerning the possibility of utilizing the appearance of the "judge" from §103 to attempt to find a way to go beyond the abstract right that governs international politics. It is unclear how this argument can function if the judge's authority (i.e., the moral recognition of and consent to the laws he or she enforces) finds its origin in the execution of the murderer. There is the possibility of punishing states that have committed war crimes, but finding a punishment with a *specific equality* is not possible. Without that there is no way for the "judge" to gain the recognition of other states in a pre-moral context (at this stage right is once again *in-itself*). Peperzak presents this argument both in *Modern Freedom* (Peperzak, 595–7) and in his article "Hegel Contra Hegel in His Philosophy of Right."
27. Wittgenstein, *Philosophical Investigations*, 79.
28. Hegel, *Philosophy of Right*, 123.
29. Ibid., 128.
30. Kafka, "Penal Colony," 150; Kafka, *Die schönsten Erzählungen*, 132.
31. Kafka, "Penal Colony," 144, 161.
32. Derrida, *Glas*, 226.
33. Kafka, "Penal Colony," 167.

Notes to Chapter 6

1. Benjamin, "Critique of Violence," 286.
2. Ibid.
3. Hegel, *Philosophy of Right*, 125.
4. Kant, *Metaphysics of Morals*, 106.
5. Hegel, *Philosophy of Right*, 130.
6. Deleuze and Guattari, *Kafka*, 45.
7. Kafka, "Penal Colony," 148.
8. Ibid., 149.
9. Ibid., 150.
10. Gills Deleuze and Felix Guattari use the term *démontage* (dismantling) to refer to the process by which the supposed transcendence of the law is exposed as the immanence of desire (Deleuze and Guattari, 45). *Désoeuvrement* (unworking) is a term used by Maurice Blanchot that becomes central to his dialogue with Jean-Luc Nancy on the question of community and the work of Georges Bataille (cf. Nancy's *The Inoperative Community* and Blanchot's response in *The Unavowable Community* as well as Giorgio Agamben's *The Coming Community*, and Jacques Derrida's *The Politics of Friendship*).
11. Kafka, "Penal Colony," 143.
12. Ibid.
13. Ibid.
14. Ibid., 148.
15. Ibid., 144.
16. Ibid., 147.
17. Ibid.
18. Ibid., 154.

Notes to Chapter Six

19 Ibid., 144.
20 Ibid., 148.
21 Ibid., 149.
22 Ibid.
23 Ibid., 150.
24 Kafka, *Die schönsten Erzählungen*, 132.
25 Hegel, *Philosophy of Right*, 126.
26 Kafka, "Penal Colony," 150.
27 Ibid., 165.
28 Ibid., 141.
29 Ibid.
30 Ibid., 144.
31 Ibid., 153.
32 Ibid., 154.
33 Socrates utilizes the story of Leontius as an illustration of the role of the "will" in his tripartite division of the soul:

> Leontius, the son of Aglaion, was going up from the Piraeus along the outside of the North Wall when he saw some corpses lying at the executioner's feet. He had an appetite to look at them but at the same time he was disgusted and turned away. For a time he struggled with himself and covered his face, but, finally, overpowered by the appetite, he pushed his eyes wide open and rushed towards the corpses, saying, "Look for yourselves, you evil wretches, take your fill of the beautiful sight!" (Plato, *Republic*, 1071)

For our purposes the spatial arrangement of this scene is significant. Like the execution within the former colony, the scene of punishment is not concealed; it is a designed spectacle, an object lesson in the force of law, and therefore the bodies are displayed in a specific manner in order to communicate a specific message. These bodies are not dressed and presented as distinct individuals, rather, they are nameless bodies piled and, in some unspecified manner, mutilated or dismembered. These corpses are placed "outside" to serve to mark the limits of the city as both a physical and a politico-legal entity. With this context in mind Leontius' reaction is even more interesting; he is at once disgusted by and drawn to the sight of the corpses, and he spatially situates each reaction within himself. In this civil war of the soul, it is his own body, his eyes, that become the site of the illicit desire to see, and he, as the rational "voice," reproaches them in anger and disgust. The spatial determination of the corpse as being "outside" structures the spectator's reaction. By seeing the exhibition of death "beyond the pale," the subject internalizes the division the law proclaims; the corpse, exhibited as "bare death," acts as a marker for the boundary both of the city and of the soul. The structural arrangement of the corpse effectively strips it of any suggestion of transcendence; it is pure body, a *corpus sans spiritus*, and, as such, it acts as a final marker between the inside and the outside.

34 Kafka, "Penal Colony," 154.
35 Ibid., 150.
36 Ibid., 140.
37 Ibid., 151.
38 Ibid., 159.
39 The term "auspices" here meaning both "under the protection of" or "supported by" and an "augur" or "omen." In accordance with its etymology (the observation of and divination from the actions of birds), the apparatus can only do its work under the sign of "justice," and yet its relation to "justice" is only maintained by

mystification. Each sentence that is written-out can only lay claim to being "just" if the condemned's silence is read as "understanding" and acceptance. It requires the work of a mystic, in that someone must "read" the look on the condemned's face. Someone must interpret it as the work of "fate." Within the "look" of the condemned, his character and his punishment must coincide as the work of necessity itself. Only this would expiate the colony and make the penal procedure "just."

40 The silence of the look functions like the silent "a" in *différance* (cf. Chapter 4, p. 17).
41 I use the term "law of power" to refer to the "rule of man" or the so-called "right of the strongest."
42 Kafka, "Penal Colony," 144, 161.
43 Ibid., 165.
44 Benjamin, "Critique of Violence," 297.
45 Kafka, "Penal Colony," 166.
46 Ibid., 153.
47 Ibid., 166.
48 Ibid.
49 Ibid., 167.
50 Benjamin, "Critique of Violence," 287.
51 Kafka, *Diaries*, 380.
52 Kafka, "Penal Colony," 140.
53 Benjamin, "Critique of Violence," 286.
54 Ibid.
55 Hegel, *Philosophy of Right*, 128.
56 Ibid., 120.
57 Kant, *Metaphysics of Morals*, 107.
58 Benjamin, "Critique of Violence," 286.
59 Kafka, "Penal Colony," 144.
60 Kant, *Metaphysics of Morals*, 108.
61 Ibid., 107.
62 Ibid.
63 Fichte, 246.
64 Ibid.
65 Ibid.
66 Kant, *Metaphysics of Morals*, 107.
67 Ibid., 242.
68 Ibid.
69 Ibid., 242–3.
70 Ibid., 243.
71 Ibid. Emphasis added.
72 Ibid.
73 Deleuze and Guattari, 45.
74 For more on this refer to Austin's *How to Do Things with Words* and Derrida's *Limited Inc*.
75 Fichte, 246.
76 Autoimmunity might be thought of as beginning with an attempt to end the play of *différance*. The desideratum of this attempt is totality (absolute meaning or the "Word-of-God"). It reads the silence of language—the "a" of *différance*—as the placeholder for that which is *yet-to-come* in the definite and final sense. That is, it reads the "a" as a temporary silence and not a condition of the possibility of meaning. It cannot simply read-out the "a" within the moment and so autoimmunity takes the

form of a project. The project systemically separates the same from the different in an effort to absolutely determine the boundary that divides the self and the other. As the distinctions between self and other (like meaning and silence) are constitutively and dynamically co-determining, its actions are paradoxical: it attacks the other as if it were itself and itself as if it were the other. It does this in order to gain the pure auto-affection of the totality. A pure "living feeling" of its self as it is *in-itself*.

77 Benjamin, "Critique of Violence," 298.
78 For more on Benjamin's "divine violence" see Chapter 4, note 54.

BIBLIOGRAPHY

Agamben, Giorgio. *The Coming Community*. Translated by Michael Hardt. Minneapolis: University of Minnesota Press, 1993.

———. *Potentialities: Collected Essays in Philosophy*. Edited and translated by Daniel Heller-Roazen. Stanford: Stanford University Press, 1999.

Antelme, Robert. *The Human Race*. Translated by Jeffrey Haight and Annie Mahler. Evanston, IL: Marlboro Press/Northwestern, 1998.

Arendt, Hannah. *Lectures on Kant's Political Philosophy*. Edited by Ronald Beiner. Chicago: University of Chicago Press, 1992.

Augustine. *Confessions*. Translated by Henry Chadwick. New York: Oxford University Press, 1992.

Austin, J. L. *How to Do Things with Words*. 2nd edition. Edited by J. O. Urmson and Marina Sbisa. Cambridge, MA: Harvard University Press, 1975.

Barthes, Roland. *Sade/Fourier/Loyola*. Translated by Richard Miller. Baltimore: Johns Hopkins University Press, 1997.

Bataille, Georges. *The Accursed Share Vol. II & III*. Translated by Robert Hurley. New York: Zone Books, 1993.

———. *Erotism: Death and Sensuality*. Translated by Mary Dalwood. San Francisco: City Lights Books, 1986.

———. *Inner Experience*. Translated by Leslie Anne Boldt. Albany: State University of New York Press, 1988.

———. *On Nietzsche*. Translated by Bruce Boone. St. Paul, MN: Paragon House, 1994.

Beckett, Samuel. *Waiting for Godot: A Tragicomedy in Two Acts*. New York: Grove Press, 1982.

———. *The Letters of Samuel Beckett. Vol I. 1929–1940*. Edited by Martha Dow Fehsenfeld and Lois More Overbeck. New York: Cambridge University Press, 2009.

Benjamin, Walter. "Critique of Violence." In *Reflections: Essays, Aphorisms, Autobiographical Writings*. Edited by Peter Demetz. Translated by Edmund Jephcott. New York: Schocken Books, 1986.

———. *Illuminations: Essays and Reflections*. Edited by Hannah Arendt. Translated by Harry Zohn. New York: Schocken Books, 1969.

———. *Reflections: Essays, Aphorisms, Autobiographical Writings*. Edited by Peter Demetz. Translated by Edmund Jephcott. New York: Schocken Books, 1986.
Blanchot, Maurice. *The Infinite Conversation*. Translated by Susan Hanson. Minneapolis: University of Minnesota, 1999
———. "Sade's Reason." In *Lautreamont and Sade*. Translated by Stuart and Michelle Kendall. Stanford: Stanford University Press, 2004.
———. *The Unavowable Community*. Translated by Pierre Joris. Barrytown, NY: Station Hill Press, 1988.
———. *The Writing of the Disaster*. Translated by Ann Smock. Lincoln: University of Nebraska Press, 1995.
Borges, Jorge Luis. "The Writing of God." In *Collected Fictions*. Translated by Andrew Hurley. New York: Penguin, 1999. 250–4.
Comay, Rebecca. *Mourning Sickness: Hegel and the French Revolution*. Stanford: Stanford University Press, 2011.
Deleuze, Gilles. "Coldness and Cruelty." In *Masochism*. Translated by Jean McNeil. New York: Zone Books, 1991. 9–138.
———, and Felix Guattari. *Kafka: Towards a Minor Literature*. Translated by Dana Polan. Minneapolis: Minnesota University Press, 2006.
Derrida, Jacques. *Aporias*. Translated by Thomas Dutoit. Palo Alto, CA: Stanford University Press, 1993.
———. *Archive Fever: A Freudian Impression*. Translated by Eric Prenowiz. Chicago: University of Chicago Press, 1998.
———. *Acts of Religion*. Edited by Gil Anidjar. New York: Routledge, 2002.
———. *The Animal That Therefore I Am*. Edited by Marie-Louise Mallet. Translated by Davis Wills. New York: Fordham University Press, 2008.
———. *Glas*. Translated by John P. Leavey, Jr., and Richard Rand. Lincoln: University of Nebraska Press, 1990.
———. *Limited Inc*. Translated by Samuel Weber. Evanston, IL: Northwestern University Press, 1988.
———. *Margins of Philosophy*. Translated by Alan Bass. Chicago: University of Chicago Press, 1982.
———. *Of Grammatology*. Translated by Gayatri Spivak. Baltimore: Johns Hopkins University Press, 1997.
———. *On Touching: Jean-Luc Nancy*. Translated by Christine Irizarry. Palo Alto, CA: Stanford University Press, 2005.
———. *Politics of Friendship*. Translated by George Collins. New York: Verso Press, 2000.
———. *Rogues: Two Essays on Reason*. Translated by Pascale-Anne Brault and Michael Naas. Palo Alto, CA: Stanford University Press, 2005.
———. *Writing and Difference*. Translated by Alan Bass. Chicago: University of Chicago Press, 1978.
Dostoyevsky, Fyodor. *The Brothers Karamazov*. Translated by Richard Pevear and Larissa Volokhonsky. New York: Farrar, Straus and Giroux, 2002.

Fichte, Johann Gottlieb. *Foundations of Natural Right*. Edited by Frederick Neuhouser. Translated by Michael Baur. New York: Cambridge University Press, 2000.

Foucault, Michel. *Abnormal*. Edited by Arnold I. Davidson. Translated by Graham Burchell. New York: Picador, 2003.

———. *Society Must Be Defended*. Edited by Arnold I. Davidson. Translated by David Macey. New York: Picador, 2003.

Hegel, G. W. F. *Elements of the Philosophy of Right*. Edited by Allen W. Wood. Translated by H. B. Nisbet. New York: Cambridge University Press, 2004.

———. *The Encyclopaedia Logic*. Translated by T. F. Geraets et al. Indianapolis: Hackett Publishing, 1991.

———. *Grundlinien der Philosophie des Rechts*. Frankfurt, Germany: Suhrkamp Verlag, 1993.

———. *Lectures on the Philosophy of Religion. Vol. III*. Edited and Translated by Peter C. Hodgson. New York: Oxford University Press, 2007.

———. *Lectures on the Philosophy of World History. Introduction: Reason in History*. Translated by H. B. Nisbet. New York: Cambridge University Press, 1975.

———. *Phenomenology of Spirit*. Translated by A. V. Miller. Toronto: Oxford University Press, 1977.

———. *Philosophy of History*. Translated by J. Sibree. New York: Prometheus Books, 1991.

———. *Science of Logic*. Translated by A. V. Miller. New York: Humanity Books, 1998.

———. "Introduction: Reason in History." *Lectures on the Philosophy of World History*. Translated by H. B. Nisbet. New York: Cambridge University Press, 1975.

Heidegger, Martin. *Being and Time*. Translated by John Macquarrie and Edward Robinson. New York: Harper Collins, 1962.

———. *The Phenomenology of Religious Life*. Translated by Matthias Fritsch and Jennifer Anna Gosetti-Ferencei. Bloomington: Indiana University Press, 2004.

Hénaff, Marcel. *Sade: The Invention of the Libertine Body*. Translated by Xavier Callahan. Minneapolis: University of Minnesota Press, 1999.

———. "The Encyclopedia of Excess." In *Sade and the Narrative of Transgression*. Edited by David B. Allison, Mark S. Roberts, and Allen S. Weiss. Translated by Allen S. Weiss. New York: Cambridge University Press, 1995. 142–70.

Hugo, Victor. *Selected Poetry*. Translated by Steven Monte. Manchester: Carcanet Press, 2001.

Inwood, Michael. *A Hegel Dictionary*. Malden, MA: Blackwell, 2002.

Kafka, Franz. *Diaries 1910–1923*. Edited by Max Brod. Translated by Martin Greenberg. New York: Schocken Books, 1976.

———. *Die schönsten Erzählungen: A Dual Language Book*. Edited and translated by Stanley Appelbaum. New York: Dover, 1997.

———. "In the Penal Colony." In *The Complete Short Stories*. Edited by Nahum N. Glatzer. Translated by Willa and Edwin Muir. New York: Schocken Books, 1971.

Kant, Immanuel. *Anthropology from a Pragmatic Point of View*. Edited and translated by Robert B. Louden. New York: Cambridge University Press, 2006.
———. *Critique of Practical Reason*. Edited and translated by Mary Gregor. New York: Cambridge University Press, 1997.
———. *The Metaphysics of Morals*. Edited and translated by Mary Gregor. New York: Cambridge University Press, 2006.
———. *Political Writings*. Edited by Hans Reiss. Translated by H. B. Nisbet. New York: Cambridge University Press, 1991.
———. *Religion and Rational Theology*. Edited and translated by Allen W. Wood and George Di Giovanni. New York: Cambridge University Press, 1996.
Klossowski, Pierre. *Sade My Neighbor*. Translated by Alphonso Lingis. Evanston, IL: Northwestern University Press, 1991.
Lacan, Jacques. *Ecrits: A Selection*. Translated by Alan Sheridan. London: Tavistock Publications, 1977.
———. *Seminar I: Freud's Papers on Technique 1953–1954*. Edited by Jacques-Alain Miller. Translated by John Forrester. New York: Norton, 1988.
———. *Seminar XI: The Four Fundamental Concepts of Psychoanalysis*. Edited by Jacques-Alain Miller. Translated by Alan Sheridan. New York: Norton, 1998.
Levinas, Emmanuel. *Totality and Infinity: An Essay on Exteriority*. Translated by Alphonso Lingis. Pittsburgh, PA: Duquesne University Press, 2001.
Löwith, Karl. *Meaning in History*. Chicago: Chicago University Press, 1949.
Lyotard, Jean-François. *The Confession of Augustine*. Translated by Richard Beardsworth. Palo Alto, CA: Stanford University Press, 2000.
Marx, Karl. *The Communist Manifesto*. Edited by David McLellan. New York: Oxford University Press, 1998.
———. *Later Political Writings*. Edited by Terrell Carver. New York: Cambridge University Press, 2004.
Nancy, Jean-Luc. *Being Singular Plural*. Translated by Robert D. Richardson and Anne E. O'Byrne. Palo Alto, CA: Stanford University Press, 2000.
———. "La Comparution/The Compearance: From the Existence of 'Communism' to the Community of 'Existence.'" Translated by Tracy B. Strong. *Political Theory* 20:3 (1992): 371–98.
———. "The Confronted Community." In *The Obsessions of George Bataille: Community and Communication*. Edited by Andrew J. Mitchell and Jason Kemp Winfree. Translated by Jason Kemp Winfree. Albany, NY: SUNY Press, 2009.
———. *Corpus*. Translated by Richard A. Rand. New York: Fordham University Press, 2008.
———. *The Experience of Freedom*. Translated by Bridget McDonald. Palo Alto, CA: Stanford University Press, 1993.
———. "Exscription." In *The Birth to Presence*. Edited by Werner Hamacher and David E. Wellbery. Translated by Katherine Lydon. Palo Alto, CA: Stanford University Press, 1993.
———. *A Finite Thinking*. Edited by Simon Sparks. Palo Alto, CA: Stanford University Press, 2003.

———. *The Inoperative Community*. Edited and translated by Peter Connor. Minneapolis: Minnesota University Press, 1991.

———. *Multiple Arts: The Muses II*. Edited by Simon Sparks. Palo Alto, CA: Stanford University Press, 2006.

———. *The Sense of the World*. Translated by Jeffrey S. Librett. Minneapolis: Minnesota University Press, 1997.

———. *The Truth of Democracy*. Translated by Pascale-Anne Brault and Michael Naas. New York: Fordham University Press, 2010.

Nietzsche, Friedrich. *Beyond Good and Evil*. Translated by R. J. Hollingdale. New York: Penguin, 1990.

Peperzak, Adriaan. *Modern Freedom: Hegel's Legal, Moral, and Political Philosophy*. Norwell, MA: Kluwer, 2001.

———. "Hegel Contra Hegel in His Philosophy of Right: The Contradictions of International Politics." *Journal of the History of Philosophy* 32 (1994): 241–64.

Plato. "Alcibiades." In *The Complete Works*. Edited by John M. Cooper and D. S. Hutchinson. Translated by D. S. Hutchinson. Indianapolis: Hackett Publishing, 1997.

———. "The Republic." In *The Complete Works*. Edited by John M. Cooper and D. S. Hutchinson. Translated by G. M. A. Grube. Revised by C. D. C. Reeve. Indianapolis: Hackett Publishing, 1997.

———. "The Symposium." In *The Complete Works*. Edited by John M. Cooper and D. S. Hutchinson. Translated by Alexander Nehamas and Paul Woodruff. Indianapolis: Hackett Publishing, 1997.

Rousseau, Jean-Jacques. *Émile, or Treatise on Education*. Translated by William H. Payne. Amherst, NY: Prometheus Books, 2003.

Sade, D. A. F. de. "*Les cent vingt journées de Sodome*." *Œuvres Complètes du Marquis de Sade*. Vol. III. Edited by Gilbert Lely. Paris: Au Cercle du Livre Précieux, 1964.

———. "The 120 Days of Sodom." In *The 120 Days of Sodom and Other Writings*. Translated by Austryn Wainhouse and Richard Seaver. New York: Grove Press, 1987.

———. "*Histoire de Juliette*." *Œuvres*. Vol. III. Edited by Michel Delon and Jean Deprun. Paris: Gallimard, 1990.

———. *Idée sur les romans*. Edited by Octave Uzanne. Geneva: Slatkine Reprints, 1967.

———. "Justine." In *Justine, Philosophy in the Bedroom and Other Writings*. Translated by Austryn Wainhouse and Richard Seaver. New York: Grove Press, 1965.

———. *Juliette*. Translated by Austryn Wainhouse. New York: Grove Press, 1968.

———. "Philosophy in the Bedroom." In *Justine, Philosophy in the Bedroom and Other Writings*. Translated by Austryn Wainhouse and Richard Seaver. New York: Grove Press, 1987.

———. "*La Philosophie dans le boudoir*." *Œuvres*. Vol. III. Edited by Michel Delon and Jean Deprun. Paris: Gallimard, 1990.

———. "Reflections on the Novel." In *The 120 Days of Sodom and Other Writings*. Translated by Austryn Wainhouse and Richard Seaver. New York: Grove Press, 1987.

Saussure, Ferdinand de. *Course in General Linguistics*. Edited by Charles Bally and Albert Sechehaye. Translated by Roy Harris. Chicago: Open Court, 1986.
Sophocles. *The Three Theban Plays: Antigone, Oedipus the King, Oedipus at Colonus*. Translated by Robert Fagles. New York: Penguin Books, 1984.
Warman, Caroline. *Sade: From Materialism to Pornography*. Oxford: Voltaire Foundation, 2002.
Wittgenstein, Ludwig. *Philosophical Investigations*. Translated by G. E. M. Anscombe. Malden, MA: Blackwell, 2003.
———. *Tractatus Logico-Philosophicus*. Translated by D. F. Pears and B. F. McGuinness. New York: Routledge, 2001.
Žižek, Slavoj. *For They Know Not What They Do*. New York: Verso, 1991.
Zupančič, Alenka. *Ethics of the Real: Kant, Lacan*. New York, Verso, 2000.

INDEX

Agamben, Giorgio, 174n11, 176n56, 188n10
Antelme, Robert, 81
Arendt, Hannah, 125–26
Augustine: authorship and reading, 60–63; conversion, 59, 66–68, 174n17, 177n75; cryptomantic, 74–78, 80, 175n53, 175n55, 176n60; *incommutabilis substantia*, 65, 69, 74, 78, 82–84, 175n53, 176n61; knowledge, 175n53, 175n55; memory, 59, 61, 71–73, 83, 174n23; reading and the word, 11–12, 68–73, 77; silence, 8, 64–66, 74, 76, 176n56, 176n61; standing still, 77–79; truth, 60–67, 70–78, 82–83; violence, 82
Austin, J. L., 104, 190n74

Barthes, Roland, 87
Bataille, Georges, 17, 19, 20–25, 80; *Acéphale*, 37, 178n79; anguish, 79; communication, 11–12, 40, 62–63, 74–77, 79, 83; community, 20–21, 23, 25, 35–37, 49, 60, 78, 80, 84, 174n11, 178n79, 188n10; on Hegel, 37; inner experience, 35–37, 42, 59, 62, 76–78, 80, 178n85; project, 33, 78–79; sacrifice, 38; silence: 74–77, 83, 87–88, 177n64; sovereignty, 35–36, 42; writing, 59, 74–77. *See also* fraternity
Beckett, Samuel, 6, 28–29
Benjamin, Walter, 8, 13, 79, 108–9; capital punishment, 108–9, 120, 139, 141, 154, 160, 184n54; and Hasidic story, 79; history, 79; language, 176n56; violence, 2, 82, 107, 120, 141, 151, 153, 161, 172n145, 184n54
Blanchot, Maurice, 15, 17, 19–21, 23, 26, 36, 49, 51, 82, 88, 91, 115, 174n11, 178n79, 180n6, 180n10, 180n13, 188n10
Borges, Jorge Luis, 73, 102, 104

Comay, Rebecca, 7, 119
community, 1–4, 6–11, 17–55, 60–63, 72–76, 78–85, 130–31, 136, 140, 163n4, 163n10, 165n46, 166n90, 167n112, 168n126, 170n134, 173n154, 174n11, 175n55, 178n79, 188n10; closed community, 10, 19, 37, 47; community, number, 4, 24–30, 44–48, 53–55, 167n112, 173n154; community-of-order, 78–82, 84–85, 178n79, 179n85; community-of-those-without-community, 17, 21–24, 42–43, 49, 51, 54, 80, 84, 85; moral community, 130–31, 136. *See also* Bataille; Derrida; Nancy

death penalty, 13, 107, 109, 111, 113–14, 129, 134, 140–42, 154, 156–58, 185n6, 186n7; execution, 6, 9, 12–13, 31, 52, 54, 92, 103, 111, 116–19, 123–27, 131–36, 143, 147–60, 171n145, 184n54, 186n8, 188n26, 189n33. *See also* Benjamin; Hegel; Kant

199

Deleuze, Gilles, 142, 180n10, 181n43, 182n73, 188n10
democracy, 1, 4, 8, 10–11, 18–23, 25, 44, 46, 53, 55, 163n4, 173n154, 177n75. *See also* Derrida; Nancy
Derrida, Jacques, 8–9, 47, 168n117, 172n150, 174n11; *animot*, 109; autoimmunity, 18–20, 109, 123, 170–71n134, 177–78n75, 190n76; on Bataille, 59–60, 63, 75; blind tactics, 4–5; community, 10–11, 17–24, 43, 49, 54, 59–60, 163n4, 170–71n134, 173n154, 178n79; democracy-to-come, 8, 18–20, 22–23, 55, 163n4, 173n154, 177–78n75; *différance*, 4, 10–11, 20, 41, 63, 73, 91–92, 114, 124–25, 159, 165n46, 170n134, 174n25, 177n75, 190n40, 190n76; force of law, 8, 119, 167n112, 182n73, 189n33; fraternity, 45, 48–49, 53–54, 163n10, 169n126, 169n128, 169n129, 173n154, 178n79; *Glas*, 137, 165n46; metaphysics of the proper, 91; more than one, 18–20, 24, 30; the One and violence, 31; remain(s), 137, 165n46; speech and silence, 177n64; *teleiopoesis*, 20–23, 43, 49
Dostoyevsky, Fyodor, 178n79, 178n85

ethics of reading, 6, 12, 136

Fichte, Johann Gottlieb, 13, 109–11, 156–59
Foucault, Michel, 2–3
fraternity, 10, 18–19, 37, 43–55, 163n10, 168n117, 168n126, 169n128, 170n134, 171n139, 171n145, 173n154

Hassidim, 79
Hegel, G. W. F., 8–9, 13, 37, 39, 42, 46, 53–54, 69, 185n4, 185n7; absolute freedom, 42, 112, 125, 187n18; *Aufheben*, 129, 132–33, 164–65n46; bad infinity, 42; crime, 131–34, 141, 154; death penalty, 13, 129, 131, 134–35, 141; finitude, 164n43; history, 126, 167n111, 183n28, 187n24; judge and executioner, 133, 135, 188n26; law of suspects, 54; *lex talionis*, 136, 154–55, 158, 160, 186–87n13; monarch, 130, 187n18; moral point of view, 186n8; murder, 131, 134–37, 141, 154, 187n24; *objekt*, 185n2; original sin, 188–89n25; punishment, 132–35, 141, 145–46, 154, 186n13, 186–87n18; right of heroes, 187n21; right of pardon, 130, 187n18; struggle for recognition, 81, 185n5; *Willkür*, 186n10; *Wirklichkeit*, 186n16
Heidegger, Martin, 19, 23, 25, 34, 36, 39, 51–52, 65, 67, 166n90, 168n126
Hénaff, Marcel, 88, 181n43
Hugo, Victor, 169n131

Inwood, Michael, 185n2, 186n16

Kafka, Franz, 1, 8, 13, 49, 105, 136–37, 141–42, 152–53, 161, 169n129
Kant, Immanuel, 8–9, 13; animal, 115, 120–26, 183n36, 184n57; compassion, 111, 117–19, 126, 155–56; death penalty, 107–11, 113, 116–19, 122, 141, 154–58; diabolical evil, 118, 124; moral law, 110–27, 156, 183n36; murder, 107, 109–11, 118–19, 141, 154, 157, 171n139; punishment, 110–14, 126, 141, 154–56, 183n23; sovereign, 111–13, 116–19, 122, 127, 167n111, 183n23; suffering, 114–16, 182n7, 183n22; sympathy, 117; Tahitians, 120–23; third critique, 37–38
Klossowski, Pierre, 96, 180n6, 180n10

Lacan, Jacques, 91–92, 169n129
law, 1–13, 49–54, 77–84, 88–90, 93–94, 97–103, 107–27, 130–35, 140–42, 145–46, 151–61, 165n54, 167n112, 177n75, 179n85, 182n73, 184n54,

188n26, 188n10; justice, 7–8, 13, 47, 109, 129–60, 167n115, 179n85, 184n54, 185n6, 186n13, 187n18, 189n39; law of the book, 89, 93; law of number, 18–19, 50; law of retribution, 107, 114; mystical foundations of law, 3, 13, 53, 153; natural law, 11, 77, 79, 88–94, 97–103, 110–11, 114, 176n60, 179n6, 180n6, 183n28. See also death penalty; Kant; Sade

Levinas, Emmanuel, 30, 125, 127

Löwith, Karl, 60

Lyotard, Jean-François, 2, 60, 65, 73

Marx, Karl, 3, 29, 33, 80, 166n63

murder, 6, 30–31, 49, 52, 93, 97–99, 103–4, 107, 109–11, 123–24, 129, 131–32, 134–37, 141–42, 146, 151–52, 154–57, 165, 168n126, 169n131, 183n22, 185n6, 186n7, 187n24, 188n26. See also death penalty; Hegel; Kant; Nancy; Sade

Nancy, Jean-Luc, 8–11, 19, 102, 166n63, 166n86, 173n153, 178n79; being-with, 25–27, 32, 39, 41–42, 46, 48, 50–51, 53, 55, 80–81, 166n90, 170n134, 173n154; *borborygmi*, 172n150; compearance, 29, 38–41, 80–88, 163n10; communion, 8, 10–11, 27–32, 34–35, 38, 42, 45–46, 53, 79–81, 171n134, 175n55; community, 8, 10–11, 17, 19–21, 23, 25–27, 29, 32–48, 51, 54, 57, 79–81, 165n46, 166n90, 168n126, 170n134, 173n154, 175n55; equaliberty, 47–48; evil, 33, 52–53, 171n139; *fasces*, 167n115, 171n139, 171n145; fraternity, 43–55, 168n126, 169n128, 169n129, 170n134, 171n139, 173n154; literary communism, 41–42; murder, 30–31, 49, 52; the political, 7–8, 11, 20, 26, 28, 57, 60, 120, 161; resistance, 9–11, 17, 19, 26–27, 33, 40, 81, 165n46, 170n134; sharing, 26, 33, 38,

40, 51, 168n126; spacing, 26, 38–39, 47–48, 55; touching, 38, 40, 163n10; unworking, 20, 24, 26, 30, 32, 120, 161, 170n134

negative theology, 21, 26, 33, 36, 38, 42, 46, 49, 55

Nietzsche, Friedrich, 18–24, 49, 163n10, 178n79

Peperzak, Adriaan, 130, 185n4, 185n5, 185n7, 186n10, 186n16, 188n26

Plato, 49, 65, 95, 148, 174n17, 189n33

resistance, 9–11, 17, 19, 27, 31, 33, 40–41, 81, 91, 95, 97, 112–13, 118, 134, 165n46, 170n134, 187n25. See also Nancy

Rousseau, Jean-Jacques, 88–90, 101, 168n126

Sade, D. A. F. de, 8, 11–12, 37; author, 11, 87, 101; crime, 88–89, 92–93, 98, 103; desire, 9, 91, 96–99; libertine, 94, 181n43; moral murder, 93, 97–99, 103–4; nature, 19, 88–90, 92, 96–98, 101–4; neurogrammatics, 90, 92–97, 101, 103, 182n73; novel, 11, 87–92, 94–102; silence, 91–92; sovereignty, writing, 87–88, 90–104

Saussure, Ferdinand de, 74, 176n61

silence, 6, 8, 52–53, 63, 67–69, 71–78, 82–83, 103, 109, 120–21, 127, 130, 139–42, 146, 148–55, 159, 161, 176n56, 177n61, 177n64, 177n75, 182n73, 190n39, 190n40, 190–91n76. See also Bataille; Derrida; Sade

sovereignty, 1–4, 32, 35, 37, 42, 47, 88–89, 91, 111–12, 135, 177n75; monarch, 116–19, 122–24, 127, 130, 187n18. See also Bataille; Hegel; Kant

violence, 2–3, 8, 11–13, 19, 31, 41, 82, 118–20, 125, 131, 135, 141, 151–61; divine violence: 82, 151, 172n145,

184n54; mythical violence: 82, 184n54; non-violence: 153; political violence: 11, 19. *See also* Benjamin

Wittgenstein, Ludwig, 177n64

writing, 4, 9, 11, 13, 41–42, 60–65, 73–77, 87–104, 136–37, 142–43, 151, 159, 180n10, 182n73; writing-out, 136–37, 141–43, 151, 159. *See also* Bataille; Derrida; Sade

www.ingramcontent.com/pod-product-compliance
Lightning Source LLC
Chambersburg PA
CBHW030320080526
44584CB00012B/635